Corporate Event Project Management

The Wiley Event Management Series

SERIES EDITOR: DR. JOE GOLDBLATT, CSEP

Special Events: Twenty-First Century Global Event Management, Third Edition
by Dr. Joe Goldblatt, CSEP

Dictionary of Event Management, Second Edition
by Dr. Joe Goldblatt, CSEP, and Kathleen S. Nelson, CSEP

Corporate Event Project Management
by William O'Toole and Phyllis Mikolaitis, CSEP

*Event Marketing: How to Successfully Promote Events,
Festivals, Conventions, and Expositions*
by Leonard H. Hoyle, CAE, CMP

Event Risk Management and Safety
by Peter E. Tarlow, Ph.D.

Event Sponsorship
by Bruce E. Skinner and Vladimir Rukavina

The Complete Guide to Destination Management
by Pat Schauman, CMP, CSEP

Corporate Event Project Management

William O'Toole
Phyllis Mikolaitis, CSEP

JOHN WILEY & SONS, INC.

This book is printed on acid-free paper. ∞

This publication is designed to provide accurate and authoritative information in regard to the subject matter covered. It is sold with the understanding that the publisher is not engaged in rendering professional services. If professional advice or other expert assistance is required, the services of a competent professional person should be sought.

Wiley also publishes its books in a variety of electronic formats. Some content that appears in print may not be available in electronic books. For more information about Wiley products, visit our web site at www.wiley.com.

Library of Congress Cataloging-in-Publication Data:

O'Toole, William, 1951-
    Corporate event project management / William O'Toole, Phyllis Mikolaitis.
        p. cm. — (The Wiley event management series)
    Includes index.
    ISBN 0-471-40240-0 (cloth : alk. paper)
        1. Special events—Management. I. Mikolaitis, Phyllis. II. Title. III. Wiley events.

    GT3405 .O76 2002
    394.2'068—dc21   2001026952

Printed in the United States of America.

10 9 8 7 6 5 4

This book is dedicated to my favorite teacher, Michael DeNoia, for his inspiration and positive influence, which set me on my path to success. Many thanks to my family and friends for their unwavering support during this effort.—P. M.

I dedicate this work to my family, Ruth and Scarlet.—W. O.

Contents

Foreword

The term *corporate event* is defined in the Wiley *International Dictionary of Event Management* as "an event sponsored by a corporation for the purpose of achieving specific goals and objectives such as entertaining customers, introducing and promoting new products or services, or providing incentives or training for employees, as well as other activities." Therefore, this simple term indeed has numerous complex meanings.

This important new book successfully transforms a complex topic into a simple and effective system that experienced or new corporate event managers may use to improve their practice. The authors have carefully and ingeniously adapted the proven principles of project management to the art and science of event management, thereby producing a new, fresh, and highly effective system for managing corporate events.

Whether you are an internal corporate event manager or a supplier of services and products for corporate events, you will greatly benefit from the authors' systematic approach to this growing field.

Each author brings more than two decades of professional experience in project management and corporate event management to this text, and their combined expertise has produced a book that will become a staple in the libraries of corporate events, communications, human resources, and other departments.

The numerous checklists, tables, flowcharts, and models will help you implement the project management principles quickly in order to ease and improve your corporate event management operations. In an age in which every worker is being asked to "do more with less," this book is both timely and valuable.

To fully benefit from this text, I strongly recommend that you use it as a training tool for your immediate subordinates as well as others in your organization. By studying and then actually teaching the principles and techniques of corporate event project management, you will soon become a master of this complex art and science.

Whether you are responsible for producing a company picnic, a sales-training program, or a multimillion-dollar new-product launch event, between the pages of this book you will find the system you have long been waiting for. By merging event and project management, the authors have developed a system that will be readily understood, embraced, and supported, not just by you but by those in other divisions, such as finance, operations, and risk management. This cross-functional approach to corporate event management is indeed one of the book's strongest points.

Within every field, there are those individuals who either on purpose or by accident invent a new theory and practice that in fact revolutionizes the field. William O'Toole and Phyllis Mikolaitis now join the short but growing list of other visionaries who have discovered a groundbreaking set of ideas that will dramatically improve the event management field. O'Toole, an Australian whose expertise is project management, and Mikolaitis, an American who is a 20-year veteran corporate event manager of one of the world's largest companies, Xerox, have brought a unique global understanding of corporate event management during the greatest period of international expansion in world history. Their close collaboration and careful merger of event and project management will be recorded by historians of event literature as one of the most significant advancements in event management during the twenty-first century.

Whether you are managing a simple dinner for 10 or an exhibition for 10,000, *Corporate Event Project Management* is the essential tool that will raise the quality level of your performance, reduce your stress level, and demonstrate to your superiors that you can successfully analyze and solve complex problems through modern event management. This book has not only broken new ground; it has built a solid foundation upon which corporate event management will rise to new heights in the future. I am certain that this book will show you that future while enabling you to benefit personally and professionally as you incorporate its important principles into your daily practice.

Perhaps after you finish reading this valuable book and share these principles with others, you will be able to craft your own new definition of the term *corporate event project management,* for in the pages of this book, a new field within event management has been conceived, and you are the fortunate beneficiary of this knowledge and wisdom.

Dr. Joe Goldblatt, CSEP
Series Editor, The Wiley Event Management Series
Dean and Professor, Johnson & Wales University

Preface

Congratulations. You have taken the next step in your advancement as a corporate event manager. Corporate event management is a young and rapidly expanding industry in its adolescent phase. It is following the paths of traditional professions such as accounting, law, and marketing and is not far behind the paths of project management and information technology. Just like an adolescent, it is bold, full of creative ideas, charming, optimistic, and reckless. But as we all know, the real world demands the qualities of responsibility, authority, and accountability. How can we introduce these qualities without ruining all that creativity? This book provides a proven and effective system that is not only accountable and responsible but also fosters the creativity so essential to an industry called "events."

There are two trends in the modern corporate event industry. The first is the drive for professionalism in response to internal and external forces, as illustrated in Figure 1, which shows in compressed form the historical process that is occurring in events. The other trend is convergence, that is, the convergence of corporate and public events. The Olympics is a prime example of this trend. The corporate hospitality events were as lavish as the actual athletic competition. In a similar way, festivals and community events are becoming more reliant on the involvement of companies through both sponsorship and expertise. This places the corporate event manager in an advantageous position. The skills developed through corporate event project management are transferable across the event industry.

Corporate event management as an industry arose out of the needs of a changing society in general and changing business practices in particular. From this chaos, the individual event manager emerged. Corporate event managers worked with the human resources, marketing, communication, and other departments of large organizations. These event managers typically exhibited a very personal style of working that included informal agreements rather than detailed contracts. Basically, they carried the event plans around in their heads.

As a response to growth both in the demand for events and in their complexity, professional event companies emerged. Due to the amount and complexity of their work, they began to standardize their methodology. The as-

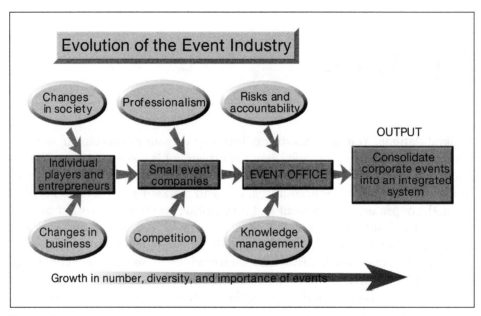

Figure 1
Maturing of the Event Industry

tounding number of events allowed these two systems—corporate event managers and professional event companies—to exist side by side.

More growth resulted in greater complexity and confusion and therefore increased risk. This was anathema to the corporations that employed the event companies. Their response was to create a new position within their organizations called the event manager or coordinator. However, each time a new person entered that position, he or she faced the same problems and repeated the same mistakes, producing no lasting improvement in the methods for managing events.

This scenario describes the present state of affairs in the corporate event industry. Most corporations have a disparate system in which internal personal assistants run the seminars, and the marketing department coordinates the sponsored events and outsources for whatever else is needed.

Corporate event management has finally reached a critical mass. And it is inefficient and therefore costly. The solution is to introduce systematic methods for researching, designing, planning, coordinating, and evaluating every corporate event. Only in this way can the corporation's knowledge be enriched by each event. Properly adapting the methodology of project management and applying it to corporate event management is one solution to this chaos. This approach enables the corporate event manager to interface with internal departments efficiently, and it measurably enhances intra- and intercompany communication, which translates directly into a higher internal rate of return on the investment in the corporate event. This book shows you how to synthesize project management and event management in order to produce that higher rate of return.

The site map shown in Figure 2 provides an overview of the topics that will be covered. At first glance, some chapters may appear not to concern the current corporate event manager. For example, the chapter on procurement may seem irrelevant to a manager who uses his or her company's procurement program. However, this may not remain the same forever. Because companies are becoming increasingly "projectized" (that is, managed as a series of competing projects), the corporate events function may soon find itself competing with other departments for funds.

First, in Chapter 1 to implement a successful corporate event project management system, it is essential to understand the corporate culture. Although

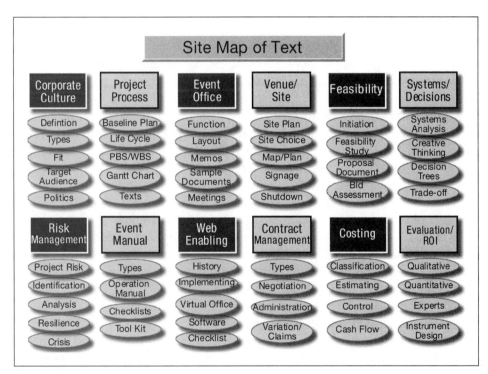

Figure 2
Site Map for the Book

the methodology of project management is seemingly independent of personalities—it's the position, not the person—it won't work without the people!
The corporate culture provides the environment, the constraints, and the opportunities—both obvious and hidden—that surround and permeate the event.

Chapter 2 introduces the basic corporate event project management process.
The model for the modern corporation is a series of competing projects held together by the corporate objectives, strategy, and culture. If there are competing
projects, then the event (e.g., a seminar, conference, product launch, or sponsorship) must show that its rate of return is better than the rate of return for other
company projects. The event now competes with such projects as product research and development, marketing, and new software implementation. It has to
demonstrate that it employs a thoroughly professional methodology and yields
a measurable outcome. Chapter 2 is designed to help you solve this problem.

Tangible proof of a profession is found in its documentation. For event
management to become a modern profession, it needs to have an efficient documentation system. The informal "jotting things down" approach is inadequate for event best practice. The right templates and their document outputs
give event management visibility within the corporate structure. Chapter 3
outlines these documents and shows how they can be simply produced as part
of the event management process.

Chapter 4 explores the importance of the venue, or event site. It does not
cover the standard areas found in other event texts. Instead, it addresses the
areas that are often overlooked, such as the venue plan, the event map, the
signage, and the venue shutdown.

The event feasibility study, described in Chapter 5, is the important initiation document used to obtain approval for the funds to plan the event. A
sound knowledge of all the areas covered in this text is vital to demonstrate
that the corporate event will result in a positive return on the company's investment. Researching the event is only one aspect of event feasibility, which
also includes comparing scenarios and developing a proposal.

Chapter 6 adapts the science of decision making and systems analysis to
events. No matter how perfect the event system is, it must still be implemented. The project management system alone will not manage the event, because that requires creativity and decision making. The theme of this chapter
is that a good system will free the corporate event office staff to make optimal
decisions and allow for more creativity.

As corporate events grow in importance and complexity, risk management, the subject of Chapter 7, has to be used across every level of the event.
This chapter demonstrates that risk management involves far more than safety
issues, and adapts the tools and techniques of risk management to events.

Contracting is an area previous corporate event managers may have had little involvement with. However, as Chapter 8 demonstrates, this is no longer the case. The best practice in risk management demands that contract management be fundamental to events. Even if the event manager does not sign the event contracts, he or she will be responsible for the results of those contracts.

The constantly changing business environment is a fundamental reason for the growth in the number and size of events. The most far-reaching change is the increased use of the Internet. Any event that is not Web enabled is disadvantaged. Chapter 9 explores the methods that can be used to take maximum advantage of the benefits offered by the World Wide Web.

The topics covered in all the previous chapters provide the content for the corporate event manual. Chapter 10 describes the variety of manuals used for corporate events and their importance to corporate knowledge management. By using checklists, the corporate event office can build on each event and create a library of best practices.

An underlying theme of this text is that an efficient system will produce a higher rate of return on an event. Chapter 11 describes the costing and procurement practices that are essential for increasing the rate of return. Procurement procedures are fundamental to project management and should be given top priority in corporate event project management.

Finally, Chapter 12 explores the overall evaluation of the event. Presenting an objective evaluation in a professional report is as fundamental to corporate event management as implementing an event management system. The event must be measured, and the measurement must be related to the corporate strategy and presented in a way that fits into the corporate culture.

The two authors of *Corporate Event Project Management* bring a stereoscopic vision to corporate event project management, resulting in a very practical and three-dimensional coverage of the topic. William O'Toole provides the text's basic structure, using his experience in both project management and event management. In particular, his work in the adaptation of project management processes and his creation of an event management body of knowledge supply the strong skeletal structure.

Phyllis Mikolaitis's wealth of experience in corporate event management provides the musculature for this structure. Thanks to her years of experience with Xerox, she brings practical information, an insider's view of the corporate world, and many "war stories" (both from her own experience and from her co-workers, vendors, and friends in the corporate community) to match the theory to reality. Phyllis was a Xerox program manager directing multiple projects simultaneously following the Xerox corporate project management process, which she now applies to her own independent corporate event management business.

This book not only describes the best practices in corporate event project management; it also allows you to prepare for the coming changes in the corporate event industry. To stimulate and develop your thinking process, each chapter concludes with an activity section entitled "Next Project." Completing these activities will put you one step ahead of your peers and leave you better prepared to handle the coming challenges you are sure to face in corporate event project management. Each chapter, similar to each corporate event project, concludes with a section entitled "Wrap Up." In this section you may wrap up and begin to use the key ideas and practices from each chapter. Since the birth of the modern corporation, organizations have depended on events to drive sales, train, motivate, and educate. Now you can further advance this progression and field using the newest discoveries from the marriage of event and project management. Welcome to the future of corporate events. Through the pages of this book your future will include greater efficiency, quality, and ultimately more successful outcomes.

Corporate Event Project Management

CHAPTER 1

Managing Events in the Corporate World

THIS CHAPTER WILL HELP YOU:

- Identify the role and scope of corporate events
- Incorporate the unique elements of the corporate culture into your events
- Describe the roles and responsibilities of a corporate event project manager
- Discuss how events are used to implement corporate strategies

---

The international corporate event market is the fastest-growing arena in the event industry. Between 1994 and 1999, The George Washington University International Special Events Society profile of event management (a biennial study) confirmed that the most frequently produced events are those within the corporate sector. Every day, trade shows, training, marketing, human resources development, sport and athletic, and other corporate events are held throughout the world. With corporations exporting their products and services to global markets, the corporate event management industry has exploded. Given the ever-increasing complexity and concurrency of events, a formalized project management process is essential for effective coordination. Therefore, the successful corporate event manager must have a thorough knowledge of formal and informal event practices and processes used by corporations around the world.

Corporate Culture

To understand the role of corporate events and the importance of formalized practices and processes, you must first understand corporate culture and the differences in culture among corporations. The culture at Xerox is vastly different from the culture at Canon, Sun Microsystems, or Microsoft, at Queensland Bank or Bank of America, or at General Electric or British Petroleum.

Before exploring the methodology discussed in this text, you must first have a clear understanding of the basic definition of culture. According to the *Microsoft Encarta College Dictionary,* culture is "3) **shared beliefs and values of a group:** the beliefs, customs, practices, and social behavior of a particular nation or people, 4) **people with shared beliefs and practices:** a group of people whose shared beliefs and practices identify the particular place, class, or time to which they belong, 5) **shared attitudes:** a particular set of attitudes that characterizes a group of people."[1]

According to Deal and Kennedy, in their book *Corporate Cultures: The Rites and Rituals of Corporate Life,* corporations encompass "a cohesion of values, myths, heroes, and symbols that has come to mean a great deal to the people who work there."[2]

The corporate culture impacts the way people think and the processes they follow in the daily conduct of their particular business as well as the way that they relate to one another. It affects every aspect of the employees' lives, and it affects how the company functions. The giants of industry and those counted among the *Fortune 500* can link their success to a strong corporate culture—their ideals, what they believe in and stand for. Companies develop their corporate slogans to communicate their philosophy to both the internal and external worlds. Consider the following slogans recently used by some major corporations:

General Electric: "We bring good things to life."
Coca-Cola: "It's the Real Thing."
Sun: "We are the dot in dot-com."
Xerox—The Document Company: "Share the Knowledge."
Zenith: "The Quality Goes in before the Name Goes On."
Delta Airlines: "We love to fly and it shows."
Visa: "It's everywhere you want to be."
Exxon: "Put a tiger in your tank."
Hallmark: "When you care enough to send the very best."
United Airlines: "Come Fly Our Friendly Skies."

However, it takes more than a slogan to weave a philosophy into the fabric of a corporate culture. Strong corporate cultures are developed over many years. Reinforcing the old or transforming to a new corporate culture takes the dedication of the senior management, combined with a strong top-down approach to all aspects of corporate life. Events are part of that process. Corporate events are used to communicate and reinforce the philosophy through such activities as training, employee recognition, and celebrations. A clear understanding of the corporate philosophy and the differences in corporate cultures enables the corporate event planner to provide value to the corporation and achieve personal success.

TYPES OF CORPORATE CULTURE

The business environment is the single greatest influence in shaping corporate culture. In some companies, there is a driving force creating a work-hard-play-hard culture. This environment keeps the salespeople selling and the competitive atmosphere keen. In other companies, the environment is very structured and strongly business oriented. The employees are focused on business from the moment they hit the alarm clock in the morning. Some companies are very process oriented, whereas others have a more relaxed atmosphere. Some companies are so well known for their culture that myths develop about how they function. For example, according to one widely circulated myth about a major corporation famous for its strict adherence to process and validation of facts, if a prospective employee salted his food before tasting it, he would not get the job. This action was deemed a sign of one who made assumptions and jumped to conclusions before checking the facts.

Contrast the structured culture of some of the established blue-chip companies with the relaxed culture of the dot-com companies in Silicon Valley. There, every day is casual day. Employees are encouraged to get outside and exercise or relax, as it encourages creative thinking. Consider how differently you would plan an event for the different corporate cultures. Although two companies may adhere to the same project management processes, their cultures will affect the elements of the plan as well as the way team members will relate to one another and to the participants.

Whether you are a project manager in the corporate event office or a vendor engaged by the corporation, when you start to plan a corporate event, you must consider the key elements of corporate culture, which Deal and Kennedy define as environment, values, heroes, rites and rituals, and cultural network. Figure 1-1 illustrates the relationship between corporate culture and the event.

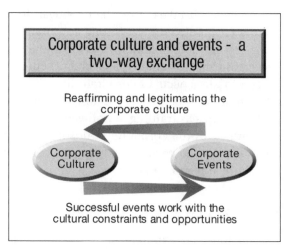

Figure 1-1
Corporate Culture and Events

This example further clarifies the two-way exchange of information and the incorporation of all the elements.

CULTURAL FIT

Understanding how the event fits within the corporate culture will enable you to be successful when planning a corporate event. Time spent gaining an understanding of the corporate culture will save hours of work, not to mention potential embarrassment, later in the project. Considering and incorporating the cultural elements connects the participants psychologically and intellectually to the corporation's core values.

A *Fortune 500* corporation and BT Event Productions, Inc., combined to assimilate their corporate culture into a major event. Bobbi Taylor, president of BT Event Productions, Inc., received three clearly identified objectives from the client:

1. To celebrate 10 very successful years and to launch into a new millennium
2. To recognize the employees' contribution to that success
3. To provide the employees and their families with an opportunity to view the broad range of products, services, and facilities of a key division of the corporation

An internal corporate committee determined that an event was the appropriate vehicle to meet the objectives. The committee evaluated the company's internal resources and decided that the scope and complexity of the event required professional assistance. Bobbi's task was to design an event that would accomplish all the objectives and fit the corporate culture. She set to work by assembling a 35-member "dream team" comprised of the top industry professionals to produce the grand event with enthusiasm, creativity, professionalism, and partnership second to none.

The first step in the process was to design a plan encompassing the state of the business, how the company operates, and the hot buttons of the corporate committee members (what's really important to the company). After many hours of research and meetings with the client team, Bobbi's team came up with a dynamite plan based on both the product and the direction of the corporate theme, including a passport to eight related destinations of entertainment, discovery, and fun for the coming millennium. This grand celebration was to light the way toward the future and highlight the broad array of important products and services that made this division a world leader.

The theme tied this division's main product to the destinations of the event, all located on the main plant's recreational grounds, with huge white tents, colorful carnival rides, game booths, entertainment, and informative product displays. Everyone in the family participated in the activities—including talent shows, team competitions, and a game show based on the corporate business philosophy—or took the opportunity to visit the employee antique car display or the laser light show that incorporated the company logo. Clowns, jugglers, and mimes entertained the guests throughout the festivities. T-shirts in packages shaped like the company logo were distributed as a memento of the celebration. A cybercafé incorporating cappuccino, espresso, and coffee with a dozen computers featuring the corporate Web site was educational, informative, and fun. Free health screenings and tours were given near the newly renovated health and fitness center. Featured on the main stage was a variety of live music acts, including the division's choir, and there were audience participation events throughout the day. For the finale, a major performing artist communicated the spirit of the event with her rendition of the division's theme song, followed by the President/CEO expressing his appreciation to those gathered, saying, "This day was for you, for how you deliver day in and day out."

All of this concluded with a brilliant fireworks display. The fireworks presentation began by launching the company logo like a rocket lighting the sky in brilliance. Sounds like a great day, but it was not without its challenges. Who would have thought that a hurricane would affect a celebration in New England? But that's exactly what happened. Half the members of the dream team and entertainers were from Florida, and hurricane Floyd was headed there just days before the event. Bobbi's advice to event planners: "Plan ahead!!

Have a positive attitude and look for solutions." Bobbi quickly used the phones and the Internet. She put out a message—leave early if you can and if you cannot fly and it is safe to drive, do just that! Members of the dream team donned their rainwear and began setting up the tents and other equipment early to get a jump on the weather. The stage was supposed to come from Philadelphia but could not be moved due to the weather, so the team obtained another from an alternate supplier. Lots of local help was enlisted due to the setbacks and deadlines being shortened because of the weather. By Friday, the rain had stopped, but team members were still in a serious situation. The corporate client helped by bringing in power blowers, mulch, hay, and other materials to sop up the water, as well as their on-site fire equipment to pump water off all of the parking lots used for event space. At 5:30 on the morning of the event, the sun came out, and everyone was set for a spectacular day of fun and friendship.

Working together as a team to produce a great event in the midst of a hurricane cemented the relationship between the dream team and the corporate client. By then, the dream team had become an extension of the corporate team. The event then won the industry's Esprit Award and a Gala Award. Matching the theme to the corporate culture and following a good process certainly was productive and effective.

Event Goals and Objectives

Corporations use events such as this one as a means of communicating corporate messages. If the company values sales performance, then it will hold an event to recognize the outstanding salesperson who accomplished that goal. If it values dedication to invention, then it will recognize those who make breakthrough discoveries. DuPont is very safety conscious and therefore recognizes employees with perfect safety records both at home and on the job.

Corporate extravaganzas are a dynamic and powerful way to connect employees to the corporate beliefs. Consider the example of Mary Kay Inc., the cosmetics company. Its annual convention is a grand affair at which Mary Kay recognizes sales, productivity, and team building. Winners are rewarded with the now famous pink Cadillac automobiles as well as minivans, furs, and diamonds. The message is clear. The event expands the employees' egos as well as their wallets.

Xerox uses the DocuWorld events, with the theme "Share the Knowledge," to educate customers about corporate communication, thus creating a connection with customers.

Events that honor corporate heroes provide role models, and honoring role models exemplifies the behaviors that employees must exhibit in order to be successful in that company. How often have you seen plaques on company walls honoring the "Employee of the Month" or the "Salesperson of the Month" or perhaps the "Recipient of the Quality Award"? These companies are sending a message: Emulate this person and you, too, will be successful. Ceremonies are often held to honor the heroes. Such events can be as simple as a long-service banquet or as grand as the dedication of a new building named after the honoree.

The internal or external corporate event planner can generate additional event projects by suggesting opportunities for management to create events that provide impact and draw attention to a particular behavior or value. A well-orchestrated event can reinforce the behaviors the corporation desires in its employees. John Daly, of John Daly, Inc., tells a wonderful story about an event used to reinforce a corporate message.

Several years ago, an international auto manufacturer contacted John to design an event whose objective was to motivate the top 75 agency owners to sell more cars, especially cars in the latest shade of blue. The client believed that an incentive event was the appropriate technique to motivate people to sell more cars. In fact, the event was not just about rewarding the top 75 agency owners; it was also about getting them to work harder during the coming year. John asked to see marketing materials to determine what was new and what were the hot items for the next year.

He found there was a new design and a new shade of blue that absolutely thrilled the manufacturer, which felt that the color would speak to current market trends. Armed with the details, John wrote a proposal for the three-day event, which would be held for the agency owners and their significant others, a total of about 150 people. It was an exhilarating proposal, written like a real page-turner. John crafted his proposal so that readers felt as if they were viewing an amazing event as they read through it. His vivid description of the proposed activities captured both the client's imagination and the contract for the business. The event included a meeting surrounded by a sumptuous breakfast, a relaxing lunch, and then a spectacular gala each day. John expertly wove the color blue throughout the whole project. He included blue in every element, down to the smallest detail. There were many subtle references to the color blue, including the theme music "Rhapsody in Blue." The attendees were not told why the entire theme was blue. To them, it was just part of the theme of the event. Six months later, the reason became evident. The client shared the statistics of the cars sold with John. The client's goal was achieved: Not only had car sales increased, but during those six months, more blue cars were sold than any other color. The attendees had no idea why the color blue had surrounded them at the event, but John knew. He had mentally associated blue with a pleasant experience. The event had been a great success. The manufacturer continues to be John's client and to recommend his services to others.

John believes that there must be a good fit between the client and the corporate event manager and between the theme and the company's objectives. He is tenacious about uncovering the necessary information to meet the client's objectives. John is fully aware that what will succeed in one corporate culture may fail in another. When dealing with a corporate client, he does not blindly repeat the approaches that contributed to his success with a previous client. He does his homework, researching the corporate culture and identifying customer requirements, before he begins to plan an event.

Successful event managers make it a practice to talk with the client about the event in order to determine the event's purpose and what message the client wants to convey. Once the objective is determined, the event manager follows a systematic process to ensure that the event will meet the objective.

Corporate events may have many different goals. A corporate event is a part of the overall corporate communications strategy. It is a management function, and it is held to achieve a corporate goal. Therefore, it will be measured as other corporate projects are measured using the same financial metrics.

The Macy's Christmas parade, a recognition event at the Field Museum in Chicago, a retirement dinner at a local restaurant or hotel, an incentive award weekend at the America's Cup in San Diego, the seventieth anniversary celebration of *Forbes* magazine, the 2000 Olympics hospitality tent, or a book signing at Barnes & Noble are all examples of corporate events. Each of these events had a goal and incorporated aspects of the corporate culture. The goal may be to increase market share through public awareness or to improve the corporate image. The corporation may spend several million dollars on an event, and in return, it expects several million dollars or more in value (e.g., increased business). Having a clear view of the corporate event's goal and the metrics that will be used to assess the level or degree of achievement is critical to the event project manager's success. Does the client expect an increase in market share? Does it seek an improvement in public relations? Does it want high attendance in order to generate increased awareness of either the corporation in general or a particular product? How do the demographics of the attendees impact the plan? Is diversity of attendees an important consideration? If lower-level guests show up, will the event still be considered a success?

The role and scope of corporate events vary, ranging from a simple individual event to multiple events under the umbrella of a unifying theme. Before starting the project management process, the event manager must determine the role and scope of the event. What is the event's fit or purpose within the overall corporate strategy? A corporate event may have one or more purposes. The primary reasons corporations hold events are to educate, provide recognition, offer incentives, improve public relations, mark an important milestone, or launch a new product.

The purpose or goals of every corporate event must be clearly stated and included in the proposal for the event. In order to evaluate the event's success, there must be a clear and measurable statement of purpose. The goals should be evaluated continually during each of the event's planning stages to determine whether the original purpose has altered in any way. If it has, the event manager can make appropriate changes to keep decisions in line with the event's goals. The theme and the clear, measurable objectives are the guide for planning a successful event. In the end, it is easy to measure success if there is a process to ensure that the plan has been followed.

Target Audience Input

The target audience influences the event's role and affects both the event's goals and how the elements of the corporate culture—values, heroes, and rituals—will be positioned in the event. Is the event targeted toward the internal customer (such as sales, production, or management) or the external customer? The event manager can obtain information about the corporate culture as well as useful factual information about production and logistics by studying client records pertaining to past events as well as records from the client's sales/marketing personnel, managers, and human resources contacts. Focus groups can identify the expectations, needs, wants, and desires of these customers, which can be included in the goals for the event. Focus groups or other qualitative research can help determine whether the event planner's perception of the customer requirements is valid or there are hidden agendas. If there is a dichotomy between the goals of the stakeholder and those of the focus group, then consideration must be given to the findings.

Ellen Martin, an event planner for a major corporation, provided an example of how the target audience and the current situation at a company can impact the plans for an event. As the event manager for her corporation's annual picnic, her experience has been mixed. According to Martin, being creative can be a challenge. "You will have some folks who want to just do the same old thing and others who like to try something different." Martin does the "something different." The different attitudes often reflect the dynamics of the organization and its impacts on the employees. In the research/feasibility phase, there must be a complete understanding of what is going on within the corporation. The employees with whom the planner is working will be the key to the event's success. If there was a recent layoff and the client still wants an event, the event management may recommend doing something that will still be fun, but low key and not too extravagant, although the budget will dictate what is feasible.

Truly understanding the organization's position will determine its attitude toward the event and how the event is likely to be received. Although it's easy to come up with a great event in good times, it's challenging to create a successful event in bad times. Martin stated that in good times, the annual picnic was held at a location an hour's drive away in a park, on a mountain with limited bathroom facilities. She arranged all different types of activities, both on land and on the nearby lake, including swimming and paddle boat races. Employees stayed past 5:00 P.M. The event was always a success regardless of the distant location and limited facilities because of the positive attitude of the employees and the positive position of the organization. In bad times, it was another story: the annual picnic was held at a fully staffed facility only a ten-minute drive away. The event was viewed as something employees had to attend in order to be seen. One employee who worked at a virtual office two hours away drove down for lunch and then turned around and went home. Employees who were not affected by particular situations were fine, whereas others just wanted to show up, eat, and leave. How does the event planner make the challenging decision about whom to focus on and how to handle such situations? Martin said that since this event was not unique and offered few activities, guests left early. Although Martin did not plan this event, the postassessment team sought her expertise in debriefing the event. They concluded that a clearer focus on the goals and objectives with clear communication might have improved the success of the corporate event.

Martin noted that sometimes the challenge is not so much designing the event itself as understanding the "union rules." When labor or trade union personnel are involved, the event manager must understand what can and cannot be done. Obtaining this information is part of the research/feasibility stage of event project management. The union steward must be part of the organization chart. This person knows the culture of the union personnel as well as the rules for working with them. For example, is there a rule about taking union personnel off the premises? Does the event have to conclude by the end of their shift? (Otherwise, you may need to pay overtime.) You may also encounter shops that work 24/7. What arrangements can you make for those union members who have to stay back at the shop and work? The event is more than just what takes place at the designated location. Be creative and develop ideas for your client to help compensate those who must work during the event.

Corporate Politics

Dealing with union employees is not the only situation that can challenge the corporate event manager. Politics is by no means limited to the government. Every corporation has its politics. Every event is political. Care must be taken to ensure that event management does not fall into the typical corporate political traps. Identifying the real decision makers is the key to success in this area. In the corporate world, there are those who behave as if they were decision makers, but they lack the signing authority for fiscal matters that is generally equated with overall project management authority. Following the direction of such individuals can have negative impacts on both the event planner and the event itself. Some clients will want to use the event to improve their position with upper management, or they may try to use the event planner as a scapegoat for any failures on their part. The corporate event office must remain neutral and objective in a political environment. Objective fact finding and following the corporate event project management process are the best ways to avoid political entanglements and career-ending mistakes.

Mitzie, an event planner at a major manufacturing corporation, provided the following example of how adhering to the established process kept her out of a nasty political situation. Marketing managers are frequently speakers at corporate recognition and annual kickoff events. Three years ago, Mitzie was managing the annual sales kickoff event. She had enjoyed a positive and comfortable relationship with Jim, her primary interface in the marketing department. Jim was very pleasant and well organized, a delight to work with. He had provided detailed information on everything, including the audiovisual equipment required for the plenary session, to be held on Monday morning of the event week. Everything was running smoothly until the week before the event—when Jack arrived on the scene.

Jack was Jim's equal on the corporate ladder, but he was younger, aggressive, and much more demanding than Jim. He was determined to make his mark and climb the corporate ladder. During the rehearsal, Jack changed his audiovisual requirements and stated that he now wanted three very large special projection screens, three cameras, and seven slide projectors for his 20-minute presentation. His was to be a dynamic show intended to capture the interest of the attending sales representatives and the attention of upper management. Jack demanded that Mitzie call and arrange to have the additional equipment delivered immediately. She checked on the details of the request and obtained two bids at approximately $10,000 each. Adding $10,000 at this late hour would have put the event over its budget. Therefore, Mitzie followed the documented process and sought Jim's approval for the rental. Jack was furious, as he felt that he had equal power and his wishes should be accommodated. Mitzie and Jim met to discuss the request. They determined that, according to policy, they would have to consult Sue, the senior vice president of product marketing, for approval of the proposed budget overrun. As time passed, Jack became increasingly agitated. Finally, Jim and Mitzie reached Sue. After an in-depth discussion with them, followed by a phone call to Jack, Sue decided to approve a modified version of the equipment that Jack had requested. Although her estimated return on the investment did not match Jack's, she did see his point that more of a splash was required to capture the audience's attention. Since Mitzie remained calm throughout the conflict, she continues to receive business from the client. Sue and Jim were pleased with the way that Mitzie had worked with them and followed the established corporate event project management and problem resolution processes. Had she not done so, Mitzie could have encountered some serious problems.

Role of the Corporate Event Planner

The corporate event manager or corporate event officer must determine his or her role in the event project management process. The title, level, and role differ from one company to another. The event-planning function may be assigned to a professional corporate planner, who often resides in marketing, corporate communications, or human resources. Or it may be assigned to an already overburdened program manager or sales executive, who may, in turn, hire a professional event planner or delegate event planning to an administrative assistant. Some people in this position who lack experience in the event management world often underestimate the effort required to produce a successful event, especially a multielement event. Others perform this function frequently and do a tremendous job. The corporate event manager is really a ringmaster, a juggler, a magician, a wizard, and a strategist all in one. Balancing the directives of the executives with the process capabilities of the vendors while staying within the budget assigned by finance is a delicate balancing act. Fulfilling any one of these responsibilities is a remarkable feat in and of itself.

Regardless of the exact role of the corporate event manager, more and more corporations are requiring that the event management function follow the same project management process used by other operating departments and be measured by the same metrics.

As management expert Tom Peters says, "You are your projects."[3] Create your own role and celebrate your successes. In the next chapter, you will discover how to further define your role and achieve consistent success.

Wrap Up

1. The international corporate event market is the fastest growing arena in the event industry.
2. An understanding of corporate culture is critical to success as a corporate event manager.
3. Corporate cultures vary between corporations; therefore, an event designed for one company may be disaster for another company.
4. There must be a fit between the theme of the event and the goals and objectives of the client corporation.
5. Focus groups or other qualitative research can assist in matching the event design to the target audience.
6. Care must be taken to ensure that event management does not fall into the typical corporate political traps.
7. The role of the corporate event manager varies from corporation to corporation.

Instruments

Deal, Terrence E., and Allan A. Kennedy. *Corporate Cultures: The Rites and Rituals of Corporate Life.* Reading, Mass.: Perseus Books, 1982.

Fast Company, Fast Company Media Group LLC, New York, New York, May 1999 Issue page 116 article The WOW Projects by Tom Peters

GE Schenectady Business News 13, no. 7 (Dec. 3, 1999). Excerpts.

Goldblatt, Joe Jeff. *Special Events: The Art and Science of Celebration.* New York: Van Nostrand Reinhold, 1990.

Soukhanov, Anne H. US General Editor, *Microsoft Encarta College Dictionary* (New York: St Martin's Press, 2001).

Pine, Joseph B., II, and James H. Gilmore. *The Experience Economy.* Boston: Harvard Business School Press, 1999.

Points for Discussion and Practice

1. Describe the values, vision points, and corporate culture of your corporate organization or others you are familiar with. How does this culture support or hinder the development of successful events? How can you enhance the positive effects of this culture and minimize its negative effects through effective corporate event project management?

2. Visit the Web sites and read the annual reports of six different major corporations and look for clues to their corporate cultures.

3. Compare the cultural elements of these corporations.

4. Find examples of corporate events in your newspaper or on a Web news site.

5. What are the goals of these events?

6. List the possible target audiences for these corporate events.

7. Interview a corporate event manager and discuss the following:
   a. Corporate culture
   b. Role of the event planner
   c. Types of events managed
   d. Typical event goal

CHAPTER 2

The Corporate Event Project Management Process

THIS CHAPTER WILL HELP YOU:

- Describe the basic concepts of the project management process
- Create a product breakdown structure
- Create a work breakdown structure
- Classify the scheduling of a task as serial or parallel
- Describe milestones and create the critical path of a corporate event

---

The central concepts of the baseline plan and the event project life cycle are critical considerations for corporate event managers. Next, basic project management methodology must be mastered. The concept of the scope of work and its decomposition into manageable units must be utilized. Finally, a discussion of the scheduling tools of project management must be incorporated and used. This methodology is described as the fundamental process of corporate event project management.

Figure 2-1

Division of Corporate Event Management into Areas of Responsibility

Management Areas

Project management as a body of knowledge has been distilled from the experience of countless projects around the world. From the campaigns of Alexander the Great to NASA's lunar-landing achievements, a systematic methodology underpins all these successes. It is only with the advent of the computer and the Internet that the similarities among projects have become so obvious. Like managers in any other project-based industry, such as construction or information technology (IT), the manager of an event must control various areas, which are listed in Figure 2-1. All these areas need planning and plan implementation. They will require different amounts of attention throughout the life of the corporate event, which is referred to as the event project life cycle. Should the event manager lose focus on any one of these areas, the event will almost certainly face serious problems.

Baseline Plan

Each of the areas of project management shown in Figure 2-1 requires a plan. Unlike most administrative management plans, the project management process requires the creation of a baseline plan. The emphasis of the administrative management plan is on sticking to the plan. A baseline plan, however, is something that can be varied, and having a baseline enables the event manager to recognize and measure any variations. Creating a baseline plan therefore implies creating a method for recognizing and controlling the variations. If the variations are large enough, they may warrant a change in the baseline plan. The budget, for example, is a baseline plan. Few events adhere exactly to their budget. Most clients recognize that there will be some maneuvering so that the event will meet the corporate objectives. Another baseline plan is the event's program. This will usually change as the speakers, vendors, talent, and so forth are contracted and the elements are fleshed out. This is an evolving process. The risk management baseline plan will need to be reviewed continually, particularly if there are any variations in the other plans. The inescapable conclusion is that the plan will change.

Event Project Life Cycle

As the event moves from concept to planning to implementation, the priorities of corporate event management will change and the focus will shift. To assist in controlling the whole evolving system, the concept of the event project life cycle is introduced. Planning constitutes a significant part of corporate event project management. It is a process of mentally fitting all the components together. It includes foreseeing any problems and their solutions. However, since the event manager cannot predict all possible problems, it is more realistic to regard corporate event planning as a method for reducing the number of problems. In this sense, the aim of event planning is to plan all the tasks that can be planned so that changes and unforeseen problems can be dealt with in a focused way. Although most aspects of the corporate event can be organized, the fluidity of event preparation means that the unexpected will always be a factor.

The basic tenet of corporate event management, then, is that changes will occur as the event is organized. The staff will grow as the event nears. Some event companies go from 2 people during the early concept stages to more than 1000 staff and volunteers on the day of the event. The concept of the corporate event project life cycle, illustrated in Figure 2-2, is a metaphor for the growth and changes that occur during the planning and implementation process.

Any type of corporate event begins with an idea or a concept. The first question to ask is, "Is it feasible?" The answer is fed back into the concept (iteration), and the concept may need to be further developed. Once the event

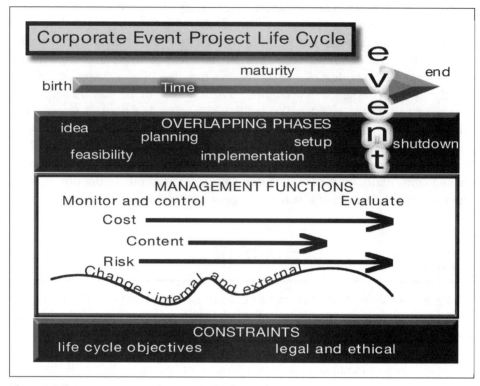

Figure 2-2
Phases and Functions over the Event Life Cycle

concept looks feasible, planning can start. This is not a mechanical or linear model. During the planning process, opportunities or risks may be uncovered that require modifying the event concept. Some aspects of the plan may be implemented while other aspects are still in the planning phase. For example, promoting the event may start well before site planning. All these processes feed into one another. Some aspects of shutdown may begin during setup. The areas of risk, content, and cost—as well as the schedule—have to be managed throughout the corporate event project life cycle. A risk may be very different over the course of the life cycle. This means that the event plan is not a static document.

The only certainty is that there will be change. Predictable internal changes include the increase in the event staff and the increase in contract management, as more suppliers become involved. Unexpected internal changes may also occur. The event company or corporate event office may take on other events while the original event is being planned. External change could involve the all-too-common change of venue, or it could occur on a grander scale, as with a fluctuation in the foreign currency exchange rate.

No matter what change occurs, the event will need to work within constraints set by the client—such as achieving the desired return on investment or making a profit—or by legal and ethical considerations. The client-set constraints establish the stated objectives within which the corporate event project life cycle functions. There may be far subtler constraints implied by the client's working environment, such as the corporate culture.

Scale

The written corporate event plan can be as short as one page or as long as a book, depending on the level of detail in the planning. The level of detail, in turn, depends on such factors as:

- Complexity of the corporate event
- Scale of the event
- Familiarity of the event management, staff, and suppliers with the particular type of event
- Legal and stakeholder requirements
- Time and other resources allocated to the planning task

The process of writing a plan aids in structuring the event. The plan is also a communication tool and a project baseline from which the event can be measured. It is not "carved in stone," however, and will need to be revised as the organization of the corporate event life cycle proceeds.

There is always a risk that the written plan will become the master of the event rather than a tool for staging a successful event. The ASSESS → PLAN → IMPLEMENT → EVALUATE procedure is an oversimplification of a complex series of overlapping processes. Corporate event planning is also a complex blend of art and science. This explains event managers' reluctance to create mission statements and objectives. In the volatile environment of event organization, these can easily become millstones around the neck of the event management staff. Although it might seem as if there were enough to do without having to constantly revisit and rework all the objectives, it is important to take the time to revisit them, as they keep the event on track. It is easy to get off on a creative tangent or become sidetracked by a problem—either of which may leave the event manager with an event that does not meet the stakeholders' stated objectives. If time is taken to ensure that the objectives are correct and current, then it will be easy to respond to requests for changes or additions. Decisions about such requests are based on how each proposed change or addition will affect the achievement of the stated objectives.

Also, there is a tendency by some authors to see planning as the panacea for all event problems, stressing poor planning as the cause for major failures of corporate events. This statement is all too easy to make and is the result of 20/20 hindsight. If planning is defined as foreseeing all problems before they arise, then, ipso facto, there has not been enough planning. This is a good example of turning a historical description into a prescription. In the real world of event organizing, change (and problems) can come from anywhere and at any time during the event project life cycle.

A regional manager or senior executive may cancel the event based on changing economic conditions, or all the event equipment may end up in Hawaii rather than Houston. Based on the recent downturn in the stock market values of the dot-com companies, several corporate event planners we know were faced with the need to cancel events and distribute liquidating damage payments to the suppliers. Although a process-oriented person might have said that such a possibility should have been considered in the plan, it was not considered because times were good and things were moving fast. No one saw the swift economic downturn coming. Also, no one knew if the Federal Reserve Board would raise or lower interest rates and what impact such action would have on the economy.

In another case, a manufacturing corporation had double-confirmed every item on its checklist for a trade show in Paris. Weekly meetings had been held with the core team members. In the last week before the event, daily telephone conferences with the corporate event planner's counterpart in Paris confirmed that all processes were in place and that the event was moving forward like a well-oiled machine. Unfortunately, the truckers called a strike just as the equipment arrived in France. With strikers blocking every road into Paris, the clock was ticking down toward the start of the event. Fortunately, after many telephone calls and lots of negotiation, the equipment was brought in circuitously by train. In this case, the incident that caused the strike was totally unforeseen.

The result of any change in a complex system made up of a fixed number of related variables cannot be predicted. For example, if setting up for an event involves 200 tasks, and one of these tasks changes or a new task is introduced, the relationships among all the tasks may change. And the changed relationships may, in turn, produce further changes, and so on ad infinitum. In other words, a small change can easily have unforeseen repercussions.

Project and Corporate Event Management

All projects have certain things in common, regardless of whether the work involves implementing a new software program, developing a new item to be manufactured, making a movie, or managing and producing an event. Therefore, the processes by which projects are managed hold a fascination for corporate event managers. Here are some of the many characteristics that projects share:

- They are time based: every aspect of a project has a time constraint.
- They are unique and involve either using new resources or using standard resources in a new combination.
- They have start and finish dates.
- They involve considerable unfamiliarity and the possibility of unforeseen risks.
- The level of activity varies over the duration of the project.
- They constitute a dynamic system subject to change from internal and external sources.

This is not to say that all the traditional methods of project management—as described, for example, in the *Guide to the Project Management Body of Knowledge*—are directly transferable to corporate event management. There are many tools to help a project manager identify the completion date of a project, which can vary slightly in the engineering and IT industries. In the event-planning field, however, there is no room for variation: the event cannot be held slightly later. An event company cannot suggest to its client that the New Year's Eve party be put back a few days. Change and dynamic decision making are far more critical in the event management field. With the speed of change in other industries, the traditional project management models are now less applicable and have been replaced by newer models, which include time to market and total quality management. However, project management tools are important and can help not only in planning and controlling the event but in evaluating and documenting it as well.

In summary, the event organization or corporate event office develops what has to be accomplished, divides it into manageable units, assigns resources, and schedules the work units efficiently. This process, illustrated in Figure 2-3, is dynamic and must continually be reviewed as conditions change.

WHY USE PROJECT MANAGEMENT PROCESSES FOR CORPORATE EVENTS?

The rapidly changing world of business is producing economies that must respond quickly to change. The traditional company model, with its pyramid structure of responsibilities and authority and functional departments, cannot

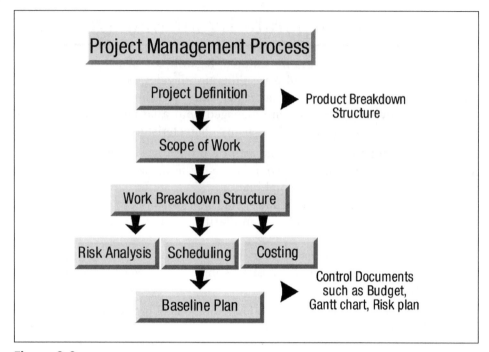

Figure 2-3
Flowchart of the Project Management Process

change quickly enough. There is an abundance of current literature on this subject. A prime example of this development is the effect of constant increases in computer processing speed, which make it a competitive disadvantage for companies to stick with their existing software and hardware. Companies must constantly be aware of new software and hardware. Of interest is the recent development of object-oriented technology. The complexity of traditional structured programming has created a need to break the overall tasks done by software into smaller units. The units, or objects, are then recombined in various configurations to produce the desired results. This pattern of breaking up the work into manageable tasks is the basis for project management. The increased use of project management is a response to the inability of traditional organizational structure and methods to deal with the new economic fluidity. Companies are now rightsizing and reorganizing into a work group structure that is more nimble and better able to respond to change.

The event industry is not immune to this situation. In part, it is fueling it. Special events are used to bring about change within a corporation, a region, or a country. The merger of two major companies is made known to all the suppliers and the press and is celebrated by an event. The event helps the employees and, in some cases, the general public to accept the change in corporate culture brought about by the merger. Acceptance of new products and new ways of doing business is strengthened through the use of special events. Conferences and exhibitions are ways to create a change in attitudes, strategies, and business methods. Factors that create the need for a systematic and accountable approach to the actual management of events include the increasing size, number, and economic importance of events; the requirement for thorough accountability to stakeholders; the complexity of events and the risks associated with them; the rules and regulations affecting events; and the cross-border status of many events. The event management process also includes the associated documentation that will facilitate communication with all parties involved in the event, including progress and justification reports to the stakeholders.

Project management offers the corporate event manager a number of advantages, which include:

- **Establishing a systematic approach to all events:** Today, the corporate event can no longer be regarded as a one-time proposition, with the techniques and skills being reinvented for the next event. Events have become an integral part of business for both corporations and governments. Having a consistent method means that the corporate event management, clients, and sponsors can learn from each event and identify areas that need improvement, thus developing better events. All the stakeholders will know what is happening and how they fit into the event as a whole. Establishing schedules, tasks, and responsibilities that fit into an overall system lets all parties involved in the event know what they have to do and when they have to do it.
- **Depersonalizing the event:** Knowledge about the event resides in the company as a whole rather than in a select few individuals. In the past, most corporate events required the full force of one personality or a small core group to make them work. The methods, deals, and skills resided in that person or those persons, and the event was a reflection of their style. This was fine when the corporate event industry was in its infancy, but the growth in the number and economic importance of events no longer allows this luxury. The planning and implementation system must be independent of any one person. This is why some event managers are reluctant to implement a systemic approach. It detracts from their power and mystique.

- **Facilitating clear communication:** Using a common terminology throughout the event and with the stakeholders enables effective decision making. Project management terms are ideally suited to communication among teams from different fields. The corporate event management team will have to communicate with the finance and marketing departments, for example, and project management terminology is becoming part of the language of those departments as well. Project management offers a transparent system for communicating tasks and responsibilities through meetings and documents.

- **Conforming to the methodology used by other departments:** Many corporations, both public and private, are undergoing some kind of restructuring, which generally is being project-managed. This means that the methodology of project management will have infiltrated most of the event's stakeholders. It will already have some presence in the company's functional departments, such as information technology, product development, and human resources.

- **Ensuring accountability:** The document outputs of the project management process mean that the corporate event will be fully accountable to the stakeholders. Event management can track a complex event, and clients/sponsors can obtain a progress report at any time.

- **Increasing the visibility of event planning:** Too often, the corporate event management team is not seen to be working. The most visible result of the planning process is the event itself. All the work that went into the event is often hidden from senior management or the stakeholders. No matter how much work was involved, if an event is successful, it may be regarded as easy to put together. A project management approach with the right reporting and documentation makes the entire process visible to the client.

- **Facilitating training:** Having a methodology means that staff and volunteers can be expeditiously trained. One output of the project management process is the corporate event manual, which can be used for training. When a system is in place, new staff members can more easily understand their responsibilities and see how their work fits into the whole picture.

- **Developing transferable skills:** Working in a systematic project management environment means that the skills learned are not only relevant to the event industry but may be adapted to other project management areas as well. When prospective staff members know they will come out of the experience with transferable skills, the event manager will have much greater success in attracting good people.

- **Establishing a diverse body of knowledge:** Project management involves the accumulation and refinement of the experience, skills, and knowledge of innumerable projects around the world, ranging from NASA's moon-landing missions to the implementation of a new software system for a local firm. Event management can learn from the mistakes and successes of all these projects.

PROJECT SCOPE AND DEFINITION

When a client asks a corporate event manager to create and manage an event, it is not always obvious what the client has in mind by "the event." Because the event may be one of a kind, specifying exactly what the event entails is the first step in event project management. This often involves a combination of objectives, some straightforward and others less obvious or covert.

A useful concept from the methodology of project management is the "project definition." It is regarded as the first step in the entire process. For event management, it means formalizing the understanding of what the client really wants—whether the client is the government, a corporation, or a charity. The project definition may be far more than the "event brief," as it includes input from the event management company or corporate event office as well as a statement of purpose from the client. It could also be called a statement of understanding plus an outline of the work, responsibilities, schedule, and budget. Equivalent terms are *project charter* or *statement of work* (SOW), the latter being a useful concept from the construction industry. These terms are used commonly by organizations in areas other than event management and are the standard terminology in modern business.

The project definition can be as detailed as necessary, although one page may suffice. It is at this stage that the guidelines—and the future directions—are set. Of particular importance will be the responsibilities of the sponsor/client and its organizations and the responsibilities of the internal or external corporate event management. If the client's resources—such as accounting, legal, and promotion—are being used to create the event, it is advisable to have some guidelines regarding how much of those resources can be committed to the event.

The guideline document may contain the following headings:

- Corporate event description—with mission statement, vision, and key objectives
- Roles and responsibilities of the principal parties
- List of stakeholders, such as marketing, human resources, public relations, government agency, or charitable sponsor

- Scope of work
- Draft schedule with milestones
- Basic assumptions (which may change over time)
- Budget with cash flow structure
- Signature authority and limitations

The statement of work cannot be expected to specify all the work involved in putting together a corporate event. However, it will provide a baseline and a memorandum of understanding from which to launch the next step in the process. It may also contain a section outlining the procedure for making any changes to this baseline.

PRODUCT BREAKDOWN STRUCTURE

A technique used in traditional project management is to create a product breakdown structure (PBS). The "product" is the corporate event itself and could include such activities as an industry exhibition, a conference dinner with entertainment, a team-building harbor cruise, or a cocktail party with networking opportunities. It is important to list the entire product and not ignore the more subtle aspects of the event. For example, the objectives of holding an event to celebrate a company opening or sponsoring a community event could be to impress the state government or to improve public relations. The product breakdown structure is a way of establishing not only client requirements in terms of the goals and objectives but also a common language for the event. As well, any hidden objectives may surface through this process. Common assumptions need to be stated and noted in the minutes or at least put on paper. It is handy to be able to refer to these common assumptions as the event is being planned and the plan implemented. Documentation is also useful when senior management wants an update or when things go awry and the culprit is sought.

The product breakdown structure can also be used to establish the organizational structure. For example, the company year-end party with a wide-ranging PBS would be managed by a committee system. This has many advantages, because committees can respond easily to growth in the event. An extra element of the event can be managed by an additional committee formed specifically to manage that element. If the event requires specialized services beyond the capabilities of the corporate event management staff, it may have to be outsourced or put out to bid. A PBS provides both the client and the event management staff with a clear view of the overall event requirements.

WORK BREAKDOWN STRUCTURE

Once the event has been defined—at least in draft form—the next stage is to analyze the work involved in planning and implementing the event. This is a process of decomposition whereby a complex project is broken up into smaller units of work that can be easily managed. The result is called a work breakdown structure (WBS). The units are commonly called activities or tasks. Hence, the process is called task analysis. A task or an activity has the following characteristics:

- It generally has a single purpose and can be managed as a discrete entity.
- It has specific start and finish times.
- It requires clearly assigned resources.

For example, activities involved in holding a sports event could include the catering for the competitors and the setup of the generators.

A corporate event may be divided into these units according to various criteria, such as by:

- Program element (e.g., what activities are scheduled at the event—an exhibition, a formal dinner, tours)
- On-site location or position (e.g., in front of the building)
- Function (e.g., finance, sound, entertainment, awards, registration)

Generally, a mixture of all three criteria is used, as the aim is to identify small, manageable units that can be assigned to subcontractors or the event staff. The treelike configuration of the work breakdown structure means that the WBS can grow or be refined as the planning nears the event date. The first-level categorization of a large event may be by location on-site, such as "venue 1: conference center," and then by function at that area of the event. Or it may be divided by event management function, such as logistics, accommodation, catering, protocol, or venue layout. Whatever first-level categorization is chosen, it should be general enough so that nothing will be left out. The right grouping or categorization at a higher level means that, as each level is expanded, it will include all the work. The aim is to make sure that nothing slips through the cracks.

The work breakdown structure can also be used to create a coding system for the whole event. These codes can be similar to the process of outlining: they define the levels of the structure. Good codes will be easily recognized by the staff and still be usable as a way of consolidating and sorting all the event data. They can be used as the cost codes for corporate finance, too. The coding can be completely numeric or alphanumeric. A training seminar and an exhibition, for example, would first be broken into S (for seminar) and X (for exhibition). The WBS for the seminar could be venue (V), presenters (P), registration (R), catering (C), and equipment (E). So the cost for the equipment for the seminar would carry the code SE.

Figure 2-4 depicts an actual example of a WBS draft for an awards night in the city. Because the event was held by an engineering company, it was especially important to get the audiovisual aspects of the program exactly right. Hence, the audiovisual component became a separate category in this case.

The WBS shown in Figure 2-4 was used as both a product breakdown structure and a work breakdown structure. It enabled the corporate event manager to scope the event with the client. In this way, "who does what" was clearly outlined at the beginning of the event planning. An important aspect of scoping is to know the limitations of the work required—in other words, what does *not* have to be done. However, the elements in Figure 2-4 were not specified in enough detail to permit all the necessary tasks to be determined and properly assigned. The next step was to expand each of those elements (e.g., "Band," as shown in Figure 2-5) to the next level of detail.

Figure 2-6 shows a piece of the next (third) level of the task analysis for one second-level task. Here, all the band entertainment is broken down into

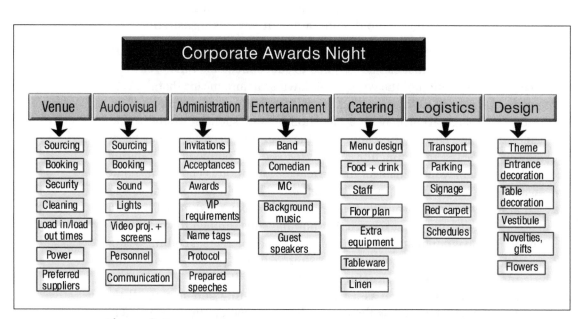

Figure 2-4
Work Breakdown Structure of an Award Ceremony

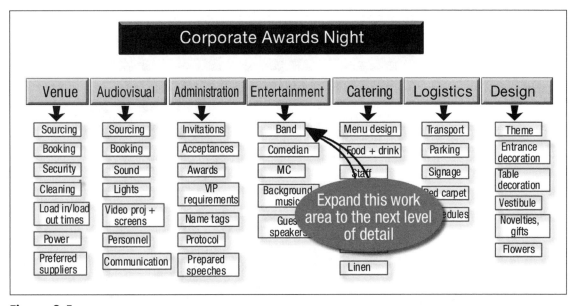

Figure 2-5
Expanding One of the Many Work Areas

separate tasks that may be undertaken by different people with specialized skills. Contracting, for example, may be handled by the legal department.

Many of these tasks can be used as cost centers, becoming the "line elements" in a budget. The costs for the entire event can then be found by adding the costs for the activities. The work breakdown structure is the basic graphical representation of event project management. It is easily understood by the corporate event staff, client, sponsors, and volunteers and gives a quick reference for any aspect of the event. Its degree of accuracy, which is indicative rather than measurable, is comparable to the changing event planning environment—that is, it doesn't bog down the plan. Note that there are various ways to divide up the work. The first division may be by physical place at the event. This is quite common when there are a number of staging areas and different teams managing them. This alternative way to divide the awards night is shown in Figure 2-7. For example, the main stage area work is divided into seven subareas of responsibility—lectern, audiovisual, chairs, décor, video projection and screens, media, and master of ceremonies and stage management. The WBS should be regarded as a tool or a means to an end and is successful as long as it captures all the work that has to be done and lets nothing slip through the cracks.

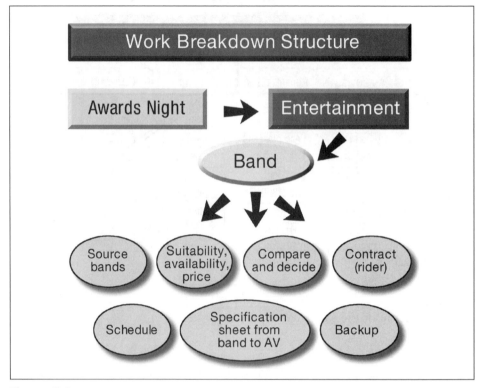

Figure 2-6
Expanding the Band Element of an Evening's Entertainment

SCOPE CREEP

An important term that will be recognized by most practicing event managers is *scope creep.* This refers to the gradual expansion of the amount of work to be done. It occurs after the work breakdown structure has been completed and often goes unnoticed by the busy event office until it is too late to change its cause or limit the damage. It can arise from the client's changing an aspect of the event—the client or sponsor suddenly decides to change the venue, for example. This can result in an unrecognized increase in the amount of work to be done by event management. Very small decisions during the planning phase can exponentially increase the scope of work. Scope creep can have external causes, such as changes in the country's law or fluctuations in the exchange rate. These are beyond the control of event management. Internal causes can be controlled by establishing procedures for any change in scope. This would include documentation, such as a change form that must be com-

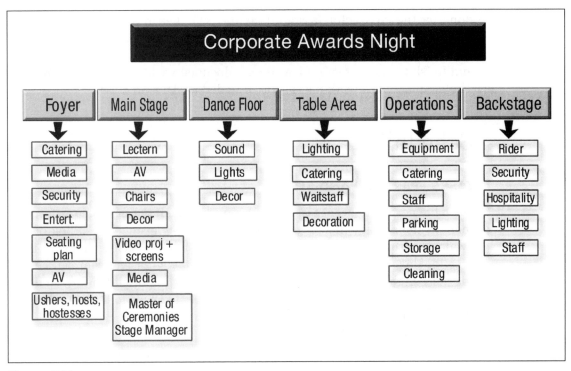

Figure 2-7
Alternative Division of the Work

pleted and approved before any change can be made. It is a trade-off decision for the corporate event management team. Is the increasing bureaucratization of forms to be filled out worth the diminution of trust and independence of the event team? Some changes are so all-encompassing that the core team must meet to discuss the ramifications of the proposed change and determine whether the change is truly necessary and whether it will impact the feasibility of the event.

WORK PACKAGE

Once the corporate event has been broken down into activities or tasks (tasks are often looked on as subunits of activities and miniprojects in themselves), they have to be assigned to a responsible person or group of people. Tasks may be grouped together to form a work package. Thus, a multistage event, such as a product launch, may have sound setup and operation as different tasks for each stage. However, they would be grouped into the one work package done by the contractor (a sound company). They represent a continuous amount of work for the contractor, which has the appropriate resources, with start and finish dates and times. This grouping of tasks with the overall start and finish times is often indicated on a document sent out to the contractors. The template for a work package is provided as Appendix 1D.

Scheduling

TASKS—PARALLEL AND SERIAL

Once the corporate event tasks have been identified, the next step is to place them in their most efficient order for the corporate event. Depending on the available resources, some tasks can be done simultaneously, whereas others must be done sequentially. For example, advertising for an event can be taking place at the same time as suppliers are contracted, provided the same person does not perform both tasks. However, the site needs to be cleared before the tents arrive.

Tasks can be divided into:

- **Parallel:** can be performed at the same time, as they require different resources and the satisfaction of different preconditions
- **Serial:** must be performed in sequence due to resource availability or necessary preconditions

The tasks must first be sorted by their immediate predecessors. What tasks have to be completed before this task can start? For instance, the audiovisual equipment can't arrive and be set up and operated until the security is in place. Given the number of tasks that may be involved in a complex event, this initial sorting process can be a daunting task in itself. For smaller events, planners often use sticky notes (e.g., Post-it Notes™)—one to a task—and place them on a large board. The notes are then rearranged to get the optimum sequence. This "system" has the advantage of being very flexible and allows planners to respond quickly to suddenly changing conditions, such as a corporate client changing its mind about the venue or preferred caterer.

Figure 2-8 is an overview of the amount of activity performed by an event company or the corporate event office. Initially, there are the tasks involved in proposal preparation, or obtaining the work. If successful in the bid, the event management goes into overdrive in both planning and preparing for the event. As all the other aspects get under way, there is a period of control, ensuring that everything is running according to plan, and the occasional flurry

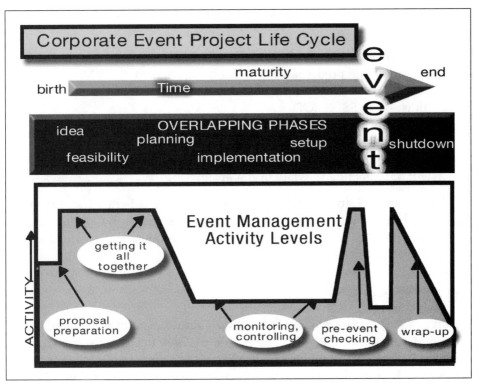

Figure 2-8
Corporate Event Project Life Cycle, Showing the Changes in the Amount of
Activity

of activity if a problem or change occurs. Just before the event, the management team needs to check and make any last-minute alterations. During the event, the manager should have little else to do except oversee the production. However, there are always unexpected emergencies, such as attendees' becoming ill, unplanned increases in the number of guests, or a change in the weather. During event shutdown, the corporate event manager's skills in controlling and responding to different conditions come into full play again.

TIMELINES

The timeline for each task must be estimated. How long will each task take given the right resources and preconditions? This duration, commonly called the estimated completion time (ECT), often has to be determined by expert guesswork! In engineering project management, there are four estimated values:

1. **Earliest start (ES):** the earliest date/time that a task can be started after its immediate predecessor task has been finished
2. **Earliest finish (EF):** the earliest date/time that the task can be finished (thus, EF = ES + ECT)
3. **Latest start (LS):** the latest date/time that the task can be started without affecting the date of the event
4. **Latest finish (LF):** the latest date/time that the task can be finished without affecting the date of the event.

The LF and LS are critical to event planning, as it is rare that the event date will change. "When will it be completed?" is one of the questions most often heard from event managers. The answer becomes more critical as the day of the event draws closer.

THE GANTT CHART

Planning a corporate event can involve an enormous number of people from different backgrounds and with different levels of education. Every extra person or subcontractor involved means that extra channels of communication are needed. In turn, this means that effective communication can produce significant savings in cost and time. Graphical displays can impart information quickly across many different work cultures. The Gantt chart, or bar chart, is such a display. If kept simple, it can show the major tasks and when they need to be completed. Such charts can be used in event proposals to illustrate the schedule or in discussions with the subcontractors to show how the success of the event depends on their punctuality. Combined with the work breakdown schedule, the Gantt chart demonstrates a management competency that enhances any event proposal.

Figure 2-9 shows a simple Gantt chart for the room setup for a seminar presentation. It contains just the right level of detail to summarize the activities for the client.

CRITICAL TASKS AND THE CRITICAL PATH

Much of the corporate event manager's skill lies in recognizing priority in a list of tasks. Some tasks must be completed on time. Other tasks have a float—that is, their completion time is not the latest finish time. Each of these types of tasks must be given its proper attention. The sequence of tasks that have

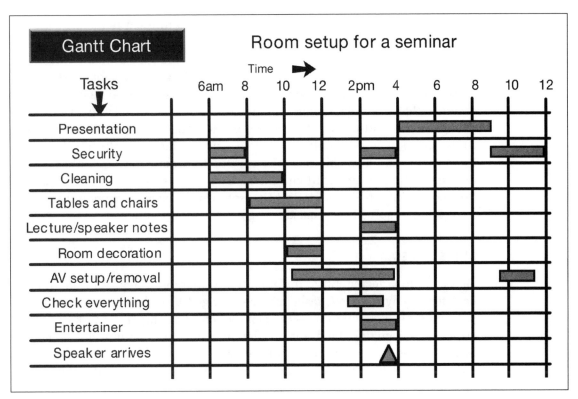

Figure 2-9
Time Chart for the Day of a Small Seminar

no buffer time is the critical path. Each task along the critical path absolutely must be completed on time, even if it costs more resources or means a change in the content of the event. At an outdoor hospitality event, so many of the tasks depend on the arrival and setup of the generator that it is regarded as a critical task. Once the generator is set up, the tents can be erected, and the caterers can get to work. While all this is happening, the decorators can do their work at the site entrance. If the generator doesn't function, the event manager is faced with a number of alternatives—all of which will consume resources (money and people's time) or change the nature of the event.

There are a variety of books on recognizing the critical path (some are recommended at the end of the chapter) through both estimation and computer software. Suffice it to say that because corporate events exist in an ever-changing environment, the tasks that are regarded as noncritical can become critical very quickly. It must be recognized that, although the critical path method is helpful, it is not set in concrete. Trying to identify the critical path by using computer software illustrates a current limitation of project management software. All the tasks involved in an event are linked in one way or another. If there are 100 tasks, then there are 5050 links. Change one task and all these links need to be updated. The resources must be recalculated. All this assumes that the links themselves remain valid. As is stressed in this text, change is part and parcel of corporate event management. Unfortunately, the fluid nature of most events is just too complex for this software. However, there is software available that will construct a Gantt chart and other critical documentation in an unlinked state. One can use elements of Microsoft Project or even create charts in Microsoft Word, Excel, or some other word-processing or spreadsheet package.

MILESTONES

Tasks are, to a degree, fluid, meaning that if there is a change in the internal or external environment, tasks may be changed to make sure the event happens on time. The milestone—the completion of an important task—becomes critical in organizing the event. In planning an event, the milestones need to be recognized and given prominence. In smaller events, milestones such as the arrival of the chairman of the board or another senior executive may be the only scheduling tool.

Influence Diagrams and Sensitivity Analysis

Influence diagrams and sensitivity analysis are tools of project management used to better understand the way change can affect the event. The influence diagram is a chart that shows, by means of boxes and arrows, what tasks are dependent on others. It is often a sketch to enable a better understanding of the many facets of an event. In particular, it demonstrates that a corporate event is a system and that a change in one area of the event can have ramifications in many other areas. For example, changes in an event's program can make a considerable difference in the security requirements. If an important politician agrees at the last minute to open an event, it will have a very significant effect on security planning.

Discovering the degree of influence that any part of an event has on the event as a whole is the aim of sensitivity analysis. In part, it is a risk management strategy: how will a small change in this area affect the overall event?

For example, a corporate event manager in Brussels decided to change one of the speakers for the opening ceremony based on a new technological breakthrough. This decision did not have a major impact in terms of resource requirements. It had a positive effect on attendance but a negative effect on the turnaround time for the programs and the associated costs. Fortunately, the change occurred before the programs were printed but not before they had been designed and set up for printing.

Outputs

The analysis involved in the project management process results in the creation of graphs, charts, and other event documents, some of which include contact sheets, responsibility charts, activity sheets, work packages, registration forms, and evaluation sheets. These documents can also be used as the basis for the event manual, as a history of the event, and as a method for comparing events.

Scalability

An advantage of the project management process is that it can be used on small areas of the corporate event as well as on the event as a whole. A common area for the use of a work breakdown schedule and the Gantt chart is in the marketing of the event. What must be done to market the event is broken down into manageable units, given a timeline, and placed on a chart. Creating a bid document or an event proposal also easily lends itself to the project management process. The setup and breakdown of the event venue, or site, is another area. All these subprocesses are then placed on a master schedule. Project management software can accommodate all these separate functional areas of corporate event planning. An outline command can be used to summarize the plan by displaying only its section headings or expand the plan by displaying all the details within the sections.

Corporate Event Program Management

An event company or a corporate event office will inevitably have a number of events in various stages of planning and implementation. This is similar to what is called program management. Unfortunately, the term *program management* has two meanings. It can mean managing a number of separate events, each of which has a different client. The only relationship among these events is that they are run by the same company or by the central corporate event office and share some of the company's resources.

Program management can also mean managing a very large event (such as the Olympic Games) comprised of a number of projects running at the same time. All the projects have their own management teams and deliverables that contribute to the whole event. The program manager's role is to keep all these "subevents" on track.

Figure 2-8 showed the activity level of an event management company or a corporate event office over the course of the corporate event project life cycle. During the monitoring period, when the office has the fewest tasks, an event company will look for more work, that is, another event. The aim is to keep the workload constant. This is an example of resource leveling.

Some large companies are becoming increasingly project driven in response to the rapidly changing business environment and the need to get products out to customers as quickly as possible. This development is having an impact on event management, because such companies are developing a project culture, in which projects within the organization compete for resources. Criteria for project selection and approval are established, and the winning projects will be those that support the companies' overall business strategy.

The core of project management is its process, analysis, and synthesis using time as the master. This methodology is consistent across the whole corporate event. It can be applied to any phase of event management and combined for the entire event. Such a methodology is necessary for the full professionalization of the growing corporate event management industry.

Wrap Up

1. The central concepts of a baseline plan and the event management life cycle are critical considerations for the corporate event project manager.

2. Creation of a baseline plan enables the event manager to recognize and control variations.

3. The event project life cycle is a metaphor for the growth and changes that occur during the planning and implementation process.

4. The corporate event plan is a communication tool and a project baseline from which the event can be measured.

5. Responding to change and dynamic decision making are critical success factors in the event management field.

6. The event management organization develops what must be accomplished and breaks it into manageable units, assigns resources, and schedules the work units efficiently.

7. A systematic and accountable approach to

corporate events is required due to size, complexity, economics, fiscal responsibility, risk, and rules and regulations.

8. Project management offers a systematic approach to all events, depersonalizes the event, facilitates clear communication, conforms to methodologies used by other departments, ensures accountability, increases the visibility of the planning effort, facilitates training, develops transferable skills, and establishes a diverse body of knowledge.

9. The Statement of Work or Project Charter formalizes the client's request and specifies what the event entails.

10. The product breakdown structure organizes the project into discrete elements. It establishes client requirements in terms of goals and objectives.

11. The work breakdown structure breaks the event into smaller units of work that can be easily managed.

12. The amount of work to be done can gradually increase, causing what is termed scope creep.

13. A work package is an activity or group of tasks assigned to a person or a group.

14. Timelines for each task must be estimated and monitored. Milestones are the completion of an important task.

15. The sequence of tasks that have no buffer time is called the critical path. Each task on the critical path must be completed on time for the event to occur on time and be successful.

16. Tools such as charts and graphs can assist the event management staff and the client in understanding the impact of change as well as create a history of the event or compare the event to similar events.

Instruments

The following project management books will provide you with additional information to improve your corporate projects.

Kliem, R., et al. *Project Management Methodology: A Practical Guide for the Next Millennium.* New York: Marcel Dekker, 1997.

Kliem, R., and S. Ludin. *Tools and Tips for Today's Project Managers.* Newtown Square, Penn.: Project Management Institute, 1999. A good dictionary of the main terms used in everyday project management.

Project Management Institute. *A Guide to the Project Management Body of Knowledge* (PMBOK). Sylva, N.C.: Project Management Institute, 2000. This 200-page document can be downloaded from the Internet and is the standard in traditional project management. To find it, enter "PMBOK" in a search engine.

Thomsett, M. *The Little Black Book of Project Management.* New York: AMACOM, 1990. A wonderful short introduction, easy to read, and it keeps within the limits of traditional project management.

Turner, J. R. *The Handbook of Project-Based Management.* Maidenhead, Berkshire, U.K.: McGraw-Hill, 1999. An advanced text with many examples.

Weiss, J., and R. Wysocki. *Five-Phase Project Management: A Practical Planning and Implementation Guide.* Reading, Mass.: Addison-Wesley, 1992. This is a good introduction to the process and uses planning a conference as an example.

The following books are for those interested in hard-core project management.

Badiru, A., and P. Pulat. *Comprehensive Project Management: Integrating Optimization Models, Management Principles, and Computers.* Upper Saddle River, N.J.: Prentice-Hall, 1995.

Schuyler, J. *Decision Analysis in Projects.* Sylva, N.C.: PMI Communications, 1996.

Points for Discussion and Practice

1. Describe how you would use the project management system to produce the following events:
   a. A corporate anniversary with two years' planning time
   b. A corporate human resources event to recruit new employees with six months' planning time
   c. A company picnic with three months' planning time
2. Discuss the limitations of using the project management methodology for event management. Will this methodology lead to an increase in bureaucratization? Is all the paperwork necessary? Will the current event staff understand the paperwork?
3. Select an event and create the following items:
   a. Product breakdown structure
   b. Work breakdown structure
   c. Schedule and Gantt chart
4. Discuss what ongoing precautions can be taken to identify and control scope creep.
5. Web research:
   a. Using a search engine, find some of the many project management sites, in particular, the site for the Project Management Institute. Do any of these sites refer to event management? Discuss the reasons for this.
   b. There are a number of project management services on the Web. Find some of these services and discuss whether any of them can be of assistance to event management.
   c. Search for information on project management portals, project office sites, virtual project management, and distributed project management. Can these techniques be used as a model for virtual event teams?

CHAPTER 3

The Corporate Event Office and Documentation

THIS CHAPTER WILL HELP YOU:

- Describe the importance and value of a dedicated corporate event office
- Describe the functions of the corporate event office throughout the event project life cycle
- Create a plan for a corporate event office and its records and filing system
- Discuss the fundamental concepts of knowledge management as they apply to corporate events
- Set up an effective documentation system for corporate events

---

The corporate event office is the organizing unit for the event. This centralized function can be performed by an outside event organization or by an internal corporate event staff. The size of the internal staff can range from a single event coordinator on loan from another department in the company to a full-time team dedicated to corporate events.

Physically, the corporate event office may be a site operations office at an outdoor agricultural exhibition, complete with mud and dust, or a room in a modern air-conditioned office building. It can even be a virtual office, with all the information residing on a computer in another country. Whatever its form,

ual, the corporate event office provides the information focal
e site for the event. Into the office come all the raw data nec-
d control the corporate event. Out of the office goes specific
rmation, highly targeted to produce the desired results. This
the office setup that enables the corporate event manage-
and implement the event effectively and efficiently. By an-
ate event office itself as well as the systems used in the of-
ct management and event management, the new manager
past successes and failures.

Functions of the Corporate Event Office

The purpose of the corporate event office is to provide centralized managerial and administrative support to the event. The event office also gives visibility to the planning, and therefore, in some organizations, it gives credibility to the event as well. It is similar to war rooms or campaign rooms and is
sometimes called the nerve center, command center, or central processing unit
of the event. Figure 3-1 shows the functions of the corporate event office and
how they evolve during the event project life cycle.

Because the range of functions can change over the event's life cycle, the
focus of the office environment will likewise change. Initially, it is a planning
office used for meetings with various sponsors and stakeholders, collecting
data, sourcing suppliers, doing project costing, and creating event scenarios.
Once the concept of the event is firmed up, the corporate event office will concentrate on contracting, scheduling, and allocating tasks and resources more
accurately. Communication becomes vital as the corporate event team expands
and the various subcontractors come on board. Just prior to, and during, the
event, the corporate event office becomes focused on dealing with operational
issues and responding to any sudden changes. Once the event is over, the office manages shutdown procedures, the handoff, archiving, evaluation, and reporting processes. All these functions must be considered when establishing
the corporate event office.

Dedicated Corporate Event Office

As corporate events become more important in the strategic plans of companies and governments, the concept of a dedicated corporate event office is
gaining acceptance. For a corporation, the event office will support its inter-

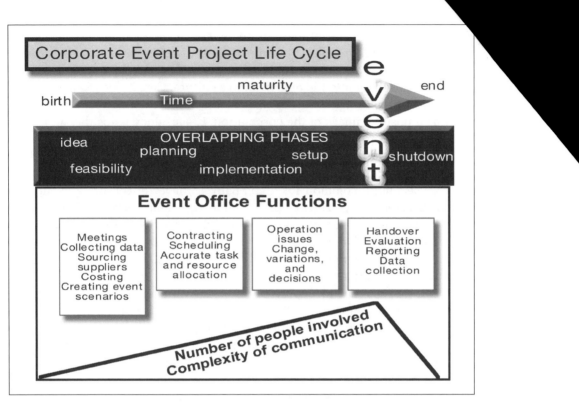

Figure 3-1
Event Office Functions

nal seminars, conferences, exhibitions, celebrations, award nights, and sponsorship events. Larger companies realize that to obtain maximum return on their investment (ROI) in sponsoring events, it would be wise to be more than mere observers of the events. Hence, they are now becoming actively involved in organizing and directing events—an undertaking that requires expertise that can be gained only by having a dedicated corporate event office.

Many major corporations in the United States—such as the Coca-Cola Company, Brach's Confections, IBM, Xerox, and Mars (maker of M&M's)—have dedicated offices to manage their events. A dedicated event staff and/or office can save costs if a company holds up to five or six large events a year. When there is a focal point with historical experience, contracts with proven vendors can immediately be reactivated, lessons learned can be formalized into new best practices, and successful processes and relationships can be reimplemented, which saves time and money and ensures successful outcomes. The staff for such an office can be expanded or contracted according to the needs of each event.

office consolidates all the expertise, skills, and knowledge that
ed throughout a company and therefore produces an economy
introduces a consistent approach to all the corporate events
em into the organization's culture. Consistency is particularly
nding. Today, events are used as marketing tools to assist in
e image of the corporation. Consistency helps the employees
ublic to form a clear view of the desired image. The event
pport for the whole range of corporate events. A key role of
the event office is to administer the sponsorship of external events.

It is becoming common for a company to have its corporate event staff work in partnership with an external event management company. This method ensures the client company that it is receiving the right promotion and that any opportunities that arise can be fully exploited. In an age of promotional clutter, having an active role in the event offers a good return on investment. An internal corporate event office can also work with other functional departments to recommend opportunities where an event would be an appropriate vehicle to communicate the desired message. Often, the demands of corporate event management, such as sudden increases in activity, are incompatible with the standard nine-to-five approach. Other departments lack the flexibility to relieve staff members of their ongoing responsibilities and dedicate them to the event project, whereas the corporate event office can shift its staff among project teams as various events expand and contract.

Physical Layout of the Event Office

As in all project-based industries, the corporate events function uses graphs, diagrams, and illustrations to communicate aspects of the event. The corporate event office is the place to display all this information. Over the life cycle of the event, the walls of the event office will be covered by an ever-changing collage consisting of any combination of the items listed in Table 3-1.

The corporate event office walls may be used to assist brainstorming and scenario building. Sticky notes with ideas, resources, and timelines can be moved around to create different scenarios. The right combination can then be transferred to paper or computer. This process is particularly useful when working out a draft schedule in a session with a small group of people. Bob, an event planner for a jewelry manufacturer, says that this process not only generates ideas and develops the flow of the event but is also fun and builds synergy among the team members. As a result, everyone in the group has bought into the final plan.

Table 3-1 Corporate Event Office Displays

Maps
- Map depicting the geographic location of the corporate event site
- Transportation maps showing airports, highways, railway stations, bus stations, parking garages, and the like
- Detailed map of the corporate event site or venue plan

Charts
- Organization chart
- Schedules, Gantt charts, progress graphs or charts, and attendee lists
- Who's who, with photos of key person(s)

Lists and Tables
- Responsibility and chain-of-command lists
- Resource requirement tables
- Delivery timetables
- Emergency procedures

Reports and News
- Progress reports
- The latest news, tidbits, and notices
- Performance targets and milestones

Communication Strategy
- Contact lists—in particular, emergency contact numbers
- Communication protocols

Corporate Event Office Filing Systems

The plan for the organization of documents—both digital and paper—must be established before corporate event planning takes place. The following subsections examine the characteristics of a good filing and records system.

EASILY ACCESSIBLE AND PRIORITIZED

The documents that will be needed in a hurry should be the easiest to find. The corporate event management team will have to decide on the initial division into folders. For large corporate events, this may be by function (such as operations, finance, and contract management) or by program elements (such as opening ceremony and award night). Generally, it will be a mixture of the two. Note the similarity between organizing a filing system and organizing a work breakdown structure (WBS), as described in Chapter 2.

SCALABLE

As the corporate event draws near, there is a significant increase in the amount of work in both paper and digital format. The filing system must be able to accommodate this increase without being swamped by paper or data. A tree structure is the most useful, because it can expand as the organization of the event progresses.

CONSISTENTLY STRUCTURED

To say that the paper and digital filing systems should be consistently structured does not mean that they must be precisely parallel. However, the approach to filing information should have a similar feel in both systems. In this way, the staff will be able to file and find information in both systems.

Marilyn, a corporate event planner for a large bank in the Northwest, recommends that the same numbering system be used for both paper and digital files, as it will avoid confusion and add structure. She described how disorganized the corporate event office was when she was first appointed manager of the team. Some items had slipped through the cracks due to the use of different numbering systems. She indicated that the clients were especially concerned because the office's lack of structure had resulted in a number of miscommunications. Because it was difficult for the planners to obtain information regarding who had been notified of changes in plans and the current number of attendees confirmed, people arrived at one particularly important event thinking that they had been confirmed, only to find out that their names had not been cross-entered into the digital system and they were locked out of key seminar elements. Needless to say, the attendees were displeased. Marilyn was able to quickly establish standards and work flow processes to ensure a more efficient and productive office, thereby producing corporate events that satisfied both clients and attendees.

Problems Faced by the Corporate Event Office

The major problem in the corporate event office is clutter. It can result from bad planning in file management, office layout, or staff training. These types of bad planning relate to the organizational design of the corporate event office. The sudden growth in activity at the office is the main culprit, and it should be anticipated when the office is set up. However, there will always be unforeseen changes, and the corporate event management team needs to be able to respond to such changes to enable the event office to continue functioning effectively.

Another significant problem is the risk of data overload. The important information can often be swamped by the unimportant and trivial. Time can be lost searching for the right information. The information needs to be kept up to date. Incorrect or outdated information will produce bad decisions, devalue information as a whole, and undermine effective communication. Ensuring the validity and integrity of all information is a high priority in corporate event knowledge management.

Focusing more on setting up the corporate event office than on organizing the event itself can also create problems. It must be stressed to all members of the staff that the corporate event office exists to serve the objectives of the event and not the other way around.

When the event preparation process is in full swing, many problems can arise, even in a tightly run and professionally managed event office. Of no small importance is the deluge of paper and how to keep it continually organized and current, so that all stakeholders are singing out of the same songbook and are on the same page.

John Oppy, PSG-Color Solutions Business Unit worldwide training manager for Xerox Corporation, states that one of his tips for success is always to put the date and time the document was generated in the footer of every document related to the event. John notes that this "version control" process has been very helpful in organizing his files and ensuring that he is always working with the latest version of any document.

Shashi Gowda, program manager at Windwalker Corporation in McLean, Virginia, established a version control process that is now used throughout the company. Until an event is over, all versions of electronic and paper documents are saved. Documents are titled according to naming conventions established early in the event-planning stage. The first draft of any document carries a "_v.1" tag at the end of its title. Subsequent versions follow in this sequence: _v.2, _v.3, and so on. All paper files and printed documents are categorized this way, and all documents contain footers with the file name and version number. This process works well using recent versions of many software packages; however, the dot (.) must be eliminated if this format is used with some software packages, particularly older versions. The important point in this example is that some standard format to identify the various versions of a document must be used to ensure that the staff is using the latest version of the document.

Meetings, Briefings, and Training

If there is enough space, the corporate event office or its associated conference room is an ideal location for meetings concerned with the event. It provides a facility in which the meeting participants can make focused, well-informed decisions. With key information about the event displayed on the walls or easily accessible in the event office's files, meeting participants can be far more effective and produce the desired results in less time than they could in a sterile environment elsewhere in the building. The to-do list developed as a result of the meeting can be immediately transferred to the corporate event system. The standard rules of meeting procedure should be followed if the meetings are to produce tangible results. An effective meeting requires a chair or facilitator to keep it on track, informed participants, written minutes, and a deadline. It is essential to have an agenda, sent out several days prior to the meeting, as well as desired outcomes or goals for the meeting. By establishing a focus and structure, the event manager will enable the participants to gather required information and properly prepare for an effective meeting. To ignore these simple rules is to court disaster.

Deborah Dunn, an event planner for a Fortune 500 manufacturing corporation, indicated that since she instituted a process for meeting preparation and procedure, her meetings have been much more productive. Deborah provides a memo and a meeting-planning form sufficiently in advance of the meeting, outlining the attendees' roles and responsibilities. She also indicates on this meeting-planning form what inputs are to be brought to the meeting and states the desired outcomes. Finally, Deborah ensures that the right people attend, thus facilitating decision making and progress. There are some excellent books on this topic, and we have included some of them in the "Instruments" list at the end of this chapter.

The corporate event office is an ideal site for media, staff, volunteer, and supplier briefings and debriefings. Because time is the real challenge in corporate event management, briefings should provide highly targeted information and, as the name implies, be brief. If the corporate event office is large enough, it provides an ideal place for training and at the same time will serve to familiarize the staff and vendors with project management and work processes, as mission-critical documents may be posted on the walls. However, the size of the event dictates the size of the staff, and training or briefing meetings will frequently need to be held in a larger conference room or even the corporate auditorium. In such cases, consider creating larger charts or foam core boards that can be set up on easels to provide information and share the feel of the event.

Corporate Event Office Library

The purpose of the corporate event office library is to store all the information related to the event. This could include the event manual, operation manuals for the office and communication equipment, software manuals, supplier catalogs, workplace safety rules and regulations, meeting procedures, past event reports, and industry association publications. The importance of data storage, easy retrieval, and archiving is apparent in the growth of the discipline of knowledge management. Knowledge is now viewed as a major factor in creating a competitive edge. Ideally, the corporate event office library would be an integrated system of information in both digital and paper form. It would be used to establish a baseline of knowledge for future corporate events. These strategic aims must be considered when designing the form and structure of the library.

Corporate Event Office Requirements

Most of the corporate event office requirements can be satisfied by standard-issue furniture and equipment. However, because event organization inherently involves a fluctuating workload that expands and contracts with varying levels of activity, the initial office setup is critical. Over the event project life cycle, the equipment, including computer hardware and software, will quickly go from a period of dormancy to intense use to virtual redundancy after the event. Therefore, the decision about whether to buy, rent, or lease is an important one. Many corporations prefer either of the latter two options rather than purchasing equipment, due to the impact on the bottom line.

The equipment and services the corporate event office will require include the following:

- Computers, peripherals, and an integrated software system.
- Internet and intranet connections.
- Filing cabinets. Even the "paperless office" must store and have access to contracts.
- Whiteboard. An erasable whiteboard is essential in the ever-changing event environment.
- Video and/or data projector for presentations to sponsors and training sessions.
- Communication system. This could be made up of a variety of communication devices, from satellite mobile phones to handheld radios, all integrated with the computer system.

- Clean and light environment. The office must be a place where people want to work, as they will be spending long hours there. It should also contain some convenience items, such as a microwave, a small refrigerator, and an electric coffeemaker, which are much appreciated, especially in the late hours just prior to and just after the event.

Additional considerations are: spare quiet rooms for uninterrupted meetings and decision making; a prominently displayed map, photo, or sketch of the event site; and space for the temporary storage of equipment. In some cases, such as for exhibitions, the event office will have a view of the event site.

Documents

It is one thing to plan the corporate event; it is another to communicate this plan to the various stakeholders. Accurate documentation is vital to managing a corporate event effectively and offers the following advantages:

- The documentation communicates the plan of the event to the staff and volunteers.
- The documents provide an ongoing record of the event's progress.
- They constitute a history of the event-planning process, which may be useful in resolving any liability issues.
- They provide a written basis for improving the methods of corporate event management.
- Standardization of documents enables different corporate events to be meaningfully compared.
- Producing the documents creates a discipline in the planning process.
- The documentation impersonalizes the plan—that is, it takes the plan out of the hands of any one person and ensures that it is separate from the individuals involved.
- The documents provide a link to other departments within a corporation, such as finance, marketing, human resources, or some other event sponsor.

One of the most common fears in event management, corporate or otherwise, is what will happen if the event manager gets sidelined ("run over by a bus," as the saying goes). As long as the details of any event are in the head of one person, the event itself is at risk. Clear, detailed documentation enables a replacement event manager to comprehend the current status.

THE MAIN CORPORATE EVENT DOCUMENTS

The documents discussed in this chapter are the results (outputs) of the corporate event project management process. Each section of the process will produce documentation, as illustrated in Figure 3-2, including various schedules, a responsibility chart, and action sheets. Each corporate event management team or independent event company has evolved its own style of documentation, with various titles such as production schedules, task lists, output matrices, timelines, run sheets, critical paths, checklists, order forms, milestone lists, show schedules, and show sequence.

The terms used generally reflect the past work experience of the corporate event manager. Xerox's John Oppy manages large training events that frequently include recognition and team-building activities. The key to John's success in managing simultaneous international events or back-to-back events is his strong foundation in organizational skills. John always builds a control book for every event, with each topic or element having a separate section in the book. He lays out the book in the order in which he refers to the materials. For example, he uses the audiovisual list frequently, so that section is in the front of the book. He tracks the budget once a month before the event and then revises it at the close

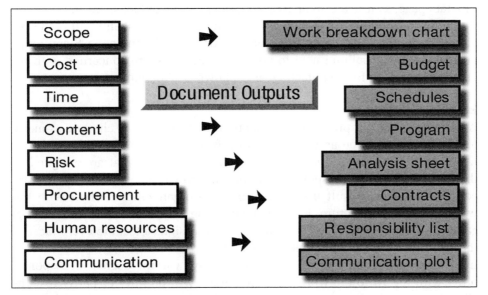

Figure 3-2
Document Outputs

of the event after the master bill is reconciled. Then he goes back to the monthly revisions as the bills are paid. Therefore, the budget and related documents are farther back in the book the audiovisual list and the contact sheet.

People new to the event management field should start out by relying on the following six main documents (see Appendixes 1A–1F) to plan and control the day-to-day aspects of the event:

1. Contact sheet, including telephone numbers and addresses (both postal and E-mail)
2. Responsibility chart, including key deliverables and dates
3. Action sheet, including the dates required
4. Work package
5. Checklists
6. Run sheet

Contact Sheet

A contact sheet may take many forms, from a concise list printed on the back of the accreditation card worn around staff members' necks to multipage lists of staff or stakeholders involved in the corporate event. Formatting the contact sheet similarly to the other documents will enable staff members to familiarize themselves with it quickly. The emergency contact sheet may be a separate page, as it needs to be located quickly. The contact sheet should have a column for codes, since coding is useful in sorting the list and will help staff members quickly find the right contacts. For example, the code S could appear in the codes column next to all the contacts that are concerned with security. A template for a contact sheet is shown in Appendix 1A.

Responsibility Chart

A basic document in project management, the responsibility chart takes many forms. It can often be as simple as a draft organization chart showing the names of the various individuals involved and the jobs that are assigned to them. A template for a responsibility chart is shown in Appendix 1B. A more complex form can result from combining the organizational chart with the work breakdown structure. Each element of the WBS is mapped onto the organization chart. Corporate event management assigns a team to every facet of the work that needs to be done to create the event. Obviously, there are sections, departments, or individuals who will have varying degrees of responsibility with regard to the work elements. Some will be fully or partly responsible for a particular element; others will have no responsibility for that element; others will have a supervisory role; and yet others will have "sign-off" authority. All of this should be displayed on the responsibility chart.

The chart can be a matrix, with the names of the persons, departments, or teams as the column headings and the tasks or areas of responsibility as the row headings. Each cell of the matrix is filled in with the level of responsibility. These levels can be coded as follows:

- **Rs:** has sole responsibility
- **Rj:** has joint responsibility
- **So:** must sign off
- **Cs:** should be consulted for advice
- **Sv:** supervises

For example, the event management responsibilities for a small client's dinner could be specified using the matrix shown in Figure 3-3.

With such a simple document, everyone can work together, knowing not only their area of responsibility but to whom they report and what tasks others are performing. These responsibility sheets can be very handy in a complex situation. They emphasize the harmony of teamwork and cooperation on a project. The responsibility matrix can be expanded by adding columns with dates as their headings. This chart should indicate when the tasks have to be completed. Although the example shown in Figure 3-3 is a small one, these documents are scalable, as is the whole methodology described in this text. They can be applied to huge, complex corporate-sponsored events such as the Olympics as well as to sections of an event such as a cocktail party.

	Ho	Ali	Frank	Mary	Xerces	Huang
Find and book venue	Rj			Rj		So
Caterers		Rj	Rj	Sv		So
Design and send invitations					Rs	So
Replies					Rs	So
Entertainment	Rj	Rj		Sv		So
Budget						Rs, So
Decoration				Sv	Rs	So
Follow-ups					Rs	So

Figure 3-3
Client Dinner Matrix

Task or Action Sheet

An action sheet is the basic element for getting things done by assigning specific task responsibility. It is a highly targeted piece of information, specifying the action to be done, by whom, when, and where. Almost all corporate event managers have a version of this sheet. However, a corporate event project management system does more than just generate a sheet to distribute to the staff. The action sheet is the finely detailed output of the system; therefore, it can be traced right back to the overall work breakdown structure. If a coding system is used, as suggested in Chapter 2, all the event information can be easily sorted and consolidated using a computer software package. A template for an action sheet is shown in Appendix 1C.

Work Package

A work package is the consolidation of the various tasks assigned to a supplier or staff member responsible for one of the event outcomes. For example, an award dinner will need various pieces of sound equipment, which would be identified when creating a work breakdown structure. This responsibility would be assigned to a sound specialist. Other tasks related to the event are assigned to people who have the skills and resources needed in those areas. Each of these people will receive a work package that describes all the tasks and resources required to enable the outcome for which he or she is responsible. A template for a work package is shown in Appendix 1D.

Checklists

The simple checklist represents the combined experience and knowledge of the corporate event management team. It is the final document output of the work breakdown structure and could be thought of as a list of mini-milestones. A checklist represents the detailed categorization of all the work that has to be done. It is the fine mesh of the net that stops anything from slipping through and escaping attention before it is too late. It is far more than a to-do list, as it can be used in future events. Anyone can read a checklist, so once the checklist is created and given to the responsible person(s), the corporate event management team can focus their attention on other areas.

The advantage of using an electronic template for the checklist is that this allows the template to be adapted easily for different events. The checklist's format can be expanded, consolidated, or rearranged to fit the size and type of each event. Chapter 10 contains various checklists that can be used as the basis for a company's event knowledge. The checklist can take many forms and be used anytime. For each corporate event element, there should be a checklist prior to the event, during the event, and during the shutdown. Once each action is completed, it is checked off the list. This means that checklists must be clear and concise, and that the actions themselves must be explicitly defined.

RUN SHEET OR PRODUCTION SCHEDULE

The run sheet or production schedule, which essentially describes who does what when, is known by many names. The terms *run sheet* and *production schedule* both refer to the corporate event itself—the actual program. They describe what must be done or what will occur during the event at certain times. Generally, a production schedule is used when the event has a significant audiovisual component, requires links with external broadcasts, or is on such a large scale that numerous components must be closely coordinated. Either way, the timing is critical down to the second. Often, there is a production book made up of various schedules—the move-in and setup schedule, rehearsal schedule, technical rehearsal schedule, production schedule, and vacate schedule. A run sheet, on the other hand, is used when the timing is not quite as critical. A word of warning, however: because corporate event managers come from varied backgrounds, they may have very different expectations regarding these documents and may use the terms *run sheet* and *production schedule* interchangeably. Whichever term is used, adherence to the schedule is of critical importance. Appendixes 1E and 1F contain both a sample run sheet and a template for a run sheet.

Vince, an event planner for a major corporation, gave an example of just how critical scheduling can be to the success of an event. A new event manager was planning a corporate public relations event in which a government official was to make a short speech between two other engagements in that city. The event had been tightly timed, and the other presenters had been advised that their speeches must run no longer than their allotted time. There was no opportunity for a dress rehearsal, as the event was merely one stop on a very busy multistate schedule for several of the key speakers. The event had been proceeding very smoothly but was gradually running 30 seconds to a minute late after several of the speeches; then a local official began running several minutes over his allotted time. The event manager signaled frantically, but the official droned on. Finally, the event manager was able to catch the official's eye and give him the "cut" signal. The planner narrowly escaped a very tough public relations situation. The key presenter almost had to leave for the next event without speaking. Carefully preparing a run sheet or production schedule and then using this document effectively is critical to the success of any event.

The event order is another scheduling document generally used by the venue management. It focuses on the setup and breakdown of the event and the various operational aspects, such as catering times, that affect the venue and its staff.

DOCUMENTATION AND RISK

Since corporate events are one-time activities, they are inherently high risk. If any problem arises, the documents are what will demonstrate that the corporate event office has exercised due diligence when managing the event. One of the indicators of professional management is good documentation, which involves not just the clarity of the documents themselves but also the way they are administered. Aside from their value for event communication and knowledge management, documents should be regarded as having a high priority in risk management. There are more than a few event managers who wish they had taken this advice.

Documentation involves more than just the event's paper trail. Many of the event managers we interviewed for this book indicated that they always carry a camera to use for documentation. Not every aspect of the event is a "Kodak moment," of course, but a well-timed picture may not only be worth a thousand words but may also save the corporation thousands of dollars. This is particularly true with outdoor events such as corporate picnics and corporate-sponsored festivals. A number of the event planners have hired a videographer as well as a photographer to document such events. The videos and photographs can serve not only as invaluable marketing tools but as hard evidence in a lawsuit as well. The videos or photos should be carefully labeled to fit into the event's overall documentation system. They can also provide the event planner with visual proof that can be shown to the client to demonstrate that the corporate event office has done what it was asked to do in its approach to the event.

GENERIC EVENT SHEETS

Over the years, newcomers to corporate event management will develop a generic event sheet that fits their management style. The basics of this type of document are shown in Table 3-2.

OTHER CORPORATE EVENT DOCUMENTS

Well-planned internal communications are critical to the success of corporate events and are the backbone of the project's life cycle. Mark Harrison, of the Full Effect, stresses the importance of communication: "The most important word is communication—at every stage from receiving the brief, to presenting the pro-

Table 3-2   Generic Event Sheets

Heading	The documents should have a heading and show the name of the corporate event. Although they may be color coded for ease of use, the color should not interfere with their ability to be faxed or photocopied.
Legend or key	It is often easier to refer to people by their initials rather than their full names. If you use this method, then you must include a legend or key showing to whom the initials refer. Also, if different elements of the event are referred to only by letters, the meaning of these letters should also be indicated in a legend.
Code	The need for coding depends on the complexity of the event. It can be helpful if tasks or work packages must be referred to quickly or if computer software is used. Even something as simple as numbering the tasks consecutively starting with "1" can make it a lot easier for readers to find a particular task quickly. Codes can also help with cross-referencing to other event areas, such as the budget.
Version number	The version number is a tremendously important part of event-related documentation. It facilitates correct communication by enabling all parties to be sure they're using the latest version of the contact sheet, checklist, or action sheet. Many mistakes could have been prevented by tracking the version number and displaying it on key documents.
Date	The date is, in part, an additional way to determine the version of a document and also helps to establish the history of changes made to a document.

posal and managing the event—without clear communication there is room for confusion. Telephone calls should be followed up with confirmation in writing. Faxes and E-mails should request confirmation of receipt and that deadlines set for a response can be met. Poor communication causes delay and uncertainty."[2]

In the following subsections, we'll consider the types of documents that comprise other internal and external communications of the corporate event office, including memos, minutes of meetings or briefings, E-mails, reports, and newsletters.

Memos, Minutes, and E-Mails

Documents such as memos, minutes, and E-mails oil the corporate event machine and should not be ignored in establishing a good internal communication system. Within the organization, they emphasize, and make public, any commitments or to-do lists. Memos and E-mails should be concise and clearly written. They have an immediacy that is lacking in the formal documents. Chapter 9 goes into some detail on the use of E-mails, their structure, and the advantages of threaded E-mails (those that display the sequential messages exchanged on a topic). Meeting and briefing minutes are another method of making public the decisions and responsibilities associated with the event. The minutes can also provide proof of due diligence in the event of litigation.

Reports and Newsletters

Written reports are a formal method for monitoring the progress of the event. They are a snapshot of the various areas of corporate event management, such as resources, schedules, and costs. The reports should compare the actual progress of the corporate event with the baseline (e.g., the work done so far versus the work scheduled) and pinpoint any apparent discrepancies.

Establishing the frequency of reports is an important concern at the start of the corporate event project life cycle. In particular, reports should be appropriate, targeted, and produced at times of major decisions—such as milestones. Informal reports and reports on the more intangible—or immeasurable—aspects of the event are also a consideration. Using a report form or template will facilitate the process of preparing the necessary reports.

Reports that are generated automatically by computer software provide only the raw data for a report and will require interpretation to evaluate the effect that any gaps may have on the event. In large, complex corporate events, progress reporting is integrated into a full project management information system (PMIS). A PMIS can be defined as a software system that provides decision-making support to the project management team. The advantages and limitations of applying these systems to various aspects of corporate event management are outlined in Chapter 9.

For larger corporate events, an event newsletter sent out on paper or over the Internet or intranet can be an effective and useful method of communicating with the client, team members, and volunteers and providing the event with identity and cohesiveness. It can be far more than a morale booster, because it can assist in solving any unforeseen developments. The style of the newsletter should reflect the style of the event, and the information must be timely and relevant if it is to be read by all the recipients.

The dedicated corporate event office in a company committed to creating and managing all its own events is quickly becoming a reality. This chapter described the best way to set up such an office and the types of documents that are most effective in supporting its goals. Rather than increasing the bureaucratization of corporate events, a correctly planned documentation system can reduce many of the risks and contribute to the development of an environment that supports creative and flexible corporate event management.

The increasing need for professionalism in corporate event management requires a systematic approach to event documentation. The "scraps of paper" approach is a thing of the past. These documents can be generated from templates that can be used for every part of every event. They are easily compatible with the Web-enabling of the event. Not only does the corporate event office contribute to the effective management of company events; it also helps the company manage and implement its overall corporate strategy.

Wrap Up

1. The corporate event office (digital or physical) enables the corporate event management team to plan and implement the event effectively and efficiently.
2. The physical layout of the event office can contribute to the communication and project development.
3. A plan for organization of documents—both digital and paper—must be established.
4. Clutter, information overload, and focusing on organization rather than organizing the event itself can become event office problems.
5. The most effective and efficient event meetings are structured and well planned.
6. Knowledge is now viewed as a major factor in creating a competitive edge; therefore, the event library, with all of the documentation related to an event, must be protected, as it is both historically and currently valuable.
7. Accurate documentation is vital to effective communication and management of a corporate event.
8. There are six main documents that can be used to plan and control the day-to-day aspects of an event—contact sheet, responsibility chart, action sheet, work package, checklists, and run sheet or production schedule.
9. Documentation can provide proof in support of the corporation in the event of a lawsuit.
10. Newsletters (digital or paper) can be an effective means of communication with team members.

Instruments

Cleland, D., ed. *Field Guide to Project Management.* New York: Van Nostrand Reinhold, 1998.

Doyle, Michael, and David Straus. *How to Make Meetings Work.* New York: Berkley Publishing Group, 1982.

England, E., and Andy Finney. *Managing Multimedia: Project Management for Interactive Media.* Harlow, U.K., and Reading, Mass.: Addison-Wesley, 1999.

Frame, J., and T. Block. *The Project Office: A Key to Managing Projects Effectively.* Menlo Park, Calif.: Crisp Publications, 1998.

Kerzner, H. *Project Management: A Systems Approach to Planning, Scheduling, and Controlling.* 6th ed. New York: Wiley, 1998.

Points for Discussion and Practice

1. Choose a specific corporate event and then do the following:
   a. List the functions of the event office over the whole project life cycle.
   b. Establish a digital and paper filing structure based on the event's work breakdown structure.
2. Discuss the advantages and disadvantages of the following:
   a. A fixed office
   b. A virtual office
   c. Having the two systems in parallel
   d. Creating a complementary system
3. Using a project management software system, create an imaginary event by
   a. Establishing a work breakdown structure and using a coding system
   b. Creating task sheets
   c. Creating a responsibility chart
4. Can the corporate event office be a part of the project office? What conflicts would this create?
5. Use a search engine to find information on the following:
   a. Project office. Discuss its relevance to the event office.
   b. Checklists.
   c. Event checklists for catering, lights, seminar and exhibition planning, audiovisual.

Notes

1. Personal interview by P. Mikolaitis.
2. Ibid.

CHAPTER 4

Venue: The Event Site

THIS CHAPTER WILL HELP YOU:

- Describe the importance of site choice for the event's success
- Analyze aspects of the corporate event in order to optimize site choice
- Assess and effectively use corporate site maps and venue plans
- Analyze the event site/venue for good signage
- Create a shutdown plan for the event

Corporate event project management must consider another significant source of potentially major constraints: those associated with the venue or event site itself. Project management in other disciplines, like information technology, faces no such constraints. Because it also deals with temporary sites, however, engineering project management has a sympathetic understanding of the challenges facing corporate event project management. Event management companies or corporate event managers often find that their competitive edge lies in their ability to design an event to maximize the opportunities of the venue. An exhibition organizer's proficiency in utilizing each square foot of space to the maximum extent translates directly into profit for the venture. Likewise, the design and layout of a corporate training function or celebration can change the entire atmosphere of the event and play a key role in its success.

This chapter explores the constraints or parameters of corporate event project management, beginning with the selection of the event site all the way through the layout and mapping of the site. The whole system has to fit into a specified physical area—and it is temporary. There is a lot of information available on choosing a venue and, to some degree, on designing the site to maximize value to an event. This chapter expands on this knowledge and examines the often-underestimated value of the site or venue map and the venue signage. Both these elements of corporate event management are basic to risk management as well as to quality management and event logistics. At this stage of the event industry's development, the corporate event manager needs to adapt information and processes from other disciplines. Software programs that assist in the project management and meeting-planning processes are beginning to become available. Each of these programs contain some information on the venue or site, although each event requires different management elements and processes.

Selecting the Best Site

With the exception of virtual events, all events must exist in a three-dimensional space. By paying close attention to the internal culture of the corporate organization, you will be able to match the event criteria to the profile for the site. When selecting the event site, you must keep in mind the atmosphere you want to create and the activities you need to plan. This process need not be lengthy. However, it must be comprehensive, as the image of the corporation is often tied to the location of the event. All the corporate event managers we have worked with or spoken to named the event site as the highest priority after determining the overall objective of the event. The medium is the message—indeed, everything about the event conveys a message in some gestalt manner. As the saying goes, the whole is greater than the sum of its parts. The foundation and backdrop for all the parts are the location and venue. Event sites may range from a specially built stadium to an abandoned garage, a museum, or a jungle clearing. We have organized events in those and many other unusual places.

The site/venue visit must go hand in hand with the event design. It is too easy to promise all kinds of experiences at an event that the venue may in fact not allow or be capable of enabling. Selecting the appropriate site can make the difference between a successful and an unsuccessful event. Therefore, most corporate event managers will not bid on an event unless they have carefully inspected the site.

Professional corporate conference organizers or corporate event managers will use the Internet, books, magazines, and networking contacts to narrow their list of possible sites to the final few. Discussions with the client will include or rule out certain sites based on the desired message. For example, the January 1999 Xerox Color Products Conference required sleeping and meeting rooms to accommodate nearly 1500 people over a two-week period as well as a large exhibition area for both Xerox and Xerox Marketing Partner products. All sales and technical support personnel in North America would be attending the event. The corporate desire was to convey an atmosphere of education and then conclude with an evening of celebration for the color production division's 1998 success. However, the event-planning team did not want to convey the same atmosphere as the President's Club sales recognition event—an incentive trip for employees who exceed their sales target. Achieving "club" status is an honor, and that goal motivates the sales force throughout the year. Therefore, certain sites, such as Florida or Las Vegas, were removed from the list even though they would otherwise have met the size and travel requirements. Chicago was ultimately selected as the most appropriate host city. It was centrally located, with large hotels and meeting rooms, and the Field Museum was an excellent venue for the celebration dinner. However, January in Chicago did not have the same incentive appeal as Florida or Las Vegas. Therefore, in this case, it was the best match to the customer requirements.

Once the client and planner have settled on the final few sites, the event planner and client representative should stay a few days in the conference hotel or site area to rate that site against their criteria. They will take into account such niceties as the distance from airports and hotels where guests may be staying, parking, ease of access to and from other related venues that guests may have to reach on foot or via some form of transportation, security, fees, quality of amenities, resources available, and so on. Table 4-1 lists the aspects that must be considered in making the selection decision. You can expand this list to include other items or concerns that reflect your needs or those of your client.

Clearly, every site provides both problems and opportunities. Many constraints are not conveyed on paper. Therefore, there is no substitute for a physical inspection of the site. We recommend that you take pictures of each site. An inexpensive disposable camera will do just as well as an expensive one to capture critical data about the sites on film. You will want to evaluate the entrances and exits relative to the number of attendees and the ease of access. Poles and posts, both indoors and out, can be a problem. For example, a major hotel once supplied us with a floor plan that failed to indicate the presence of posts in the center of three of the rooms we planned to use. In our case, these rooms worked well for hospitality suites and specialized exhibition rooms rather than for educational sessions. A physical visit to the sites

Table 4-1 Venue/Site Selection Decision Table

Event scope:
Number of people:
Resources required:
Special requirements:
Theme:

Subcategories	Factors	Event requirements		
External	Location Transport External access		**PHYSICAL**	**CONSTRAINTS**

Internal	Room size
	Accom.
	Floor loading
	Entrances
	  and exits
	Internal access
	Power
	Other
	  facilities			

Budget			**NONPHYSICAL**	

Resources
  Human
  Equipment				

Time				
Brief	Sponsor Client			
VARIABLES	Service			
	Entertainment			
	Room/site configuration			
	Staff			
	Audiovisual			
	Catering			
	Changes over time (e.g., building work)			
	Other			

and a few photos will help you recall the feasibility of each venue when making your final evaluation.

When considering hotels for events that include activities for subgroups attending particular presentations or meetings, it is a good idea to physically walk the path for these breakout sessions. For example, the Hyatt Hotel in Chicago is an excellent site for corporate meetings and exhibitions, but additional time should be allowed for travel between its two towers if both areas are to be used for breakout sessions for the same group of attendees.

Large plenary sessions today often include complex multimedia extravaganzas or other unusual physical requirements. Take the Mary Kay Inc. annual convention, at which Cadillacs and minivans are brought onstage for presentation to the outstanding sales representatives. This type of ceremony is integral to the corporate culture. As Deal and Kennedy said, in their book *Corporate Cultures,* "Properly done, ceremonies keep the values, beliefs, and heroes uppermost in employees' minds and hearts."[1] Thus, the venue selected must make this key event element possible. To ensure that the venue will support the ceremony, the path to the stage and the weight-bearing statistics are included in the site selection criteria.

Different yet equally important were the space and technical requirements for an event produced by Kaleidoscope Productions with the technical services company Entolo, both of New York, for Glaxo Wellcome at the Mandalay Bay resort in Las Vegas. The focus of the event was to inform and motivate the company's sales force and ultimately generate sales for its latest addition to its prescription drug line of business. The team designed various special effects to meet the client's requirements, including a stage that appeared to collapse to the accompaniment of pyrotechnics and sound effects. A confetti shower and a "burning" sign spectacularly concluded the high drama of the finale.

Numbers of people, variety of equipment, and types of activities drive the physical requirements for site selection. As you can gather from these examples, a solid plan and a detailed list of physical requirements are essential to successful site selection. David Sorin, CSEP, president of Current Events International, suggests using a checklist compiled by the vendors to include all their requirements. Signing a contract before all requirements are identified can lead to an overbudget situation. A map is also beneficial to ensure that nothing is missed. Graphics can highlight what may get lost in the written documentation.

Once the site selection has been confirmed and the contracts signed, the planner can map the other details of the site. Whether the event is a company picnic or a formal celebration ceremony with presentations and after-dinner dancing, a map or floor plan is essential to good event design and logistics.

The more detailed the plan, the better. The event manager needs to be "map-literate" when it comes to the plans. A simple matter of overlooking the way a door opens, for example, can cause considerable problems during the setup of the event. For example, a corporate event planner had received incorrect, unclear information from a hotel sales office regarding the hotel's floor plan when designing a training conference for more than 2000 attendees. She had to spend 40 additional planning hours remapping logistics, simply because she had not been told that, even though the main ballroom could be divided into eight rooms, the four rooms on the east side were only accessible to the attendees from an airway in the room divider. The hallway shown on the hotel map turned out to be a service-only hallway—off-limits to the attendees—and that detail led to scheduling errors for sessions with different start and end times. The lack of clarity and of complete information on the hotel map could have been disastrous if the event planner had not made a site inspection trip to the hotel about 6 weeks prior to the event. If a clear, comprehensive floor plan is available, it can provide the basic blueprint for all aspects of the event, including lighting plots and soundscaping, as well as the flow of equipment and attendees.

A site map is a means of communicating with everyone involved in the event. Graphical information is both immediate and nonlinear. A supplier can get far more from a simply sketched map than can ever be explained in words. The old saying that a picture is worth a thousand words is just as true in event planning as anywhere else. (A later section of the chapter presents detailed information on creating effective site maps.)

The site map can also be used as a means of promotion. For example, a version of the site map specifically designed for the attendees can indicate areas where food or gifts may be purchased. It may also indicate the location of fee-based activities. Colorful depictions on the map along with clear directional information can generate additional revenue at an event. If revenue generation is not an objective, the focus can be changed to encourage attendees to participate in activities that make the event more exciting and enjoyable. The Walt Disney Corporation uses the site maps of its theme parks both to promote the purchase of film, food, and memorabilia and to provide directions to the top attractions.

The type of events that can be held in a particular venue often depends on the history of the venue. If the venue has been used for conferences, then it stands to reason that much of the workload will be reduced. The venue can provide historical information regarding the number of people that can be accommodated, the types of activities included in past events, and the types of permits required. For example, a well-known hotel in San Diego has been used for many corporate meetings and celebrations. One company decided to ensure that weather, though usually fantastic, would not be a factor in its annual sales achievement celebration. The planner also wanted to facilitate the award presentation portion of the event by taking advantage of the stage, sound, and lighting elements available in the ballroom. "Reward and relaxation" was the theme of the entire event, and the final award celebration was no exception. The planner brought a beach party indoors, complete with real sand castles and beach games like limbo and volleyball. Since the hotel had previous experience with the precautions necessary to keep sand from being tracked throughout the premises and the requirements for a speedy cleanup, staging this type of event was no problem. Likewise, the use of pyrotechnics, wild animals, manufactured snow, laser beams, and the like can be facilitated if the venue has had previous experience with such special effects. Corporate event planners frequently feel more at ease with an independent event planner or production company with experience in special effects.

All the preceding discussions illustrate the value of creating and using a site map. However, the map is effective only if it can be understood. Later in this chapter, you'll find a checklist to help you create an effective map, together with examples of site maps for your reference.

SITE CONSTRAINTS AND OPPORTUNITIES

As previously stated, the corporate event manager should walk the site and review the checklist with the venue representative to ensure that the venue will support and permit the planned experiences. The types of venue constraints can be classified as follows:

- **Physical:** Physical constraints (entranceways, poles and posts, weight-bearing capacity of floor or stage) are the most obvious ones. This is particularly true with large exhibitions or outdoor events.
- **Legal:** This category covers local, state, and federal laws and safety regulations. The site's ability to support pyrotechnics and the availability of the required licenses and permits were high on the list for the Glaxo Wellcome corporate production team that staged an event featuring elaborate special effects. Glaxo Wellcome required proper legal documentation as well as a map indicating the distance of the attendees from the spectacle. A fire marshal can quickly squash the most elegantly developed plan. The safety of the attendees is his or her number one priority, so before the contract is signed for the site, the ability to secure a permit must be investigated and a map indicating the location of the pyrotechnics relative to the audience must be developed. In terms of project management, the permit

acquisition is linked to the site selection elements. Many of the computer-based programs, such as Microsoft Project Manager, permit such linkage and flag any attempt to move forward without taking the proper steps to secure the necessary permits.

- **Historical:** The event history of a venue could have considerable effect on what can happen during the actual event. It is safe to assume, for example, that holding a conference would require less work if the event manager chooses a venue that has traditionally been used for conferences.
- **Ethical:** Is the venue appropriate for the event?
- **Location:** This does not refer just to transportation and parking but also to the region. Is it safe? Are emergency services readily available?
- **Environmental:** Environmental constraints are becoming an increasing concern and deserve special consideration.

Due to the litigiousness of today's society and the risk of a political incident in the case of international events, the corporate legal department must be involved in approving plans and reviewing contracts. The legal department will want to determine the liability associated with the contract and will assist you in protecting yourself and your corporate client. Consider the following real-life experience of Martin G. Greenstein, CSEP, of Enchanted Parties, operating in New York City. Greenstein states, "Unfortunately, most people, companies, committees, and groups that are getting ready to have an event think that by renting a space and selecting a menu for the day they want the event guarantees success. Boy, have they positioned themselves for a possible rude awakening! The venue is only concerned with selling the space and the food! Anything after that is an unexpected bonus." Marty's first rule is, "Don't book the space until the event is designed." If you book the space first, the event must be designed around the space, as opposed to the space's being selected to complement the event design.

No one plans to fail, but all too many fail to plan. Planning is the key to knowing what should be included in the contract. A number of years ago, Marty's company planned an intriguing event at a local catering hall. He had been presenting events and entertainment at the selected venue for more than 20 years, and he knew every room like the back of his hand. He knew what he needed included in the contract. Why should he do a site inspection? It seemed like a waste of time. However, the site inspection was critical. The event he would be presenting featured a magical theme with an exotic luncheon show. He was planning to use his unique "Enchanted Entrance," a wonderful visual show about the honoree with special scripting to be projected on a very special giant screen. The audio parts were to be performed by the honoree and his family to a montage of music selected to enhance the program. At the conclusion to the program, the honoree would step out of his photograph and into the event.

This particular luncheon performance was to be a major illusion show designed to culminate with the honoree's stepping into a giant cage, disappearing, and being replaced by an 850-pound Bengal tiger. Greenstein conducted the site inspection, received permission (written into the contract) to bring the tiger, arranged a safe and appropriate place to keep the tiger, and all was ready to roar—or so he thought! As Marty put it, "The *oy vey* factor was about to drop in!"

He thought he was safe. Every facet of the event fit together perfectly. Everything was in place. The tiger, named Meetra, arrived at Enchanted Party's warehouse on Friday for the photo shoot with the family. The "Enchanted Entrance" program was ready, Marty's team arrived on time at his warehouse, the trucks were loaded, he had the blowups of the photos with the tiger, and the team was on its way to the venue with plenty of time to spare. No problems had arisen—yet.

Forty minutes later, they arrived at the venue. An air of excitement surrounded the team members as they began the load-in process. Greenstein went to the room to make certain the floor plan was in place so the team could begin decorating and complete the rest of the setup.

When Greenstein entered the room, he said, "Death would have been a kindness. . . . The *oy vey* factor exploded with a vengeance!" The room had completely changed! The ceiling had disappeared—replaced with a glass ceiling! The place where the tiger was supposed to hide was now a beautiful waterfall. The place where they were supposed to show the "Enchanted Entrance" slide presentation was under the glass, and the sun was shining. Thoughts raced through his head. "Why didn't I do a final site inspection a week or two before the event? Why didn't the venue call to relate the changes as per the contract?"

Fortunately, Greenstein and his team were able to make changes, and the show went on, albeit a little differently than planned. They died a little, they laughed a little, they growled a little at the venue manager, but they survived because of cool heads, a world of experience, and an embarrassed venue management (with a boss who wanted his picture with the tiger).

But Greenstein and his staff, the venue, or the entertainment company providing the tiger all could have been sued. Instead, they walked away with the war story to end all war stories. They were all very fortunate, but they learned the cardinal rules: get it in writing in the contract, get someone to sign off, and conduct a final site inspection!

Ethics also plays an important role in site selection. What is the message communicated by the venue? At times, the corporate client will have preselected the site and the independent event planner or the corporate event office must find creative ways to maintain the corporate image and message in a site that may be less than perfectly aligned with them.

For an example, Julia Rutherford Silvers, CSEP, was hired to organize and manage a company picnic for a large bank. The bank had already booked the site—a water park with a very large swimming pool—because it was one of the few venues in the area able to accommodate a group of this size. The challenge for the Silvers was to devise a way to keep guests out of the pool. Why? The bank's conservative culture dictated that swimwear would be inappropriate, so the bank's management did not want any swimming. Silvers designed a cruise theme and roped off the sides of the pool with wooden posts strung together with heavy rope like a pier with each post decorated with a bright life preserver. At the end of the pool, she designed a cruise ship facade created with draping, large smokestacks, and strings of colorful pennants suspended over the pool. The theme incorporated the attributes of the water park while establishing the desired dress code.

Location does not just refer to the suitability of the venue to the corporate culture or the transportation and parking; it also refers to the region. Is it safe? Are emergency services nearby? This element bears serious consideration, particularly in the case of outdoor and international events. Let's first discuss this constraint in terms of outdoor events. According to a survey in the January 1999 issue of *Successful Meetings* magazine, today's corporate incentive events are an example of the experience economy. We are sure you have noticed the increase in experience activities, such as theme parks, rock climbing, and white-water rafting. Today's corporate events, especially outdoor events, frequently include such experiences, hence, the need for the corporate event planner to include a review of safety issues in the project management process. Careful review of the available safety resources can prevent a legal battle from becoming the final unpleasant note to an otherwise successful event.

One corporate event planner had several beach venues on his short list for a corporate family picnic event intended to promote camaraderie and pride in the division. Although a site on an island just off the coast would have provided the quiet, space, and exotic atmosphere desired, he opted for one just slightly less exotic and much closer to fire and health services. A small fee to the local fire and rescue squad was money well spent. The event planner was complimented on his foresight and skill when the need for emergency services arose: a senior citizen experienced chest pains, and a small child tripped on his shoelaces and broke his arm. Unhappy endings for the event planner as well as the corporations in both instances were averted, due to a quick response from the on-site emergency medical technicians.

Equally important with international events is a thorough check of the current and projected future political situations in foreign countries. Although travel into exotic areas may begin with excited anticipation, it could end in terror. Kidnappings and bombings, as well as disappearances, are not uncommon in many areas of the world. A call to the embassy or the state department can determine the feasibility of a particular international site for your event. Some of the many questions to ask when putting together a site map of the event are: Who will be reading it? The attendees? Are they map-literate? What sort of maps can they be expected to be familiar with?

You may have to put yourself in the attendees' shoes. Maps are a form of visual communication. It is up to the event manager to make sure the map reader understands the information. When and where will the map be read? Before the event, during it, or both? Will it be used as the attendees wander the site? How robust should the map be? Is it a stationary "you are here" map? Will it be on the Web so the attendees and suppliers can familiarize themselves with the layout in advance?

Please be aware of the advantages and disadvantages of using computer-aided design (CAD) for map preparation. It is not a neutral technique. All maps are a summary. Some things need to be left out and others highlighted. The wonder and ease of CAD can often obscure what it leaves out. There are no straight lines or perfect circles in nature, and a map so created may not be a good communication tool. A hand-drawn map with illustrations may be far better at communicating with your target audience than a precision CAD map. Also, an attractive, artful map may be used to set the mood for the event as well as more accurately describe the site.

WHAT SHOULD BE INCLUDED IN THE VENUE/SITE MAP

In their text *Festival and Special Event Management,* McDonnell and O'Toole suggest the following items should be included in the venue/site map:

Scale and direction (north)
List of symbols used on the map
Entrance and exits
Roads and parking
Administration center
Information booths
First-aid areas and emergency road access

Lost-children area
Electricity and water outlets
Rest room facilities (toilets)
Food and market booths
Tents and marquees
Equipment storage areas
Off-limits areas and danger spots
Greenroom
Maintenance area
Pathways
Telephones
Electronic funds transfer, point of sale, and automated teller machines
Media area

Not all these items may need to be on a single map, however. Effective communication can easily be hindered by visual confusion. It could be preferable to have a master map and several derivative maps—one for the suppliers, one for the attendees, and another for use on the Web. A number of outdoor events use an aerial map as the basis for all the maps.

In the following subsections, we'll take a detailed look at each of the items on the preceding list.

Scale and Direction (North)

Although you, as the corporate event manager, may already know which direction is north and see no reason to put it on your site map, it is the universal reference. In outdoor events, in particular, the direction can be your last-minute way of communicating with emergency services. If nothing else, having a universally accepted direction on the site map is a sound risk management strategy.

The scale of the map may depend on the type of map. A map aimed at marketing the event may have a variable scale, and the illustrations will never be to scale. Cartoon-type maps have little need for an exact scale. If, on the other hand, the map is aimed at suppliers and setting up the venue, then a scale can make the difference between having the operations run smoothly and having your suppliers arrive with a truck too big to fit into the loading dock or with a generator whose cable is too short to reach the stage.

List of Symbols Used on the Map

Often called the legend, the list of symbols is of utmost importance when running events with attendees who have different "visual" languages. A common visual symbol language must be chosen. The symbol for danger spots may be obvious to you, but it might not be to all the attendees.

Ingress and Egress

There may be different entrances for suppliers, emergency vehicles, and attendees. Who enters where should therefore be clearly specified. The entrance for audience members with special needs may have to be marked on the map as well.

Roads and Parking

Often a smaller map is included—called a locator map—to show where the event is situated on a road map. Entertainers, coaches/buses, and general attendees may all use different parking areas, so the area designated for each group must be indicated.

Administration Center

The construction industry traditionally situates the administration center—or site office—where the project manager can view the work in progress.

Information Booths

Putting the information booths on your site map is an obvious way to assist the attendees and minimize confusion on the day of the event.

First-Aid and Emergency Road Access

The first aid area is a good example of retrieval of information being important. In the construction of large stadiums or multiuse arenas, an emergency road is generally part of the peri-track, or perimeter track, system. This system consists of a number of concentric supply routes around the main arena, with one designated for emergency vehicle access. In many outdoor events, the emergency road access circles the event and may have a cross-site diagonal. Showing these access roads on the site map may assist in keeping them clear of obstructions.

Lost-Children Area

Anyone who has organized and coordinated a family event knows the critical importance of the attendees' knowing the exact position of the lost-children tent or meeting spot. Indicating this on the corporate event map can reassure potential attendees that the event is child-friendly. If child-care/baby-sitting services will be provided, it is important to specify those areas, too, on the maps for attendees.

Electrical and Water Outlets

We have never seen a site map for the suppliers of an exhibition that did not have the electrical connections clearly indicated. It is also important for most events that the suppliers—in particular, for catering and audiovisual—be aware of the location of all the connections and the amount of power available. Care should be taken to determine this early in the project management process. The corporate event planner for a high-level global communications meeting hosted on an island off the coast of Korea had to rely on good resources and quick thinking to recover from a near disaster in this area. He had planned for an island picnic to conclude with native dancing and a photo opportunity with the entertainers. Just an hour before the arrival of the guests, the planner tested the electric grills, which were powered by a generator. Much to his dismay, he found that there was insufficient power to illuminate the setting and prepare the food simultaneously. The planner sped into action and reversed the order of the activities. The attendees were delighted with the native dancing and photos by torchlight as a welcome. Meanwhile, a small plane flew to the next island and secured additional generators to enable the food preparation to proceed. This is only one example of how a small item on the project management list can make the difference between success and disaster.

There can be two kinds of water outlets—for cleaning water and for drinking water. Indicating each type on the map will help both suppliers and attendees obtain the type of water they need.

Rest Room Facilities (Toilets)

Even though it always seems as if there are never enough rest rooms, their location must obviously be indicated prominently on the site map.

Food and Market Booths

It is very important to advise stallholders of the exact position and size of the food or market booths assigned to them. This almost always becomes a problem at events where vendors will be selling their wares, because some stallholders tend to take up more than the allotted space. Event management is therefore asking for trouble if it fails to specify the position and size of the booths.

It is also important for the general attendees to be able to determine where the booths are located and what is sold in each one. Specifying the type of food on the map—for example, halal or Chinese—may help cross-cultural marketing.

Figure 4-1 shows a wonderful sketch map prepared for use in a winery promotion. Such sketches can be drawn quickly and still impart a maximum of information.

Tents and Marquees

It is important to indicate the setup position for tents and marquees on the map that is given to the suppliers. A detailed description of what goes where within a tent is not much use if it's impossible to find where the tent should be set up in the first place. Large corporate celebration events may require

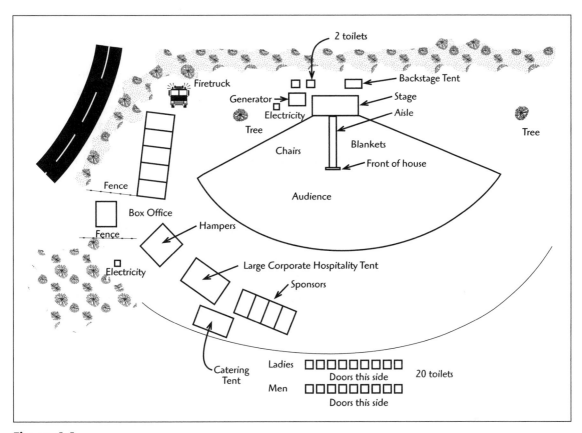

Figure 4-1
Winery Promotion Map

multiple tents to enable the preparation and serving of food, as well as attendee activities. Some outdoor events have more than 20 tents and marquees.

Equipment Storage Areas

For exhibitions, sporting events, and large festivals, the area reserved for the storage of equipment must be shown clearly on the map provided to the suppliers. In the case of exhibitions of manufactured equipment or events involving an intricately themed design, a staging area is frequently required as well. This enables the project team to preassemble items requiring many hours of setup and then disassemble and pack the items following the event. This is particularly beneficial in conference hotels and convention centers, where the move-in and move-out times can be minimal.

Off-Limits Areas and Danger Spots

Identifying dangerous areas such as creeks and blind corners on the site or venue may require the skill and expertise of a variety of people. In particular, if you lack experience in managing events attended by large numbers of children, then it is very wise to ask someone with this kind of experience. This is not a consideration to be overlooked when planning a family picnic at the corporate location. Also, areas that are off-limits due to the sensitive nature of the information kept there or sites that include manufacturing areas can pose additional security/safety challenges. Identifying these areas should be part of the corporate event risk management strategy.

Greenroom

Entertainers and speakers will need to know the exact location of the greenroom facilities, where they can wait and relax during the event.

Maintenance Area

The location of the maintenance area will be of interest primarily to the suppliers and to the operational staff at the event.

Pathways

If you stand at any one point in a large multifunctional event, you are likely to see a passing parade of attendees, performers, participants, suppliers, security personnel, staging equipment deliveries, emergency services, and much more. All these people use the pathways around a site, so paths must be clearly indicated on the map. Planning the actual layout of the pathways is a science unto itself, because the paths will both direct the attendees and help create their event experience. For some corporate events, pathways are deliberately laid out to wind and snake around the site so that every turn becomes a surprise for the attendees. Make sure the pathways are wide enough for the amount of traffic expected.

Telephones

Even with the widespread use of mobile phones, landline phones are still important at an event, so their location should be indicated on the site map.

Electronic Funds Transfer, Point of Sale, and Automated Teller Machines

Electronic funds transfer (EFT), point of sale (POS), and automated teller machines (ATMs) enable attendees to easily obtain funds and use their credit cards. Clearly indicating the position of these machines is an obvious plus for events that rely on attendee spending for their success.

Media Area

The location of the media area should be specified for the benefit of members of the media as well as for entertainers, VIPs, or other "media talent." The media area may also be the site for a related press conference.

Event Signage

The operational element often left until last is the signage at the event. When we asked a number of event managers what they did with regard to signage, they said it was obvious. This probably accounts for why the signage at many events is unsuitable, inadequate, illegible, or incomprehensible. To our knowledge, with the exception of books on airports and parking areas, very little seems to have been written on the topic of temporary signage.

Some events need only a few signs, as the audience is already "event site-literate." An annual corporate function held at the same venue would require only a few signs compared to many other events. This is because the suppliers, attendees, performers, and speakers are already familiar with the site and its facilities. The point here is that the amount, position, and style of signage depends on the event history and the needs of the target audience.

As with most aspects of the event site, the signage is temporary. When combined with the fact that the attendees will be unfamiliar with the site, this means that the models of sign design found in fields such as architecture and national parks have to be adapted. There can be no mistake with the signage during setup and the event. Then, once the event is over, the signage is taken down and, in most circumstances, is completely useless. However, in the case of annual events or events that move from city to city, the signage can be reused if the theme remains the same from year to year or from one location to the next.

Four types of logistical signs are used for events:

1. **Directional:** Directional signs include both off-site signage pointing out the event's location and signage at the site itself (e.g., "REGISTRATION THIS WAY").
2. **Operational:** Operational signage includes information signs and maps (e.g., "YOU ARE HERE").
3. **Statutory:** Statutory signage includes signs displayed in accordance with legal regulations (e.g., "FIRE EXITS") as well as special warning signs like "SLIPPERY FLOOR."
4. **Facility:** Facility signage includes identification signs such as "ENTRANCE," "REST ROOMS," "BAR," "STAGE 1." The sign used for the entrance

is especially important, because it creates the attendees' first impression of the event site and establishes the type/style of signs in their minds.

Other signage may include sponsors' signs, promotional signs, signs for the registration area, notifications, and signs of a more general nature (e.g., "COME BACK NEXT YEAR!").

CHECKLIST FOR CORPORATE EVENT SIGNS

Planning
Map showing the location of signage that will be needed at the site/venue. Where are you going to put the signs? What types of signage are permitted? Types of signs needed, such as:

- Parking/transportation/access
- Directional
- Safety/security/first aid
- Informational
- Promotional
- Sponsorship
- Facilities

Placement of signs, such as:

- Prior to arrival:
  —Transportation (buses/trains)
  —Parking lot or garage (for staff, participants, and attendees)
  —Location of entrance
- At the entrance:
  —Entrances for staff and participants
  —Entrance gates and ticket booths for attendees
- Location of facilities within site/venue
- Location of site map ("YOU ARE HERE")
- At the exit:
  —Public transportation
  —Parking lot or garage
  —Taxis
  —"LEAVE ANYTHING BEHIND?"

Assessment of the resources that will be required for signs

Implementation
Design: size, color, legibility from a distance
Restrictions: size, type, location, mounting method

Supply:
- Manufactured or rented
- Cost (competitive quotes)
- Arrival, storage, pickup schedule
- Maintenance and replacement ("turnaround time")
- Placement on site (including when and in what order), mounting method
- Removal from site

Responsibility for implementation

GUIDELINES FOR THE USE OF SIGNAGE

Data Confusion

Presenting too much information can be as dangerous as presenting too little. Good event signage must achieve an effective balance between thoroughness and legibility. Similar to the event manual and the event map, signage is about communication. If the "message" is confusing, cluttered, ambiguous, or unfamiliar, the signage has failed. Moreover, poor signage can create far more problems than the signage was supposed to prevent. The event manager needs to understand the event audience. What is their history of "sign reading"? Acronyms and symbols should be used only when all the attendees can be expected to understand them. Although too much information can be a problem, too little can be a problem as well. We are now a global economy, and many corporate events include attendees from other nations. Providing key information in the primary languages of the attendees can eliminate miscommunication and ensure that attendees arrive at the various functions on time.

Sign Placement

It might initially seem obvious where the signs need to be placed, that is, in locations that are away from obstructions, visible, prominent, and that have a neutral background. As well, the event manager needs to consider where the signs are placed so that the event audience will become sign-literate at the event. In airports, railway stations, and parking garages, signs are placed in similar areas so if passengers need information, they will "instinctively" look to a certain area for signage. It is also worth considering other paths that attendees may use at an event. For example, families with children in strollers may not use the most common path and may therefore miss the signs if the signage is confined to the most heavily trafficked areas.

Sign Design

For most corporate events, there should be uniformity in the design of signs. It enables the audience to quickly become sign-literate. However, for some events, the uniformity of the signs may backfire (as has now happened with banner ads on Web sites) and lead to their being ignored.

As with the other elements in an event, the signage should incorporate the event's overall theme. Interesting signs may grab the audience's attention, thereby achieving exactly the effect intended by the event planner.

Sign Color

Subway systems—such as the RTA in Sydney, Australia, and the Metro in Washington, D.C.—often color-code their signs. Green signs mean something different from blue signs. Such a system can be used as a subconscious means of communication. For example, different colors can be used for directional signs and statutory signs. However, care must be taken with the use of certain colors, as a certain percentage of the general population is color-blind.

Including graphics, particularly internationally recognized graphics in the case of multicultural or multinational events, can be a big help in avoiding confusion.

Sign Mounting

How are the signs to be mounted? What types of mounting are permitted? What resources are necessary for this? Are the signs durable enough to last for the duration of the event? Will they be stolen as souvenirs?

The issue of mounting may seem trivial, but it could prove costly. Take the case of the event planner who had spent a considerable sum for the design and manufacture of signage to match the theme of the event, only to find that the required mounting was prohibited by the hotel at which the event would be held. Fortunately, the sign vendor was able to modify the signs, but not without additional cost, which put the event planner overbudget.

Turnaround Time

If the signs are damaged or stolen or more signs are needed, how long will it take to manufacture and deliver new signs?

Event Theme

The signs should reflect the overall event theme. The style of signs used at an airport might not be appropriate at a formal recognition event or a beach party. Corporate event managers must always consider how to get the audience, suppliers, and participants to read the signs at the right time. This requires placing themselves into the attendees' minds, in order to determine, for example, whether the signs should be unobtrusive and restrained or flamboyant and eye-catching. Nor is this just a matter of audience comfort; it is a priority in risk management.

Credibility

Signs should be error-free, since the impact of a single error can quickly be compounded by the number of people who are misled by the error. Beware of any last-minute changes in the event, as the signs may need to be quickly updated. One erroneous or outdated sign can reduce the credibility of all the other signs at the event.

Emergency Services

The importance of signs is never more evident than when emergency services are called to an event. Just as with house street numbers, the design and placement of event signage must be considered from the viewpoint of emergency personnel.

Navigation

The method by which people find their way around in an unfamiliar environment is now almost a new field of study. It has been helped along by the need for navigation in virtual space, such as on the Web. Fortunately, the knowledge that is being gained is applicable to corporate events. The key word here is *unfamiliarity*. One of the lessons to be learned for the corporate event manager is that, for some events, it is wise to have signage that explains the scope—not just what lies around the corner but all the points of interest to be found down a given path. Instructions for signage at national parks in the United States, with recommendations for all the preceding points, can be found on the Web.

A field story best communicates this discussion of venue and site layout. For a retail stock analysts' field trip, Julia Rutherford Silvers, CSEP, and her team were required to coordinate and manage 25 events in a period of two and a half days. These 25 events included meal functions, retail outlet tours, and presentations by various corporations showcasing to these analysts. Each corporation, of course, needed to make the best impression possible.

The mandate from the brokerage firm hosting the trip was that, with the exception of the morning breakfast, all the events had to be beyond walking distance of the headquarters hotel so that none of the stock analysts could "slip back to their rooms for a nap." In other words, the analysts needed to be a "captive audience."

Each day's agenda started with a corporation making a presentation at breakfast in the headquarters hotel, followed by buses going to a retail outlet in the vicinity, followed by a presentation at a different hotel, followed by another outlet tour and presentation, followed by lunch and a presentation at another hotel or club, followed by another outlet tour, followed by a presentation at another hotel, followed by another outlet tour, followed by dinner and a presentation at a restaurant venue, followed by "free time" at an entertainment venue.

Such an agenda required selecting and procuring ten venues for food and beverage functions, half of which were only for break-food service and an audiovisual presentation—not a lot of revenue for a venue. In addition, these venues had to be in close proximity to both the preceding and following retail outlets on the tour. Adding to the challenge was the need to ensure that each food and beverage menu was different from all the others as well as the need to meet the image requirements of the individual corporate hosts. See Figures 4-2 and 4-3 for examples of the different themes and layouts.

An integrated plan was also required for the numerous audiovisual presentations, both at the hotel and restaurant venues and at the various retail outlets. To further complicate matters, the presentations involved a variety of media, including computers, film, slides, and multimedia. Silvers's team worked with its AV provider to rent just enough equipment, which was installed and dismantled in a progressive manner according to the agenda route.

Preplanning was, of course, critical. The agenda route had to be carefully planned for efficient travel. The only way this event could really run smoothly was to have one member of the team stay with the tour and another serve as lead person. As soon as the tour arrived at a given venue, the lead person would depart for the next venue. This approach allowed Julia, as the lead person, to scope out the traffic situation en route and radio back to her partner to make alternate route recommendations to avoid trouble spots. It also allowed her to alert the hosting company personnel to the tour's imminent arrival, so its staff could line up for an impressive greeting when the motor coaches pulled up.

It also allowed Julia to make any last-minute changes required before their arrival. For example, before the final luncheon event, about 15 of the analysts left the tour to catch early flights home, leaving several tables empty. She was able to have these tables removed and the room rearranged, making the luncheon appear full.

Two floor plans for venues used in this event are included at the end of the chapter. These floor plans provide you with excellent examples of the effective use of event space and the incorporation of the theme in the floor plan

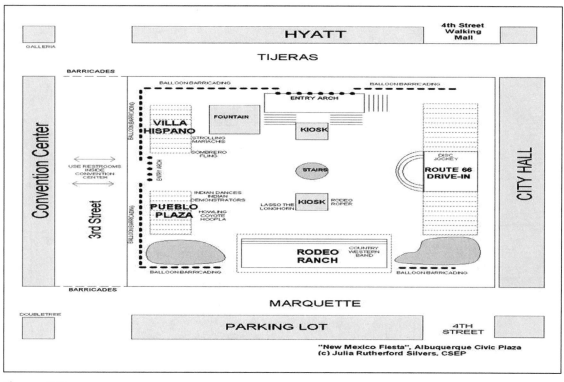

Figure 4-2
Civic Plaza Floor Plan

layout. Note the configuration of the tables in Figure 4-3. Pay particular attention to the tables near the dance floor and stage. Such a configuration would enable the removal or addition of tables without affecting the symmetry of the design. The event planner could then expand or contract the number of seats available based on the actual number of attendees. (Note this is not the actual venue referred to in this paragraph but rather an excellent example.)

Silvers and her team had to communicate with 25 different corporations; manage separate contract arrangements with each to provide the venue, food and beverages, and audiovisual equipment; plus receive shipments and deliver collateral materials and hospitality gifts. They needed to ensure that each presenter had the correct equipment and sufficient rehearsal time, as well as control the agenda so that the tour would stay on the (very tight) timetable. And of course, each corporate participant needed to feel that its function was "the best."

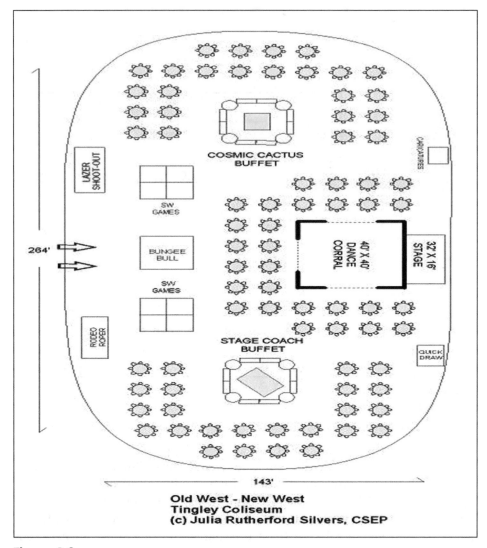

Figure 4-3
Arena Floor Plan

It was truly critical for Silvers's team to understand the goals and objectives of all the corporate participants—and know just how vital it was that they make a good impression on the analysts. While the retail outlets had complete control of their environment setup, Silvers's team had the responsibility of finding and coordinating venues that would enhance the presenters' quality and branding objectives. It was critical, too, for Silvers's team to understand the experience for the analyst attendees—providing efficient transportation routing, menu variety, quality presentation environments, plus a bit of the flavor of the destination's indigenous culture.

In this instance, Silvers's main client, the brokerage firm, declared it the best stock analysts' trip the firm had ever done, primarily because of the agenda control. All the firm's other trips had consistently run behind schedule and been fraught with delays due to service delivery problems and miscommunications, leaving its corporate participants dissatisfied and its analyst attendees frustrated. And that doesn't meet anyone's goal.

Utilizing a formal corporate event project management process for selecting, laying out, and mapping an event site can minimize the risks and maximize the opportunity for a successful event.

Site Shutdown Procedure

The corporate event manager needs to be aware that the event is not over until the event has been "shut down." The conclusion of an event is a time of high activity for the event management. On site this will include the outflow of all people and equipment, and the cleaning and storage of other equipment and facilities. Also, there will be a general cleaning of the site. This represents only part of the event shutdown. Shutdown also includes contract acquittal, venue handover, and many other tasks listed below.

The preparing for the event shutdown process includes:

- Creating a work breakdown structure
- Establishing timelines
- Assigning task responsibilities
- Creating an effective reporting procedure
- Performing a security analysis

This is the project management process as set out on this text. The amount of work to be done in shutting down the event is divided up and given a time when it is to be done. The order of the tasks will be important so that an efficient process can be created. A precedent diagram may need to be made showing what tasks need to be completed before others can begin. For example, the dismantling of staging lights at a venue can create a major problem if there isn't an alternative source of light. As the tasks are completed, the event manager needs to know that they have been done (or, just as important, that they haven't been done), so a reporting procedure must be put into practice.

Judging by reports from many corporate event managers, this is the time when equipment is stolen. This can range from the decorations at an office party to computers at an exhibition. The movement of equipment and people and the general exhaustion of the staff and volunteers creates a perfect environment for theft.

Below is a series of headings with both a checklist and an explanation.

CROWD DISPERSAL

In most situations, there is not much that can be done on-site until the crowd has left. The mix of moving crowds and moving equipment is a recipe for disaster. The provision for crowd management at the end of an event needs to be part of the initial event planning. The last impression can often be the dominant impression for an audience member. There are endless solutions for removing large numbers of people from a venue—the most obvious being to inform the local transport authorities (and the taxis). The correct programming of an event can assist in the shutdown process. For an event with many staging areas, each area can be packed up in sequence as the performance is finished. Ending all activities simultaneously and causing everyone to exit into the surrounding area at once, putting a strain on the transportation system, can be diminished by staggering the entertainment. It is not just a large crowd that needs attention; removal of VIPs and politicians requires as much thought and care during the shutdown process as the rest of the audience.

EQUIPMENT

At exhibitions, a careful schedule needs to be created so that docks are accessible, and this needs to be adhered to. A truck arriving late or going to the wrong dock can be amplified throughout the entire shutdown process. Support equipment needs to be on hand, such as forklifts and cranes.

The event manager may find it more cost-effective to buy or make the equipment necessary for the event and sell it afterwards. Small equipment is a problem, as it can easily get lost or stolen. The handheld two-way radios are often left on the stage after use. To stop this from happening, a system of signing on/off for the equipment is used in many events.

Removal of huge equipment requires special thought. At a recent Mining Equipment Exhibition, almost all work had to stop while one of the huge trucks in the show was removed from the site. Barricades at events need to have a schedule for being dismantled, as they can create bottlenecks in traffic.

Entertainment/Guest Speakers/Star Players

One of the most common comments from entertainers is that once the performance is over the event management virtually forgets about them. Many artists do not have the "invoice cycle" of large firms and therefore need to be paid as soon as the performance is finished rather than after 90 days. Thank-you letters are always appreciated, and they should be just that and not contain any other material. The artist/speaker may like to use the letters as reference in order to obtain further work.

HUMAN RESOURCES

The termination process on-site may require special staff. Often, the event staff will be tired after working all day, and a new team may be needed. Also, specialists may be required, such as forklift drivers, riggers, and computer technicians. For some events, the human resources people are the main resource. The people working on the event can supply the corporate event office with all kinds of information to ensure greater efficiency and effectiveness for the next event.

Generally, the event manager will be in charge of the thank-you party at the conclusion of the event. This needs to be integrated into the event planning.

LIABILITY

Event shutdown includes collecting all the data to prove or disprove any liabilities. Videos and photographs of the event may be difficult to obtain months after the event.

ONSITE/STAGING AREA

Generally, the staging area is the area most thought about when we talk about event shutdown. The cleaning and hand-over of the venue must be in a condition that is in accordance with the venue contract. The "idiot check" is the last look to see if anything has been left behind. At exhibitions, the removal of all signage is an important consideration.

CONTRACTORS

The shutdown process is not just about site issues; it also includes contract acquittal. This is part of the contract management process, as described in Chapter 8. Also it is polite and wise to send a thank-you letter to all the subcontractors.

FINANCE

All the bills should be paid as soon as possible after the event. This must be arranged with the accounting department—as difficult as that may be. For some special events, the volatile event environment means that it is easy to forget payments and invoices. So this is best done in the week immediately after the event has shutdown, while details are still memorable. It is also a courtesy that all the subcontractors be paid as soon as possible after the event.

MARKETING AND PROMOTION

There are many companies that can take care of collecting all the media information about the event. Don't forget to collect any notices on the Web. An idea for some events is to politely ask why the invitees didn't come to the event. This can give the corporate event office some invaluable advice.

SPONSORS AND GRANTS

Most, if not all, grants require that a report be presented as to how the money has been spent. Just after the event—when everyone is still excited—is a very good time to meet the sponsors or event partners and arouse some enthusiasm. At a recent event, a number of children who took part in the event came to the postevent briefing. Not all sponsors see the results of an event, so the children were able to show sponsors how much it meant to them. Also, they were given a computer disk along with the name of the Web site and photos of the event.

CLIENT

Most successful event companies will provide a glossy report to the client of the event. To create such a report requires that a photographer attend the event, and this needs to be planned.

EMERGENCY SHUTDOWN AND CANCELLATION SHUTDOWN

Emergency and cancellation shutdown are all part of the risk management plan. In particular, what are the venue's arrangements for emergency shutdown? Do these correspond to the event office's plans?

Conclusion

There are a myriad of factors involved in site or venue selection. This is all the more reason to go about the selection of a site or venue in a methodical way. Once the venue has been selected, the event layout has to be designed. An essential tool in this is the site plan or site map. It is also used as a communication device to the stakeholders. If correctly drawn, the map can show the scope of the event and the specific location of event elements. The other important communication device is event signage. Finally, the shutdown process is considered. These three elements—the site map, signage, and shutdown procedure—often are overlooked in event literature, but they are essential for a professional approach to event management.

Wrap Up

1. The event site must match the corporate culture and the event criteria.
2. There is no substitute for a physical inspection of an event site.
3. A table or chart and photos should be used to document and evaluate possible event venues.
4. A map or floor plan is essential to planning good event design and logistics.
5. A site offers constraints and opportunities—physical, legal, historical, ethical, location, and environmental.
6. Checklists are helpful to ensure that important information is included on the event map.
7. Sufficient, clear, and legible signage using familiar terms or graphics is an important factor in a smooth-running, successful event.
8. The event is not over until it has been shut down physically and contractually.

Further Reading

Simms, M. *Sign Design*. London: Thames and Hudson, 1991.

Graham, S., J. Goldblatt, and L. Delpy. *The Ultimate Guide to Sport Event Management and Marketing*. Ill: Irwin, 1995.

McCabe, V., B. Poole, Weeks, and N. Leiper. *The Business and Management of Conventions* Brisbane: John Wiley & Sons, 2000.

Gray, C., and E. Larson. *Project Management: The Managerial Process*. New York: McGraw-Hill, 2000.

Note

1. Terrence E. Deal and Allan A. Kennedy, Corporate Cultures: The Rites and Rituals of Corporate Life (Reading, Mass.: Perseus Books, 1982), p. 63.

Points for Discussion and Practice

1. Create and fill in the site selection table for a variety of events such as a large seminar, an awards night, a sponsored public festival, a staff party, a product launch.
2. Select a specific event.
   a. Discuss the physical constraints and the variables.
   b. Design the layout and draw a sketch map.
   c. Design the signage and discuss the placement of signs.
   d. Create a shutdown schedule.
3. Web research:
   a. Obtain the floor plans for event venues, such as:
      i.   Sports arena
      ii. Ballroom
      iii. Entertainment venue
   b. Compare the floor plans and discuss the aspects that are missing.
   c. Look up signage and way-finding using a search engine. Find the National Park site and research their signage methods.
4. Develop a comprehensive site inspection checklist for the following corporate events:
   a. Three-day new-product launch attended by 500 salespeople
   b. Two-day conference for 30 computer software users
   c. One-day exposition with 100 exhibitors and 3,000 buyers

CHAPTER 5

Feasibility, Bidding, and Proposals

THIS CHAPTER WILL HELP YOU:

- Conduct a feasibility study
- Evaluate the feasibility of a corporate event
- Use the corporate event feasibility tools
- Prepare a proposal/quotation
- Determine if an event is feasible

The project initiation phase in corporate event project management answers two questions: (1) Is the event feasible? and (2) Is this the correct approach to achieve the desired results? The output of this phase becomes your specific plan for the corporate event.

The three areas—feasibility, bidding, and proposals—are examined simultaneously, as they are often intertwined and they represent time and resource commitments to an event. The corporate event manager needs to know how to efficiently put together the three documents related to these three areas. In the past, the corporate event manager rarely had to submit a proposal. However, the global movement toward management by projects means that the event team has to compete for funds with the other projects in the company.

The event must meet the desired level of a return on investment just as a product research and development project would have to demonstrate. For example, in the case of events for human resources, the corporate event team would have to demonstrate that the event was a better return on investment than an alternative solution to achieve the stated goals, such as a CD-ROM or a course book. This requires the event office to conduct a solid, fact-based feasibility report for the proposed event.

Role of the Event Manager

It is rarely possible to have a full dress rehearsal of an event to determine if the event is feasible and if the elements work together to achieve the desired goals. Therefore, it is important to conduct a feasibility study and report the results to the event stakeholders. An event feasibility study is a detailed exploration of the alternatives for an event to ensure that the event meets the client's objectives. An outcome of a feasibility study is the event proposal. An event proposal is a detailed recommendation for an event.

With the change in focus of organizations to outsourcing and yet at the same time creating a corporate event office, the event manager may have three roles:

1. **Event initiator:** The corporate event manager suggests events for approval by senior management of the division or corporation. In the project-based corporation this method will be standard for all departments. Events, just like other projects, will have to meet the selection criteria of the company.
2. **Event partner:** Each participating organization sends its event manager or a core team to become part of the overall event team. The various hospitality events surrounding the Olympics were an example of this organizational process.
3. **Event assessor:** When the corporate event management is completely outsourced, the organization has to assess the viability of the event and monitor its progress.

In all these situations, the organization has to understand event feasibility and proposals.

The event manager may be in one of two positions when considering bidding. The manager may submit a bid or proposal, or may create a request for proposals (RFP) and assess the results. The relative position is illustrated in Figure 5-1.

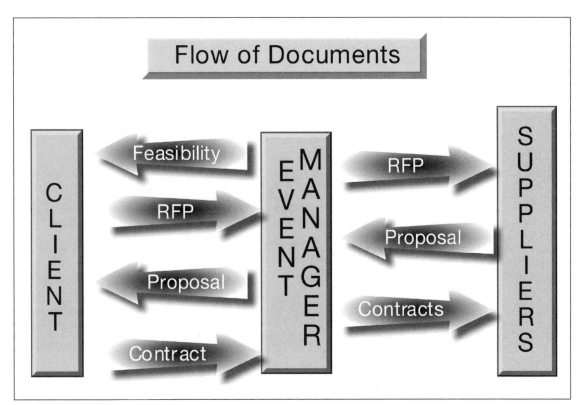

Figure 5-1
Flow of Corporate Event Documents

Feasibility Study

A formal feasibility study is generally done for larger events. The major purpose of a feasibility study is to provide a choice of various models for the event and to present the cost and benefits of each. The outcome is a decision-making document on which the pros and cons of the event can be assessed. In the case of an internal proposal, the feasibility study should address all the known selection criteria. Table 5-1 shows the headings that may be used in a study.

The most important section of the event feasibility study is the comparison of the event models. This section will necessarily contain some approximation, but it can give a quick overview of the points made in the study. The comparison must use the same aspects of the event and they must be a like comparison, that is, "apples with apples."

Table 5-1 Headings for the Feasibility Study

- Introduction: Description of the goals of the study and the objectives of the event as well as how they fit with the strategic objectives of the sponsor or client
- Choice of time and place
  - Factors in site/venue choice, including financial and political
  - Draft of suggested places
  - Factors in the choice of date
- Logistics
  - Sourcing
  - Transportation
- Estimating project cost
- Revenue
  - Funding sources—department budgets, partnering sponsors, foundations
  - Payment schedule or funding transfer
  - Invitation or ticket distribution
  - Registration, ticket scaling
- Event content
- Event options or models
- Comparison of event models
- Administration, including contracting and organizational structure
- Assessment of similar events
- Recommended option
- The next step
- Attachments
  - Model matrix
  - Overall flowchart
  - Draft schedule
  - Draft budget

An option or event model matrix, with the type of event across the top and the elements of the event down the side, allows a quick comparison. These elements may be primary costs, target audience, promotion opportunities, possible partners or sponsors, and significant risks.

Visualizing the event is an important part of a feasibility study, and any graphs, photos, videos, or charts can help. The two major constraints of event management need careful attention. Time is shown by the schedule and choice of date, and the venue is illustrated by a location map, site plan, or floor plan. Time and tasks can also be visualized by means of a flowchart. This will help establish the sequence of tasks and their primary dependencies.

A flowchart illustrates why certain decisions can have such long-range consequences. Because it is important not to get lost in the details, only the information necessary to make the important decisions needs to be included. Figure 5-2 shows a simple flowchart for a promotional event. The stakeholders can immediately see what the event involves.

In the example shown in Figure 5-2, the project leader or responsible senior manager first divided the responsibility and management of the event into three areas, as each area required different skills and resources. The output document became the draft of the work breakdown schedule. The actual event for the attendees was only one part of the work for the event management team. The promotions and the innovative Webcast took up much of the resources. This method of laying out the schedule enabled the client to quickly see that, for example, the live event could not go forward without first selecting the site. Although the promotion and Webcast would also depend on the site selection, the flowchart shows only outlines. Too much data can be as

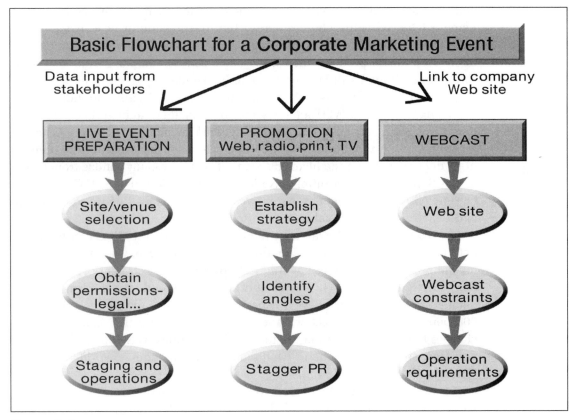

Figure 5-2
Flowchart for a Corporate Promotional Event

much a problem as too little. The senior management can get a quick summary of what work needs to be done and the approximate order of the work, without being confused by the details.

TOOLS FOR FEASIBILITY

Event feasibility can draw on the tools used in other disciplines. Particularly useful are the SWOT analysis from marketing, gap analysis from planning, and the cost-benefit analysis from finance.

SWOT Analysis

The SWOT (strengths, weaknesses, opportunities, and threats) analysis is an effective tool in the feasibility study. It is familiar to most corporate event managers and other stakeholders and provides a framework for describing the elements of the event. The choice of the date, for example, can be compared using a table with the choices across the top or column headings and the SWOT down the side or row headings. If the event is a launch for an ecologically sustainable product, then three dates can be compared such as World Environment Day, Earth Day, or a day to be decided by other criteria.

Leslie Hayes of Hayes & Associates in McLean, Virginia, provides an excellent example of a SWOT analysis and the decision-making processes. Their client was Animal Planet, a television network owned by Discovery Communications, Inc. Animal Planet wanted to create a special event for the premier of its documentary on the historic arrival of two new giant pandas from China to the Smithsonian Institution's National Zoo in Washington, D.C. The film chronicled the young pandas' early lives, the months leading up to their trip, and their celebrated arrival in the United States.

Hayes and her staff evaluated the options against the SWOT criteria and determined that the National Zoo, the pandas' new home, was the best setting for the premier. Initially this would not appear to be a straightforward event. So, you might wonder why Hayes and her team would take the time to do a detailed SWOT analysis of every aspect of the event, if the guest list was only 500 persons. But best practices and instinct told Hayes that there would be changes to the scenario. After all, the previous pandas were the darlings of the Zoo for visitors to the nation's capital as well as the hometown FONZ crowd (Friends of the National Zoo).

Hayes and her staff always use a SWOT analysis to determine the strengths, weaknesses, opportunities, and threats associated with changes. They had many issues to consider as they worked through the process. What were the strengths? Well, first, the National Zoo has a natural setting for the pandas, and they would be comfortable there. Second, the National Zoo is large and can accommodate many people, is accessible to public transportation, and has good parking facilities. The Zoo also has a film theater and can support several areas for serving food. It is a very picturesque location and thus offers good photo opportunities for the press. What are the weaknesses? What would they do if the guest list grew? How would they handle security issues related to the pandas and the numerous VIP guests expected to attend? The staff in charge of the well-being of the pandas determined that there could be no more than 250 people in the panda exhibit at any one time. The Washington, D.C., fire marshal would allow no more than 500 people in the theater. Where and how would the team move the crowd so that it never appeared that they were being shuttled from area to area in order to keep the flow of traffic moving? How could they keep the Animal Planet film the focal point of the event and the balance of the activities, secondary?

Certain items had to be constructed for the event, and they had to coexist with the established environment for the animals. For example, all communication had to be conveyed by signs or people, as there could be no loudspeakers or loud noises, as the noise would impact other animals. Given that guests would include U.S. and Chinese government officials, there was also the issue of protocol and international faux pas to be considered. Not all Far East décor would be politically correct. Hayes & Associates had to ensure that the décor was Chinese. Any hint of other cultures, such as Japanese or Korean, would be cause for concern.

What were the opportunities? For Hayes & Associates, of course, future business from the client or an attendee would be one opportunity. Also, there was the opportunity for Animal Planet to gain more recognition and to grow their business. On the political level, it was an opportunity to build stronger ties with the United States and China. And, of course, it could be great press for the pandas and the National Zoo.

What were the threats? Exceeding the limits required by the Zoo officials or the fire marshal could close down the event or could cause distress for the pandas. Of course, there was also the possibility of someone wanting to make a political statement against the National Zoo, China, or one of the attendees who included the Chinese ambassador to the United States. There had to be a plan, and it had to be flexible.

What actually happened, and what were some of the decisions? Well, as expected, the list of attendees grew to 1500. This required an expansion of the planned strategy to move people. Fortunately, the SWOT analysis enabled Hayes and her crew to respond to that requirement with plan B. They gave color-coded tickets to the attendees. The ticket color corresponded to a specific schedule that included a children's area, where guests could make panda bookmarks and hats; several food areas; viewing of the pandas; and, of course, the main event, the viewing of the film. Each group moved through the activities in a different sequence. For example, 250 people were served food on the roof of the Panda House while others were watching the film. Everything was double- and triple-checked to ensure the requirements for the Chinese panda theme were met. Even the writing on the linens was authenticated by an expert to ensure that it was in Chinese and not Japanese. No detail was left to chance.

The theme and the invitation that would attract the desired attendees required an in-depth look at all of the parameters. Discovery Communications, Inc., wanted to attract a very high-level audience, including Administration employees and local government officials from the Washington, D.C., area. Hayes and her team were very creative. The theme of the event was "Take a Peek at the Pandas." The invitation was a box that the prospective attendee opened; lying on the green paper grass inside was a pair of binoculars with the Animal Planet brand and an invitation that said, "Take a Peek at the Pandas." When the guests arrived at the zoo, if they forgot their binoculars, that was not a problem—Hayes and her team had a box of them waiting.

The point of this story is that a SWOT analysis and the construction of a plan enables the event planner to make informed decisions regarding the feasibility of an event and allows flexibility so that the event planner can make changes as required as the event develops.

Gap Analysis

Gap analysis is a risk management tool that, in this case, looks for gaps in the feasibility study and event best practice. It is best conducted during the drafting of the study because the process of compiling the study may uncover areas that have been left out. A gap analysis can be carried out by using checklists or by comparing elements to previous events. As the event management may be too far immersed in the study to recognize gaps, it is wise to have another corporate event manager or an independent event planner review the study.

Cost-Benefit Analysis

The event manager should prepare a rough cost-benefit analysis on whether to conduct a feasibility study. Depending on the size and uniqueness of the event, the feasibility study may take a week or longer to complete. International events may require more time to conduct a feasibility study. Researching and compiling the data into a usable form takes time. Also time is required to prepare a presentable document. It can depend on the level of detail necessary—that is, the coarseness of the information, and the number of alternatives suggested. As well as the dollar cost, the cost in time and resources that need to be redirected to this task should also be considered. This may be costed in terms of lost opportunities. However, the results of the feasibility study help the client and the event manager determine if the event has an acceptable return on investment. Over time, the feasibility studies can save the corporation millions of dollars by eliminating events with a poor ROI or payback and directing funds to those events with the greatest return on investment.

Initial Client Interview

The initial client interview is critical to the success of every event. John Daly, CSEP, president of John Daly, Inc., says people don't prepare themselves for the proposal and the initial interview with the client, and yet these steps are extremely important in the process to ensure a fit between the client and the event planner or the corporate event management team.

When John receives a request for an event, he interviews the client as much as she interviews him. He knows that nobody writes a check because she wants to write a check; she wants a return on the investment. The client wants to do an event because she believes that it is the best vehicle to achieve the corporate objective. John begins the initial interview by asking, "Why are you doing this event? What message do you want to convey?" He looks at the way that the client works and determines if he has what she needs and if she has what he needs. He asks himself, "Is there a match?"

John and his team want to become a partner with the client. The integration between client and planner should be seamless. However, many event planners or event offices do not look at the business as a partnership. They consider instead how much they can get out of this client. They ask themselves, "What kind of event can I do for them so I can look good?" They should be looking at the opportunity as what they can do for the client so the client looks good. If the event planner makes the client look good, then the client will do business with the event planner in the future.

Ninety-seven percent of John's business consists of repeat clients. He believes that his philosophy of ensuring a fit and making the client look good has been a critical success factor. When John's clients hold events in other cities, they don't call a stranger. They call John and bring him and his team with them all over the world. The clients are confident in John's knowledge of their culture and their process. He is accustomed to working with them, and he fits into the way they work. Why should they risk failure or spend the event training another person on how they work and what they want done? They have a known success factor in John and his team. John has enjoyed long-term relationships with his clients because they have a special working relationship. He has become a part of their companies. It is as if he is an employee on call for them, expanding their resources when required and then contracting back when the job is complete. This fits the clients' requirements perfectly. They have an excellent resource, but they do not pay for the resource when it is not actively required.

Proposal Documents

In marketing terms, an event proposal is far more than a document selling a service. This highly targeted document contains dense information providing a solution within the client's specific requirements. The form and content of the document must reflect the professionalism of the corporate event management staff. It should demonstrate the event management's unique knowledge and experience as well as a commitment to the client and the event objectives. This document will be read on many levels.

The document may be a one-page proposal, a detailed folder, or a presentation. In most cases the proposal for the event management is presented in person; however, in the case of subelements, government requests for bid, or certain corporation regulations, the bid is submitted via mail. The in-person presentation or mail version of the proposal can be supplemented with a version on an internal or a secure external Web site. The advantage of the Web is that the stakeholders can access it at any time, just about anywhere in the world, and the hypertext allows quick navigation to areas of interest to the user. The proposal can then have various levels of detail according to the needs of the user. However, the mail or Web version loses the impact that an in-person presentation of the proposal can have on the decision maker.

Larry Lubin, event producer, related a great example of the impact of an in-person presentation of a proposal. Larry received a request from a client with specifications that created a real challenge for his team. As they pondered how to address the client's request, they struck upon the idea of using *Mission: Impossible* as the event theme. Larry decided to generate interest and to demonstrate his firm's creativity by using the theme before the actual presentation of the proposal. Several days before the proposal was due, Larry purchased a book with a hollow center from a spy store. He had a local disk jockey tape-record a message with the *Mission: Impossible* music playing in the background. The message used the *Mission: Impossible* format, but it was directed to the client rather than to Mr. Phelps as in the television series. An employee of Larry's firm delivered the book in an official-looking package to the front desk of the client corporation. The client's secretary could not imagine why someone sent a book on Chinese culture, until curiosity got the better of her and she opened it and heard the message.

The next step was the delivery of the first-round bid document. Larry hired an actress to deliver the document to the front desk in the main lobby of the client headquarters at exactly lunchtime of the due date. The lobby is situated above the corporate cafeteria. She was dressed to fit the part: slim skirt, leather jacket, slicked-back hair, and wraparound sunglasses. An elegant leather briefcase handcuffed to her wrist contained the treasured document. She asked for the client, and he loved the approach. Larry and his team made the first-round cutoff. They were into the final four.

On the day of the proposal presentation, the team arrived early to set up the conference room. They locked the door and placed an appropriately dressed guard outside the door. The team transformed the room into a control center complete with clocks showing the time in various parts of the world, monitors with appropriate spylike information, and lots of charts and cryptic notes on the wall. When the client arrived ten minutes early, the guard refused him entry. The excitement grew, and the client wondered what Larry and his team were planning. When the guard gave the signal at the appropriate time, the doors opened and the fun began. The presentation was delivered like a *Mission: Impossible* story. Larry and his team won the bid hands down. So, the main point is that the delivery can be more powerful than all of the words on the page.

SELF-GENERATED PROPOSAL

A proposal does not have to be in response to a request. It can be developed from a perceived opportunity. The event office may see an opportunity to enhance staff relations though an inter- or intracompany sports event. Or an event may be an opportunity to improve a company's public relations with the local community. For example, the relationship between mining companies and their surrounding communities is always very sensitive. The suggestion of a festival involving all the local communities and showcasing their cultures may help to create a mutual understanding. This has been tried successfully around the world. In some countries, these issues, if left unattended, can lead to the nationalization of the mine and the expulsion of the company.

STANDARD VERSUS CUSTOMIZED GOODS AND SERVICES

Whether to use standard or customized goods and services is fundamental to proposals and feasibility studies. In ongoing administration management, a large part of the business stability is the result of using standard goods and services. The quality, price, delivery times, and risk can be estimated for standard resources. These resources can be simply sourced and compared to obtain the best deal. Project-based industries are the opposite. They rely on customized goods and services. Often these have to be created from scratch. The staging props will need to be built and the decorations constructed. At the end of the event, some of the staging equipment and other event assets will be sold, donated, or recycled.

Many of these decisions about using standard or customized goods and services will need to be made well after the proposal is finished. The combination of these resources is unique. To estimate all of this for a proposal is a difficult, but necessary, process.

Many corporations use a single repetitive theme for multinational or cross-country events. They are then able to reuse some of the goods and services. For example, in the Xerox DocuWorld event of 1998, the theme was high tech with a lot of metal and pipe grids to direct the attendees through an elaborate exposition featuring all of the available digital and networked products. The same theme was used in various countries participating in the worldwide event. The setup for the Sao Paolo, Brazil, portion of the global event was carefully packed and shipped north for use in an internal sales training event in Chicago. Neither group saw the other setting, so the décor was new to each group. It maintained the theme the corporation wanted to convey, and it saved thousands of dollars.

THE CONTENTS OF THE BID PROPOSAL

A response to a request for proposal is a common way for an event company to obtain work. In some cases, it is the only way a new event company can enter the field. Government agencies are required by law to put their needed supplies and services out to bid. Most private companies will do this as a matter of good business to make certain they are receiving competitive quotes. The event industry is no different. An event company will put together bid documents in much the same way as any other supplier. Depending on the quality of its work, the event company may be placed on a preferred corporate supplier list, where it will regularly be asked to put in a bid. Preparation of a bid response can be an arduous task, as the event company does not want to be removed from the preferred supplier list. However, the company may not want the work for any variety of reasons, including a crowded schedule or an event that is not in the company's area of expertise.

Below is a checklist of what may be contained in the event proposal:

- Cover letter
- Title page
- Proprietary notice—cautions about unauthorized disclosure, which should always be at the front of the proposal for legal reasons
- Table of contents (TOC)
- List of abbreviations
- Executive summary
- Body of proposal
  - Profile of the event company
  - General, including mission, background, credentials
  - Specific, including previous similar events and resources available
- Project partners and their profiles
- Event-specific information
  - Objectives
  - Scope of work
  - Stakeholders
  - Themes, design, and ideas
  - Site/venue assessment
  - Resources required: AV, entertainment, catering, staff, and suppliers
  - Marketing and promotional services required
  - Budget—corresponding to functional areas of program elements
  - Control management—reporting processes, organization structure responsibilities
  - Schedules—planning, transportation, running order, promotion
  - Environmental impact—natural environment, traffic, transportation
  - Appendices

PROPOSAL PREPARATION

Preparing a proposal can be viewed as an unenviable task or as a chance for the event management team to focus all its skills and knowledge on an event. Either way, it is a main responsibility of the event management team. It is the first step in actually getting an event organized.

Team formation for the preparation of a proposal is a project unto itself and requires the correct team configuration. It may be internally sourced or use consultants and partners. Once the proposal team is established, all the right information needs to be collected and assembled. With these inputs, the proposal preparation can be broken into manageable units and divided among the team members. Finally, the proposal preparation schedule is decided with enough buffer time for any contingencies.

Figure 5-3 shows the inputs to a proposal team and the outputs necessary to create an effective proposal. The inputs include information about similar events and this specific event. It is wise to find out who the decision makers are for the proposal. Is it a board, a committee, or an individual? Is their background financial or marketing? The proposal should be written in response to

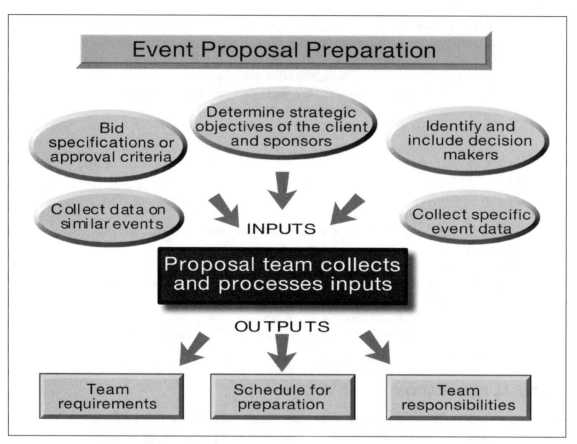

Figure 5-3
Proposal Preparation

the objectives of all of the event stakeholders. If the proposal is in response to a request for quote (RFQ) or request for proposal (RFP), the correct quote or proposal specifications have to be addressed. The specification or the selection criteria will provide the template for the proposal's structure. To support the assessment of the proposal, it should address the points in the same order as found in the RFP or RFQ. A proposal that is a multipage document should have an executive summary, page numbers, and identification such as a header and/or footer on every page. Using the template will also ensure that all the criteria are fulfilled.

Below are a few hints with regard to creating the proposal.

Clarity

The proposal must be clearly written. The opening paragraphs of the proposal should invite the reader to turn the page. The use of graphs and tables will be particularly helpful in communicating the proposal. As with all event documents, such as reports, meeting minutes, and risk analysis tables, the proposal is a medium for communicating the concept of the event and the abilities of the event management to the reader. If it goes unread, then it fails its primary purpose. It is best to get an idea of who will be reading and evaluating the proposal. Obviously, marketing will have different priorities than finance. This is why the Web is a good support vehicle for proposal presentation, as the document can be available later for review or for inspection of a particular element or section. However, it has the usual drawbacks of new technology—the target has to be familiar and comfortable with its use. Also, the Web should not be the only vehicle for proposal presentation, as mentioned previously.

Requirements

Whoever assesses the proposal will have a priority list of criteria. This can be a point rating system with the requirements as a row heading and points rated from 1 to 10. The essential or core requirement will be the first-level filter for the proposal. If the proposal does not meet these, then it will be immediately discarded. Next, the point system will be used. Often extra advantageous features offered in the proposal will win extra points.

Alternative Support

A multimedia presentation can be an addition to the proposal document. A video, CD-ROM, special Web page, or computer presentation can all assist the acceptance of a proposal. Needless to say, this has to fit in with the style of the assessment team.

Cultural Differences

The proposal should be sensitive to the various cultures, both corporate and community, that may be involved in the event. The wording of a proposal can easily offend if these sensitivities are not understood. More obvious ones are the differences in dietary requirements by different cultures. For example, suggesting a South Pacific or Maori Hungi event—where a pig is roasted—would offend many culture groups.

Now This! an improvisational entertainment supplier for corporate events doing business in the Washington, D.C., area, related this example about dealing with corporate clients and corporate culture. Carol Nissenson, Lisa Sherman, and Jeanne Ann Williams agree that most people in the event industry feel that corporate clients are generally easier to deal with than social clients. The corporate client usually knows what it wants, its budget, and any constraints related to the event. By the time Now This! has a contract, the client has checked out the entertainment supplier thoroughly and knows that it is a good fit for the event and the client. Corporate clients tend to micromanage less and let the supplier do its job. So, the employees of Now This! were surprised when a meeting planner at a large electronics firm grilled them endlessly every step of the way as they worked on the show for the annual kick-off meeting. Then they learned that the previous meeting planner was fired because of the entertainment at the last annual meeting. Apparently, a comic had used some rather sexist humor, which actually resulted in harassment charges filed by a female employee. Now This! indicated that the reason the company is contracted for a lot of work in the corporate world is because it understands that what it leaves out is as significant as what it puts in the show. That means not only being politically correct but also finding out the company's sensitive area or "hot button" issues and even political leanings.

Informal Help

It is wise to have an informal communication channel with the decision-making organization. An insider can help by suggesting a good time to present the proposal and investigate why no action has been taken on it.

VENUE-USE PROPOSALS

The event office may have to submit a venue-use proposal. For example, a seminar, conference, or symposium held on campus at some universities will have to complete a proposal document. This can be a very detailed form with such topics as compliance with university bylaws, insurance coverage and other risks, sponsor supporting statements, and how the event would benefit the university.

Bidding Assessment

Long before a proposal is prepared, the corporate event office has to decide whether to bid for the event. This may be an internal company bid. Competitive bidding is increasingly being used to ensure that internal departments of organizations are efficient in their practices.

The factors involved in this decision include:

1. Is this a real request, a requirement of the organization, or just a feeler? It is not uncommon for an RFP or RFQ to be a way of collecting event ideas or just seeing who is in the marketplace. As unethical as this might be, it is a reality in the event business and has to be considered.

    Equally, the submitted proposal may not be a real one but just a way of staying on the firm's approved vendor list. Most companies have a list of preferred suppliers and will send out an RFP or RFQ only to approved vendors. To keep on those lists, in the loop, can be very important to an events company.

2. How much time and energy will be spent on the bid? It could be a large proposal document. Is the opportunity worth the effort? Getting together a proposal can take up a lot of resources that could be better used in other areas. Large proposals may take weeks to prepare. Site visits and other research require focus in order to be effective.

3. Can you deliver if you win? What will you lose—other accounts? Opportunity cost must be estimated if the proposal is successful. Working on one event to the exclusion of others can leave an event company or the event office without the resources to handle different kinds of events. The company may lose a supplier that has been carefully nurtured over the years, if there is no work for them. As the industry is so volatile, current information provides the company a competitive edge, and focusing on one event may leave the event management team "out of the loop" on current trends.

4. Who is the likely competition? Identifying the competition and their advantages and disadvantages as well as their possible influence should be considered. All of the factors need to be covered in a SWOT analysis. Within a corporation the competition will be with other projects for funding.

5. What's in it for me? The bid must ultimately benefit the event management team as well as the client. If you cannot fulfill some specifications, then you may have an opportunity to go back and try to change the bid specifications. After all, people who know little about events often create the bid requests, and professional event management input may be welcome.

In the increasingly projectized business environment, the corporate event office will be expected to submit event proposals. These could be solicited either informally or formally as an RFP, or unsolicited as a self-generated proposal. Whatever its reason for creation, the proposed event will compete with other projects for the organization's resources. To enjoy early success, the proposal or feasibility findings need to be structured as a serious business document. A basic knowledge of the feasibility study and proposal preparation is essential for the successful corporate event manager. By understanding and adapting the methods of project management, the corporate event manager can create a consistently professional product.

Wrap Up

1. Events must compete with other projects in the corporation for funding. Therefore, the event must show a desired level of return on investment (ROI).
2. A feasibility study is a detailed recommendation for an event.
3. Charts, graphs, photos, and videos in a feasibility study can help the client visualize the event.
4. The corporate event manager may have three roles: event initiator, event partner, and event assessor.
5. A SWOT (strengths, weaknesses, opportunities, and threats) analysis, a gap analysis, and a cost-benefit analysis are effective tools when one is conducting a feasibility study.
6. Proper preparation for the proposal and initial client interview is critical to ensure a fit between the client and the event planner and for the success of every event.
7. A proposal is a detailed and specifically targeted document that provides a solution to the client's requirements.
8. The form and content of a proposal must reflect the professionalism of the event management staff.
9. Before the proposal is prepared, the corporate events office must assess the event and decide whether to prepare a bid.
10. Factors in a bid assessment include the following: Is it a real request for a bid? How much time and energy will the event require? Can you deliver if you win? What will you risk if you win? What is in it for you?

Instruments

Cleland, D., ed. *Field Guide to Project Management.* New York: Van Nostrand Reinhold, 1998.

Marsh, P. *Successful Bidding and Tendering.* Brookfield, Vt.: Gower Publishing Company, 1989.

Porter-Roth, B. *Proposal Development: How to Respond and Win the Bid,* 3rd ed. Central Point, Ore.: Oasis Press, 1998.

Reid, A. *Project Management: Getting It Right.* Boca Raton, Fla.: CRC Press, 1999.

Turner, J. R. *The Handbook of Project-Based Management.* New York: McGraw-Hill, 1993.

Points for Discussion and Practice

1. Using the executives of your own corporation or one of the *Fortune* 100 companies as the target audience, create ideas for an event and draft a proposal.

2. With so many aspects of an event subject to change, is a feasibility study out of date before it has been completed?

3. Research the legal side of bidding and probity. What are the risks and legalities surrounding partnership with other companies to collaborate in bidding?

4. Why do some event companies get most of the event work—even when it is put out for bid?

5. Discuss the advantages of outsourcing as opposed to in-house event management for your company.

6. Using a search engine, research the current RFPs that are on the Web.

CHAPTER **6**

Systems and Decisions

THIS CHAPTER WILL HELP YOU:

- Use a systems approach to manage a corporate event
- Incorporate systems analysis tools as a resource in corporate event management
- Apply decision-making processes and use them in corporate event management
- Identify indicators of deeper problems in the event project life cycle

---

Event management, as in any project management, should be viewed as an ongoing process of risk control. A significant factor is the ability to identify problems that might arise. What are possible changes? How can we deal with them? Do we have the resources?

The best resource is the skill to make effective decisions. The basis for making effective decisions is understanding how each element of an event is related, however remotely, to all the other elements. Every decision has a "flow-on effect" on other decisions. The effect of a decision will be felt in areas of the event that may not be directly apparent and in areas not directly connected to the decision made.

As with other aspects of corporate event management, traditional management practices and procedures can be adapted to event management.

Systems analysis processes can be applied to overall event planning. The practices used in decision analysis can assist in the ongoing choices that every corporate event manager needs to make. As the event industry matures, systems theory can be adapted to provide a language and a method for effective event management.

The Corporate Event as a System

FROM TACIT TO EXPLICIT

Systems thinking in one form or another is as old as Aristotle's philosophy. It must go hand in hand with decomposition and analysis for the event manager to truly remain in control and make effective decisions. Systems thinking is recognizing the interdependence of all event elements, and understanding the basic concepts of feedback loops and emerging properties. Like many of the processes put forth in this text, this knowledge is often tacit and second nature to an event manager. A characteristic of a mature industry and of corporate event management as a profession is that the tacit knowledge becomes explicit.

DYNAMIC SYSTEM

Event planning and implementation can be described as a dynamic system. Each functional area of event management is dependent on and influences all the other areas. This bewildering arrangement is made more complex by the element of change. Whether this mutual influence is strong or weak will depend on the type of event and will vary over the event project life cycle. In other words, if there is a splash in the calm waters of one area of the event, the result could be a dissipating ripple or a tidal wave that can't yet be seen. The art of corporate event management is to anticipate these changes and to realize their effect on the event. This is the realm of risk management as outlined in Chapter 7.

Systems Analysis

In thinking of the event as a system, it follows that the tools and techniques used in systems analysis can be applied to corporate event management. It is often a prerequisite for the implementation of event management software. The theories used in systems analysis are similar to the Web-enabling analysis described in Chapter 9 and illustrated in Figure 6-1. Systems analysis is a

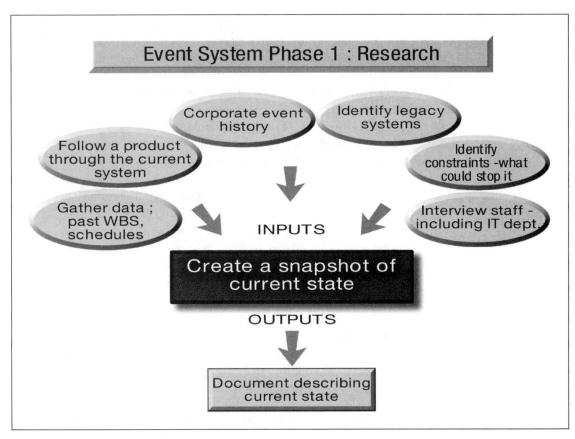

Figure 6-1
Phase 1: Research

critical factor in effective corporate event project management. Because systems analysis affects every aspect of management, this is sometimes referred to as systems engineering.

RESEARCH PHASE

Identify Current System

The first phase of systems analysis is to research and identify the current system in use. It may not be obvious and certainly will be unstated, but for the event to function properly, a system must be in use. Modern technology demands it. The work breakdown structure and the organization chart are necessary but not sufficient for identifying the system. These two charts do not show the methodology currently being used. The formal and informal processes and procedures are all part of the system. A method of illustrating this point is to follow one element in corporate event management through the event's life cycle. This method is similar to examining the life cycle of a product from its design state to its manufactured state.

The task of sourcing a keynote speaker is common to many events. Some of the processes involved are researching who is available (which now includes searching the Web) and making a record of this process, that is, documenting the process. Finding a speaker has various constraints—the type of speaker, availability, fee, and so on. Most events have a standard procedure for this, as well as one for comparing different speakers. Alternatives have to be identified and recorded. These records can then be used for sourcing other speakers for other events. It all has to fit in with the overall event and be accountable to the client or sponsor. In other words, it is part of a system. Even if this is done on the back of an envelope, it does not diminish the fact that it is an integrated process—a system.

Many Existing Systems

Within corporate event management, a variety of these systems, formal and informal, covert and overt, tangible and intangible, grow organically over the years in a seemingly natural progression. They eventually become the corporate culture—or the "way things are done here." This hybrid system absorbs new methods and fits it all together. In software project management, one result of this hybrid system is something called spaghetti code—code so convoluted that it is hard, if not impossible, to find a simple pattern.

Determining what current systems are in place includes identifying legacy systems. The methods that underlie the current management may be a constraint or can be used to leverage in the new project management approach.

Personalized Management

The system for managing events is described as robust if it can absorb changes without affecting basic foundations. Many event companies are currently run following the personal style of the president or top official. These types of organizations are what Henry Mintzberg (1994) describes as the "entrepreneurial organization." With the right personality at the helm, this type of organization can be very robust. However, if the dominating personality creates too much stress, and not enough inspiration, those supporting the event goal will most likely focus on an easier-to-accomplish, and shorter-term goal.

A robust organization has strong charismatic leadership and engenders those in it with a sense of personal responsibility and empowerment. The corporate environment has worked diligently to embrace this style of management because it works; this approach gets successful results. However, this system relies on the merits of its leadership, often just one person.

Today's trends in adopting professionalism, accountability, and risk management, in accommodating stakeholder interest, and much more, has resulted in a change from the entrepreneurial focus to a belief that management should not be chained to any one personality.

Using system analysis methodology is a key enabler to this goal.

IMPLEMENTATION PHASE

The second phase of systems analysis, as illustrated in Figure 6-2, is to analyze the existing and required tasks, processes, and functions for the next event. The *systems approach,* combined with the other methodologies

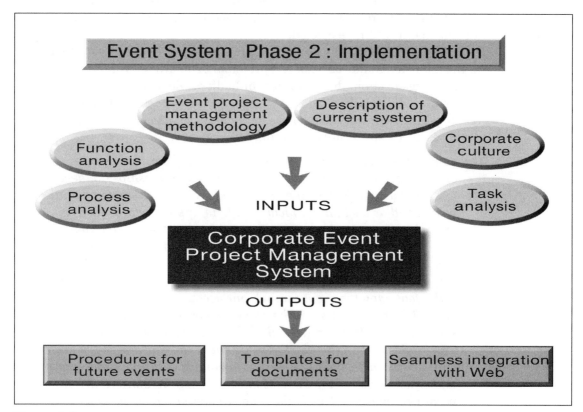

Figure 6-2
Phase 2: Implementation

described in this text, can be integrated into the one project management system. *Functional analysis* is deconstructing and describing the various functional areas of the event office, both current and future. *Process analysis* looks within the functions and at the various processes used. Finally, on the micro level, *task analysis* reviews the tasks of past and future events to determine how they might adapt to the project management system. The goal here is to first identify the current event methodology (or haphazard approach) so that the project management methodology can be implemented. For example, one of the functional areas of corporate event management is risk management. The current processes are probably "all around the shop" and include undocumented opinions and experience. A task analysis would look at which activities are commonly carried out with regard to risk. The results of such an analysis, when input into risk management practices, results in a new system that, when implemented, is integrated with all aspects of the event.

The existing corporate culture will, of course, have constraints on the implementation phase. However, as discussed earlier, project management is becoming the corporate culture, so the project manager may find more support for this than is at first expected.

Let's now see how the systems approach is used by a successful manager in this industry. Mark Harrison is a principal of an award-winning event management organization, the Full Effect of Bedford, England. Although Harrison does not use the terminology that we have just introduced, it is apparent from reading this case history that he has found and uses a management system that produces successful results. According to Harrison,

> *an event is born with that first telephone call from the client requesting assistance. This is the stage where relationships are developed and a good feel for the client's requirements needs to be established, and as such, in an ideal world, an appointment is fixed to meet the client to extract this information from them. From the outset an event is allocated a project number, which tracks through its life, from brief, to proposal, to confirmed event, to archived file. This project number assists with logging and filing information, and also with identifying the event through our accounting procedures. All event files, no matter what the size of the event, are set out in the same order, and should read like a book, so that any member of staff could pick up the file and understand the progress of the event and the next actions due. An event action list forms the front piece to the file. Once the brief has been established we move to the proposal-writing stage. This is the point where our creativity comes to the fore. We have a team of designers—scenic and lighting, choreog-*

raphers, and writers—who brainstorm to develop an event which will meet the brief and come to life in a way which will totally involve the guests in an unexpected way. This element of surprise makes an event memorable, to stand out from the many others that an often sophisticated audience encounters in this day and age. Whilst it is important to present a proposal which completely meets the client's brief in terms of cost and creativity, we will often also show enhancements, an opportunity for us to upsell the event. Frequent meetings between the operations team working on the event and the operations managers ensure that everything is on track and that no small items are slipping through the net. Site visits, meetings with the client and suppliers, including production meetings with all relevant parties round the same table, also ensure that every smallest detail is attended to, all the t's are crossed and i's dotted. A working document, containing every detail of the event from first delivery to final invoice, is the insurance policy that rules out any last-minute panics. The team sits down and "walks through" the event in minute detail, recording what should happen, when, by whom and who is responsible for ensuring that it happens. The working document is checked and double-checked by the whole team, and is meticulously followed throughout the event. A detailed contact list with telephone, fax, mobile telephone numbers, and e-mail address ensures that lines of communication cannot be broken at a vital moment. There is nothing more frustrating than knowing how to solve a problem, but not having the information available to make contact with the person who can provide solution. In all the above the most important word is communication—at every stage from receiving the brief, to presenting the proposal and managing the event—without clear communication there is room for confusion. Telephone calls should be followed up with confirmation in writing. Faxes and e-mails should request confirmation of receipt and that deadlines set for a response can be met. Poor communication causes delay and uncertainty during the corporate event management process.

Distributed Expertise

One of the advantages of having a well-thought-out methodology is that team members can use it across the company and around the world. The concept of distributed teams and distributed expertise will really work only if a common system will be used. Project management in civil engineering now has evolved to accommodate working with people from different backgrounds. A large construction project in South Africa will require people not only of different work backgrounds but also with different languages, even within the one country. Once again we meet the concept of a system that is scalable and transferable. By adopting a system for event management, a corporation can use that system worldwide. Indeed, the exhibition and conference industry already does this with their event manuals placed on a company's intranet so that staff around the world can create the same kind of event.

Knowledge Management

A further advantage of using systems analysis methodology in corporate event management is that the effort in creating a management system likewise helps to create a knowledge bank for the organization. One of the functions of the corporate event office is to be a repository for the cumulated knowledge gained from past events. How many times do we see that each event has to start anew because the event manager has left the firm and taken all the expertise? A proper system for capturing and storing information should be established before event planning takes place. Such a knowledge system should seamlessly integrate with the overall management system, that is, the project management methodology and the event office.

Knowledge management is more than just creating a library. It must consider the following:

1. Integration with the current organization's knowledge management system (if in existence) if the event office is part of a corporation.
2. Knowledge retrieval. This is particularly important for events, as time is of the essence.
3. Absorption of past event knowledge and its evaluation. Also called knowledge aggregation and mining.
4. Future growth of the system and its expansion and contraction over the event project life cycle.
5. Simplicity of data entry. Information entered should automatically go into various areas rather than having to be input a number of times. For example, the WBS becomes the basis of the risk documentation and accounts.

Creative Thinking

ANALYTICAL THINKING ASSISTS CREATIVITY

To see the introduction of systematic thinking as the death of creativity is a mistake. Certainly, a danger exists of allowing the simplicity and elegance of a system to become more important than actually organizing the event. The analytical approach outlined in this chapter is an aid to creative thinking. Some people believe that those who have to think on their feet are the creative thinkers. When a well-thought-out system is not in place to assist decision making, the corporate event management team will be continually solving problems, putting out the grass fires. Problem solving in a state of panic requires a certain amount of creative thinking. However satisfying this may be when it all works out, it is no substitute for creatively thinking in an ordered and calm environment. Knowing that most problems have been solved before they occur is a wonderful way to focus on the creative process.

INFORMAL TOOLS

A number of tools can be used to assist creative thinking. Perhaps the most recognized is the ability to draw from a variety of experiences and skills. Some event managers purposely attend lots of events that have little to do with their specialty, and others will read widely. A creative idea can come from surprising sources. The book *Claudius the God,* written by Robert Graves, provided one event manager with an idea for the launch of an environmentally friendly product. In the book, the Basques dressed as birds and walked on stilts through the swamp in order to scare the Celts. The event manager built on this idea and had people dressed as birds walking on stilts during the event.

Creative thinking means frequently making those connections that are hidden from view but once exposed cause everything to fit into place. The connection can be found through synthesizing different ideas or looking at the same idea from a different perspective. For example, one event manager conducted a construction firm's Christmas party at the construction site, which was a large hole in the ground. The guests were lifted in by crane. Another event manager located a medieval-themed dinner in an old parking lot, a connection that worked because the brick-walled parking lot already had a medieval feel to it.

FORMAL TOOLS

More formal methods to assist creative thinking use the decomposition of a problem or situation into its attributes and the recombination of the attributes to provoke a different way to view the situation. The morphological box is a technique whereby the attributes are listed on the top (column headings) and side (row headings) axis of a matrix. The combination of attributes can provide innovative solutions to problems and provoke creative thinking.

For example, Table 6-1 shows the attributes of a product launch.

This type of attribute thinking was used to launch an ecologically friendly forklift. Buyers from around the world were flown to an outdoor park location. The forklifts arrived down the road in a procession with stilt walkers. The forklifts danced with the stilt walkers, all carefully choreographed to the music of steel drums, in order to demonstrate the maneuverability of the forklifts. The creativeness of this kind of event added enormous value to the function and reflected the client's expertise in choosing the right event management company.

STORYBOARDING

Storyboarding is a common method for stimulating creativity in corporate event management, as well as for presenting an event proposal to the stakeholders. In storyboarding, the ideas and problems are graphically represented and placed on a board so that different arrangements of the attributes or ideas can be discussed. It is common method used for drafting a sequence of tasks. The tasks are placed on small notepaper and pinned to a board. In this way the optimal sequence of tasks can be worked out.

Table 6-1 Morphological Box

Product	Unveiling	Demonstrating	Food and Beverage	Venue	Logistics
Actual product	Coming from smoke	Straight demonstration	Buffet	Inside hotel	Clients arrive by bus
Model	Rise from ground	Dancing	Theme to product	Outdoor park	Clients fly to venue
Picture	Lowered by helicopter	Vocalizing	Cook your own	Parking lot	Limousine
Laser image	Delivered by van	To music	No food	On an island	Product delivered to client

TRIZ (A RUSSIAN ACRONYM FOR THE THEORY OF INVENTIVE PROBLEM SOLVING)

TRIZ, an integrated method developed by Genrich Altshuller, is a way of describing and analyzing creativity and problem solving. Originating from a close study of engineering innovation, TRIZ is now used in many business applications. The method is too involved to go into in this text, as there are numerous principles and inductive laws derived from the features and functions of inventions throughout history. However, TRIZ is far more than just the usual combining of attributes, and it approaches a science of creativity. The event office looking for new ideas should follow up this text by researching TRIZ on the Web.

Making Decisions

Most people realize that the important decisions are made at the beginning of the event project life cycle (EPLC). As the EPLC moves toward the event itself, the number of decisions will rise. The effect of all those decisions, however, will not be felt until the actual event occurs. This is the reason for using a tried-and-tested methodology and for considering what tools can assist the corporate event manager in making decisions. This section of the chapter describes aspects of decision analysis applicable to an event project environment. Decision analysis not only assists the event office in making decisions, it also documents the decisions and is a step toward corporate event management becoming a recognized profession.

SPECIAL CHARACTERISTIC OF THE EVENT ENVIRONMENT

Making a decision requires making a choice between alternatives. This definition assumes a relatively stable environment in which to make the decision and a straightforward link between a choice and the result of the choice. This is the case only with some standard corporate events. This definition also assumes that the choice and its consequences are fully understood. In a complex system this is almost impossible. Decision making for events is more a matter of reducing the uncertainty of a course of actions. The decision will not be hermetically sealed from the other parts of the event. It will be affected by decisions made elsewhere. For example, the carefully thought-out decision to use a particular venue can be annulled by a choice made by the client or CEO or any major stakeholder. Any decisions in this fluid situation imply that the decision maker will strive to make them work.

TYPES OF DECISIONS

Many decisions are made over the life cycle of a corporate event. They will all be within the constraints of the strategic objectives of the stakeholders. They can be classified as:

1. **Project decision:** The go/no-go decision to take on the event at all. In an ideal situation it will be based on the results of the feasibility study. It will concern issues such as the capacity of the corporate event management to achieve the objectives, the resources available, the time required, and other factors. These are listed in Chapter 5 as part of the event feasibility.
2. **Comparison:** The fairly straightforward decisions made by comparing alternatives. For example, a supplier will be compared to other suppliers. It assumes that the comparison is made on commensurable factors.
3. **Event value:** The decisions based on the future value of a choice to the event objectives. For example, the event sponsor might determine the future value of including an extra sponsor.
4. **Configuration decision:** The trade-off between the three variables of cost, content, and time. For example, if certain tasks of the event exceed the time allotted, the event manager will have to decide which of the variables to change.

DECISION TREES

The decision tree was developed to assist the process of deciding in times of uncertainty. Constructed graphically to represent the choices and their consequences, the decision tree is particularly helpful in sequential decisions. The advantages of using this tool are:

1. It can clarify a complex problem by ordering the process.
2. As a graphical representation it is easily understood and can be discussed with a group of people.
3. It is a record of the decision.
4. It is a standard procedure used in other areas of business.

Figure 6-3 shows a simple decision tree for an outdoor event, a corporate dinner for clients in a remote wilderness. Part of the event experience was getting to the event site. Due to the inclement weather—it had been raining and hailing—on the morning of the event, the event manager had to make the following choice:

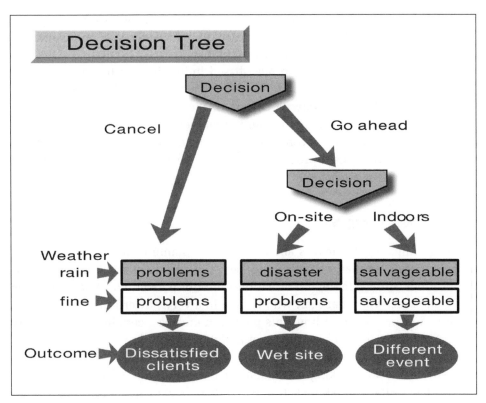

Figure 6-3
Decision Tree

1. Cancel the event.
2. Have the event, either at the outdoor site or at the indoor alternative.

Some of the factors to consider were:

1. The event site was already set up.
2. Communicating the change of plans would require immediate action.
3. The weather could turn fine.
4. Some invitees had already traveled a distance to attend the event.
5. The indoor alternative would require a large workforce to get it all together on time.

Given that the objective of the event was to satisfy the stakeholders, the event manager consulted the stakeholders. A number of them said that the rain may clear, but based on the probability and consequence of the outcomes, they decided to hold it indoors. The decision enabled the event manager to concentrate on the tasks at hand and immediately focus the staff on the event—that is, create a slightly different event indoors.

The decision trees used in project-based industries can be very complex, and estimating a probability value for the consequence of choices can be difficult. Some of the more stalwart sectors of the event industry, such as conferences and exhibitions, benefit from the mathematics of statistical analysis. However, many aspects of events are more related to project management of research and development programs and therefore are too fluid to be captured with mathematical precision.

MAKING NO DECISION

Although much of this text is about clarity in communication and documentation, some event managers prefer to keep the decisions vague and the communications stifled. In such a situation the only person who knows what is going on is the event manager, who is then in a very powerful position, as the event would not occur without this person. It creates a certain mystique. Any company employing such people is at a high risk of failure.

Keeping decisions vague should not be confused with the genuine decision strategy of not making a decision. It is a valid way of solving a crisis. Making a decision and taking action when there is inadequate information can be worse than doing nothing.

In particular, the ability to trust the event staff to solve problems before they reach the threshold of importance is a vital part of project management. A robust management team is one that enables its members to make decisions and to take responsibility for them. Regardless of the outcome of making a choice, the team needs to feel that, by using the right process in decision making, they have the full support of the event management team. It is important not to confuse a lucky result with a well-thought-out method.

TRADE-OFF ANALYSIS

Trade-off analysis concerns the configuration of the three variables of cost, content, and time. In a closed system—that is, one without any external input—any decision will mean a change in the configuration of the three variables. In practice this is all too familiar to the event manager. The project management methodology gives the event manager a way to express this, based on the triangle of project management as seen in Figure 6-4.

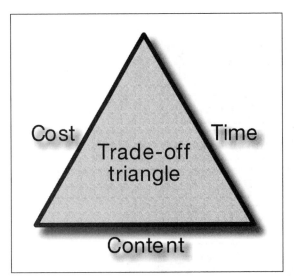

Figure 6-4
Corporate Event Project Management
Triangle

Basically, any change in one of the sides of the triangle will require a corresponding correction to the other sides. Put metaphorically, the area of the triangle must stay the same. If this relationship is explained to the client and the other stakeholders in these terms, then the decision becomes a clear choice independent of the personalities involved. When such problems arise (inevitably), the professional event manager should have a systematic method to use. Figure 6-5 illustrates such a method.

When a problem arises, the corporate event management team has to assess whether it is a real problem, a perceived problem that seems very important to some people but has little consequence for the event, or a perceived problem that could become a real problem. For example, bad publicity for an event may upset some people associated with the event, but will it impact on the event itself? When these situations occur, the event office has to determine the time that can be spent on solving the problem and what will be sacrificed. It is essential that the problem be clarified: What will it affect? Will it lead to a secondary problem? Can the problem be better defined? Small situations can easily be magnified, particularly when the event is set for the next day.

If the problem gets past this filter, the next step is to review the objectives of the event. These will be a mixture of the stakeholders' objectives, and these create most of the constraints on the event—such as costs and the deadline. This review will give the corporate event management team an understanding of the current decision environment. At this point alternatives have to be discovered, and they will mean a trade-off between the variables.

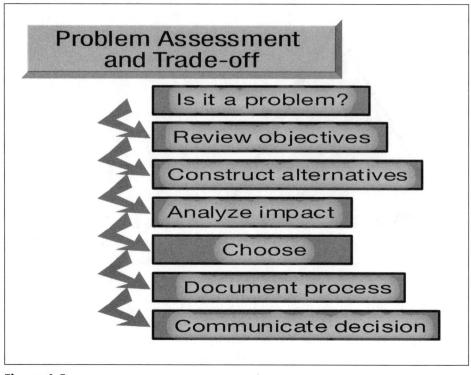

Figure 6-5
Trade-off Process

Given that the greatest constraint is the deadline, then a change in the content of the event (i.e., what is on the program) will mean an increase in cost and resources. Organizing an event entails constant trade-offs. The more time spent on one task means that other tasks will require extra resources to be completed on time. When the alternatives and their impacts are listed, the event office can decide on the optimal solution. Although all this seems very formal, corporate event management may, in fact, be doing it all on the back of an envelope. But what will happen when the event managers are called on to explain their decisions? Documentation of this process is essential for best practice in corporate event management. Of course, once the decision is made, then it must be communicated to all the interested parties. This can be done effectively only if a system is in place for handling variations from the base plan. A communication plan for an event has to take into account these types of changes and how the various parties will be told about the change in time to affect their decisions.

Decoupling and
Object-Oriented Philosophy

A recent development in software systems provides a useful analogy to assist the implementation of a project management methodology to events. As computer software grew more complex, developers became aware of a growing problem. The style of programming was one of a large single system or structure. If a new feature was added, the original software had to be rewritten. With the pace of software development, this rewriting became impossible. To accommodate the rate of change in software, a new approach was needed. In this approach, the task the software must perform is broken up into objects—separate units that have their own characteristics. The only information the overall program needs to know is the inputs and outputs of these objects. The program knows that it provided an input to the software unit and that it received an output from the unit of software. But, how the unit of software accomplishes a particular task is hidden from the overall program. This is similar to the black-box view of management discussed in Chapter 8.

The concept of hiding is called encapsulation. Among the benefits of encapsulation is that objects can be used from other programs, and if a new feature is to be added to a program, it may require only a different configuration or pattern of the objects.

This is precisely the same methodology for corporate event project management. Our objects are the suppliers, teams, and individuals. All that the event manager needs to know are the inputs, such as the specification, and the outputs, the results of the work. The event manager is in charge of the pattern, configuration, or coordination of these work units. In the ideal situation the only time the event manager needs to make decisions is when a problem occurs that the units cannot manage—that is, when the problem goes beyond a certain threshold of importance and the skills and resources of the team or supplier are unable to solve it. This method is often called management by exception.

Heuristics

Heuristics are advice, sayings, or informal rules learned though experience. They are often prefaced by "the best way to do things is" or "this is how we do it around here." They are closely aligned to the corporate culture and reflect the work style of the event company or the corporate event manager. The event manager uses heuristics to teach the event staff. In the complexity of shifting priorities that occurs in actually organizing an event, heuristics can be a powerful tool to convey essential meaning that cannot be expressed by guidelines. For example, one event manager tells his staff, "If there is a problem, just tell me. I can understand mistakes but won't tolerate being kept ignorant of the situation." Another corporate event manager tells his huge staff to "keep the preevent briefing brief—tell them only the relevant information or they will lose concentration quickly and forget everything."

A professional corporate event manager will collect these heuristics because they make the whole event run smoothly. No matter how thoroughly the project management system is implemented, often the more human and informal parables make the event work. The following story is an example of how one event manager continues to satisfy her clients through solid event management processes and the use of contingency plans.

Mona Meretsky, CSEP, of COMCOR Event and Meeting Production, Inc., of Fort Lauderdale, Florida, runs a tight ship. Several years ago, Meretsky had a relatively new staff member who had spent many years in the industry but was managing an event on her own for the first time since joining the firm. Meretsky's policy was for the event coordinator to call all the vendors one or two days before the event to confirm their arrival times and respond to any questions or concerns that they might have about the event. When the employee called the band two days prior to the event, she got no response—not even an answering machine saying the voice message system was full. Finally, on the day prior to the event, the operator came on the line and said the phone had been temporarily disconnected. The event coordinator called Meretsky, who was in another city managing another corporate event, to ask what options she had. Meretsky indicated that the client was new to her firm and she could not afford to disappoint the client. Always having a contingency plan in mind, she told the planner to engage a second band. In the event both bands showed up, the event coordinator would have to pay for both bands but have the first booked band actually perform.

On the night of the event, all was ready. The décor and lighting were enchanting, and the food was a wonderful sight and absolutely a culinary delight. But where was the band? The event planner had booked two bands, and now none was in sight. With the guests due in an hour, what was the planner to do? She called Meretsky for advice. Coolheaded as ever, Meretsky suggested she rush to the local record store and buy a stack of CDs of the same type of music that would have been played by the band and then have the music tied into the venue's audiovisual system.

Shortly thereafter, the event manager's cell phone rang. It was the leader of the second band. They had been taking the train, and it had struck someone on the tracks. The police were interviewing the passengers and crew to determine if there were any eyewitnesses. They would arrive two hours late, but they would not disappoint her. A few moments later, the first band showed up. When the event planner asked why they had not contacted her to confirm their appearance and why the phone had been disconnected, the leader replied, "We've been playing in Jamaica for several months. We know Meretsky knows we are incredibly reliable, so we felt there was no need to call." A much-relieved event coordinator breathed a welcome sigh as the band set up to greet the guests due to arrive momentarily. The second band was late but did show up, and the planner paid both bands. Paying for two bands and buying CDs cut into the profits, but Meretsky and her crew were assured that their reputation would remain intact.

Meretsky recommends that the corporate event manager do everything possible to ensure that the client's expectations have been met. Meretsky says having a contingency plan or two for every possibility enables her to remain calm under pressure. She also feels making the right decision for the client ultimately pays off, even if it costs you extra at the moment. Meretsky has continued to receive business from that client because she committed her professionalism and her dedication to what is right for the customer.

Event Problems and Symptoms

The event manager is always looking for early warning devices to indicate the presence of a problem. As time is always the master, just looking for a solution to a problem is a difficulty and will take away time from other tasks. Many event managers talk about having a gut feeling of a problem about to happen. However, on closer questioning, this feeling is a result of some trigger. The trigger may be subtle, but it indicates a problem waiting to happen. Below is a list of some triggers:

Staff and vendors unaware of tasks or responsibilities: This is an indicator of a lack of a communication plan or a proper responsibility list.

No return phone calls or E-mails: Often if there is a problem, the staff or supplier will hope that it will be solved before they have to tell the event manager.

No progress reports: The event team must know that whether an assigned action has been done or not, they still have to report back. Most staff is reticent to report failures.

General lack of enthusiasm: Events are supposed to be interesting. They are not ordinary occurrences. A lack of enthusiasm could be an indication of management problems.

High event staff turnover: The event staff is the most valuable asset, therefore, any changeovers can be a real problem for the event and will often indicate a deeper problem.

Lack of personal responsibility for decisions: The corporate event team members have to feel that they can make decisions and be backed up by the event office. If the team is to be empowered and therefore be independent, then they must be proud of their involvement in the event.

Lack of cooperation from the other departments: The ability to work with the other departments within a company is an art form. Even with the support of senior management, all kinds of obstructions can cause the event to fail.

Argumentative suppliers: Suppliers who know that they can't deliver what is specified on time will often bring up minor issues to cover for the major problem.

Staff concentrating on event management rather than the event: When members of the team are not 100 percent dedicated to the event, they may resort to bureaucratic exactness at the expense of running the actual event. This can result, for example, in beautiful and large Gantt charts rather than a well-organized event.

The event, whether it is a client's dinner, an exhibition, a sponsored festival, or a product launch, is a system. Within the system the event office needs to make decisions that optimize the benefits to the stakeholders. Through the use of systems analysis the event office identifies the current systems used and establishes a project management methodology. The dynamic system can be controlled and optimal decisions made using the tools of decision analysis. This whole process allows the corporate event management team the freedom for innovative thinking, problem recognition, and creative solutions. All of this is an imperative for the professionalization of the event industry.

Wrap Up

1. Systems thinking is recognizing the interdependence of all event elements and understanding the basic concepts of feedback loops and emerging properties.
2. Systems analysis methodology is key changing from an entrepreneurial focus that is dependent upon one person to a focus on professionalism, accountability, and risk management.
3. A well-thought-out methodology enables team members to use it throughout the company and around the world. It also creates a knowledge bank for the corporation.
4. Analytical thinking assists creativity. There is

no substitute for creative thinking in an ordered and calm environment.

5. There are formal and informal tools that can assist in creative thinking, including synthesizing ideas, using a different perspective, brainstorming, decomposition and recombination, storyboarding, and TRIZ.

6. Decision analysis assists in decision making, documents the decision, and is a step toward corporate event management becoming a recognized profession.

7. Decision making for events is a matter of reducing the uncertainty of a course of action.

8. There are many types of decisions made over

the life cycle of a corporate event, such as those involving the project, making comparisons, the event's value, and configuration.

9. Decision trees assist the process of decision making in times of uncertainty.

10. Trade-off analysis includes cost, value, and time.

11. In an ideal situation, the event manager should only be required to make a decision when the unit cannot manage the problem. This is management by exception.

12. The corporate event manager must be alert to early warning signs that indicate that a problem might exist.

Instruments

Ash, D., and V. Dabija. *Planning for Real Time Event Response Management.* Upper Saddle River, N.J.: Prentice Hall, 2000.

Kerzner, H. *Project Management: A Systems Approach to Planning, Scheduling, and Controlling,* 6th ed. New York: Van Nostrand Reinhold, 1998.

Kirkwood, C. *Strategic Decision Making: Multiobjective Decision Analysis with Spreadsheets.* Belmont: Duxbury Press, 1997.

Kleindorfer, P., H. Kunreuther, and P. Schoemaker. *Decision Sciences: An Integrative Perspective.* Cambridge, UK: Cambridge University Press, 1993.

Mintzberg, H. *The Rise and Fall of Strategic Planning.* New York: Free Press, 1994.

Modell, M. *A Professional's Guide to Systems Analysis,* 2nd ed. New York: McGraw-Hill, 1996.

Perlman, W. *No Bull: Object Technology for Executives.* Cambridge, UK: Cambridge University Press, 1999.

Satzinger, J., and T. Ørvik. *The Object-Oriented Approach: Concepts, Modeling, and System Development.* Danvers: Boyd & Fraser Pub. Co., 1996.

Schuyler, J. *Decision Analysis in Projects.* Upper Darby, Pa.: Project Management Institute, 1996.

Tiwana, A. *The Knowledge Management Toolkit: Practical Techniques for Building a Knowledge Management System.* Upper Saddle River, N.J.: Prentice Hall, 2000.

Points for Discussion and Practice

1. Construct a decision tree for a new product launch event.
2. Create an attribute table for a company picnic.
3. Create a trade-off triangle for an event element such as a board of directors dinner.
4. Research a previous event and investigate how decisions were made.
5. Create a morphological box for a corporate hospitality event at a trade show or exhibition.

CHAPTER 7

Event Risk Management

THIS CHAPTER WILL HELP YOU:

- Articulate the value of corporate event risk management
- Create a risk management plan for a corporate event and communicate it with the event team
- Apply the standard tools of corporate event risk management.
- Articulate the importance of documentation to corporate event risk management
- Prepare for a crisis within the corporate event management process

---

This chapter describes the fundamental knowledge a corporate event manager needs to assist himself or herself in managing risk. Risks can occur anywhere in the event management process and therefore must be continually under review. Hence, the life cycle approach is recommended. Two types of risk are discussed. The first type of risk is one that creates change and can jeopardize the success of the event. The second type of risk relates to the physical risk that can put the corporate event planner and the corporation in a legal situation. Since today's society is litigious, large corporations are particularly vulnerable to lawsuits. The concept of a risk-resilient organization is introduced. The chapter describes the various tools that can help in identifying risks and communicating the risk management plan. No matter how much work is done to identify and control risks, a crisis may occur; therefore, crisis management is also described.

Risks Are Integral to Special Events

What is risk? It is the measure of the probability and consequence of not achieving a defined event project goal. Ideally it can be expressed mathematically. However, whether that is practically possible is a risk itself.

In a time of change, staying exactly the same is a risk. One has only to consider the state of many computer companies to see the risk involved in modern corporate life. The great advantage of the event industry is that risk is an integral part of it. If there is one industry that is used to the roller-coaster ride, it is the event industry. Ticketed events, such as concerts, depend for their income on the financial risk involved in promoting events. This risk keeps the number of competitors in the industry to a minimum. Corporate-sponsored sporting events such as the Xtreme games depend on an element of danger as their attraction. This very fact results in an industry that is very careful when it comes to risk. If a corporate event manager is risking a large sum of money on the success of an exhibition, then in just about every other area of the event, the risk has to be determinedly reduced to a minimum. Within a company the event office takes responsibility for the company's sponsorship of large events or works in partnership with the marketing or public relations department because the event office has the knowledge and skills to ensure the event maximizes the opportunities and minimizes the risk to the company. To leave this responsibility solely to any other department within the company is also a risk.

In particular, one-time events are, by their very nature, a high risk. If anything is special, it is out of the ordinary, and people are used to responding to the ordinary. With the changes that are happening in the general business environment such as deregulation, globalization, and the pervasive growth of information technology, a detailed plan for a special event can be out-of-date long before the special event actually occurs. The measurable objectives, so carefully thought out, can quickly become constraints and strangle the creativity needed in a changing environment. For example, a major speaker engaged for a conference may become a constraint if that speaker gets bad publicity prior to the conference or if that speaker is no longer the right fit for the event.

The value of the project management process with clear objectives is demonstrated in how a *Fortune 500* corporation was able to respond to a major change that could have spelled disaster for a large multielement event. The corporation had planned a combined training and celebration event for its highly successful sales staff. The event management staff started the planning process six and one-half months prior to the event. This enabled them to book a major hotel in the southwest that could provide the required number of sleeping and meeting rooms.

One of the key elements of the event was a kickoff meeting spectacular featuring the senior vice president of the division. The event office spent a considerable sum to create a video hosted by the vice president, touring his worldwide operations and acknowledging his successes in each area. They also planned dynamic special effects using pyrotechnics and split video screens for his entrance at the kickoff meeting. The event staff was already on-site making the final preparations for the event, when three days before the kickoff, the corporation announced a reorganization. The senior vice president around whom the opening spectacle had been designed was moving on to an assignment in another division of the company and a new senior vice president would be taking over the reins.

Although the objective for the overall event remained the same, the objectives for the kickoff had to be adjusted to reflect the change in circumstances. The event staff took a few hours to recraft the objectives, and they formed the foundation of a new plan for the kickoff. The team was able to move forward making good business decisions regarding the positioning of the elements. The video was repositioned to describe where the corporation had been and what it had accomplished. This was followed by the passing of the torch to the new senior vice president, who then discussed the future direction under her leadership. The happy end result was a very successful event. Structure and process helped the corporate event office manage the risks surrounding the unexpected change.

Life Cycle Approach

AN ITERATIVE PROCESS

The management of risks is an iterative process; it is continual across the life cycle of the event. Some risks may come to prominence only as the event planning moves into implementation. Risks that have a low priority may quickly become important over the course of the development of the event. In other words, risk management is an ongoing process. Recognizing and understanding these changes and developments are important. The project management method is used to create a baseline plan.

RISK ASSESSMENT MEETING

At the beginning of the event planning process, a risk assessment meeting is convened and a baseline plan established. The meeting needs to have guidelines so that it is kept on track. These guidelines will include parameters such as time frame and people involved. Many companies now follow the total quality management process or some other established meeting guidelines format.

The agenda for the initial meeting should allow the team members to describe a mixture of their experiences at other events, to establish various risk scenarios, and, by means of the tools below, to identify the unique risks to this event. This meeting is in part a brainstorm session, because various combinations of event elements will need unfettered creative thinking to help the process.

The outcome of the meeting is a draft risk analysis sheet that identifies strategies to manage the risks. (A sample risk identification sheet provided by Explosion Lighting is located in Appendix 2.) At this stage the analysis document may designate who will own the risk (i.e., who will be responsible for managing the risk) at specific times during the event. The importance of documenting the event project management process is emphasized throughout this book, and it is as important here as in all other areas. Should a change or even a crisis occur, access to documentation would make dealing with the situation much easier.

THE MEETING STRUCTURE

The meeting can be divided into groups according to the event management function or the major categories of the work breakdown structure. For example, the risk analysis meeting for an international conference may be divided into marketing, registrations, on-site issues, special effects, logistics, finance, protocol, and administration. Each of these groups should contain a mix of personnel from different departments. Traditional lines of authority in this situation may hinder the identification of problems. People can be so immersed in their roles that they are oblivious to the risks. Also, the meeting should bring out everyone's experience in attending events—not just organizing them. Each of these groups would look at the risks involved in the one area and produce a risk analysis sheet. These are collated to produce a risk baseline plan. This process is also helpful to train the staff in the terminology of risk management. An outline of this process is shown in Figure 7-1.

RISK RESILIENCE

An important responsibility of the corporate event office is to create a risk-resilient organization. Resilience is the ability to withstand changes and keep the event on course. Such an organization is characterized by:

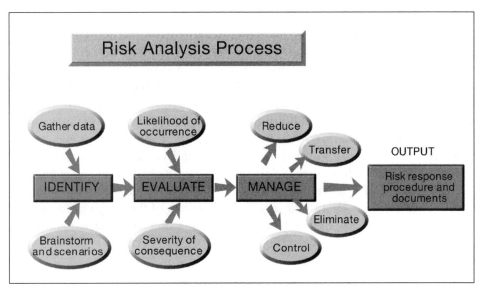

Figure 7-1

The Inputs, Process, and Outputs of Event Risk Analysis

- Recognition of the importance of having all staff members manage risk
- Procedures in place to identify risks and deal with them
- Informal mechanisms to identify risks and bring them to the attention of corporate management (called "constructive insubordination" in the army)
- Full integration of the risk management process into the corporate event management process
- Use of risk management terminology as part of the overall corporate culture for the event
- Thorough documentation for all of the above

RISK MANAGEMENT PROFESSIONALS

When using the services of professional risk managers, the corporate event manager has to be aware of their viewpoints and work histories. For example, if an event will take place in public, the local government may require their risk management department or an official such as the fire marshal to undertake a risk analysis. This is only one small part of a true event risk analysis. A town council or other local government will be concerned with liability issues for the council, such as fire or safety, and not the overall risks that may be faced by the event manager, such as the star performer becoming ill or a lack of attendance. Insurance companies often have a risk manager who can assist the corporate event manager. However, the same warning applies as with the government official. The insurance company representative is only evaluating the risks associated with the insured elements, not the overall event. The insurance company representative's work culture is to look for standard insurable risks. A condition of leasing venues from large institutions may be that the corporate event management staff or independent event company uses the in-house risk management specialists. Once again this is not enough. To have such a narrow risk analysis and present it as the event risk analysis can result in an unrealistic expectation of protection or sense of security. Therefore, the event manager must be aware of the scope of the expertise of the risk management professional. Experts in several areas may be required to cover the full scope of the event.

Special Circumstances of Events

In the event field, as in many project-based industries, the identification and management of risks is a high priority for management. Some of the special circumstances at events that add to the importance of risk management include:

- Large numbers of attendees
- Use of volunteers and inadequately trained staff
- Untried venues and sites
- Quick decisions and inadequate time, particularly as the event gets closer
- Complex and specialist activity
- Thrills and Spills (i.e., activities that are meant to seem like it is a risk)
- Need for good community relations
- Untried communications
- New independent event organization or newly formed corporate event management office
- The high-risk period just prior to the start of an event, due to the lack of time to make well-considered choices and the cost of making any changes
- Subcontractors and suppliers who are not influenced by the promise of possible work in the future.

In the last bullet above, the event manager cannot control the suppliers by saying "We won't continue to hire you" as an event is not continuous work for a subcontractor there is little incentive to do a good job for possible future work. Company A may have three major events a year. The supplier on the other hand may supply three hundred events per year. So, if the supplier doesn't perform properly the risk is really to company A not to the supplier. This work relationship is what separates event management of subcontractors from a company that can offer a lifetime of work to an employee. The promise of future work, of a promotion, and of a career path is the incentive that most ongoing organizations offer. This is not to say that the supplier is not concerned with providing a good product but, rather, that the risk is greater for the company than for the supplier.

When combined, the above points provide a very good reason to identify and control as many risks as possible.

Risk Management

The management of risk is more than identifying and controlling risks. It entails evaluation, identifying the context, and communicating the risks. In other words, it is the steps of identification, analysis, control, and reporting. The aim is to minimize losses and maximize opportunities. It is not a negative process; risk management can find areas of potential benefit to the event. It may be a stimulus for creative activity, as in this example. A recent corporate promotional event was unable to use a particular venue, and the event had to be moved at the last minute to a local sports arena. As part of the event planning process, a thorough risk management plan had been constructed for the event. The corporate event manager knew the alternatives and therefore was able to focus on any opportunities that might arise. Local artists were asked to decorate the bland arena and worked all day to produce a temporary mural. The event management realized that because of the change in circumstances, an opportunity emerged to raise money for a local charity. The mural was auctioned at the event for a large sum of money. In this circumstance, a risk was turned into an opportunity.

Risk Identification

Part of the knowledge gained by a person with event experience is the ability to identify risks. Asking those people with the most experience to provide input throughout the life cycle about potential risks makes sense. In many cases, these experienced people are the subcontractors and suppliers. Although the event may take a year to plan and be over in a day, the suppliers are continually working at various events, and their knowledge is invaluable to the corporation and to the corporate event manager. Often, experienced people in the industry can identify potential risks at the concept stage, and the event management team can avoid the costs and associated problems.

Other methods of identifying risk are:

- Meeting with event stakeholders
- Employing risk management experts
- Raising the issue at staff and volunteer meetings
- Consulting the local authorities, including the fire and police
- Asking the emergency service suppliers
- Brainstorming risks, for either the whole event or just particular sections

The use of test events, event modeling, and "event incubating" are other methods for risk identification. The Olympic Organizing Committee carries out a detailed schedule of smaller events that test aspects of their overall plan. As yet there is little computer modeling of events for risk management. However, simple financial scenarios, using spreadsheets and project management software, are used as a method of risk identification. On a larger, more scientific scale, events can be "incubated" in a controlled environment or on a small scale, and the finished plan can be used as the basis of a larger event or franchised to other regions. The cocktail party organized the night before a conference, seminar, or exhibition is often used as a test event to identify and take care of any last-minute issues.

Risk Identification Tools

The basic tool used in risk identification and analysis is the work breakdown structure (WBS). The method of creating a WBS is shown in Chapter 2. Basically, the work needed to create and manage an event must be broken down into separate manageable units. Each unit has its own resource requirements, such as equipment and skills. A WBS chart can be used to identify the risks associated with each unit. For example, an area of event management that requires special skill and resources is promotion. Certain unique risks are associated with promoting the event. Perhaps the most common risk is misrepresenting the event. The promotional material can easily exaggerate the positive aspects of the event, all in the cause of presenting the best image to the press. The result of this could be attendee dissatisfaction because the event did not live up to the promotion. Today, this can result in litigation for loss of enjoyment. The WBS can also assist in finding who will own the risk, that is, which person or what department is responsible for the management of that risk.

The corporate event manager must work with the owner of each unit to look for possible problems or undesirable outcomes associated with an activity or a decision and to determine what could be the cause of a problem or an undesirable outcome. You must look forward to the possible result of an activity or a decision you have made, and you must determine what action or decision would cause an undesirable outcome. In other words:

Cause to effect: What is the result of possible causes (actions or decisions)? For example, what happens if the invitations are not delivered to the attendees by a certain day? There is a possibility that no one will attend the event.

Effect to cause: What is the worst result and what are its possible causes? For example, a terrible result may be that an attendee or a corporate partner is dissatisfied, and so the corporate event manager needs to investigate what might have caused this dissatisfaction.

FAULT TREE

One method for the "effect to cause" identification is to construct a fault tree. This starts by deciding on a bad outcome, such as the event losing money or running over budget, and working through the various areas of the event to identify possible causes. The diagram in Figure 7-2 illustrates an outline of possible causes for reduced attendance at an industry trade exposition. There may be deeper causes that result in those listed in the tree. The listed causes may be the surface results of an unsuitable organization structure or a bimodal authority—that is, too many cooks!

This tree can expand to other areas of the event—for example, event administration. Also each of the branches (boxes) can further expand. For example, "Entrance difficult to find" can branch into:

Lack of signage
Unreadable signage
Entranceway obscured
Poorly written or drawn communication

Such a process helps the event manager and staff identify "trigger" events. These are actions or lack of actions that indicate a future problem.

Promotion	Theme/Content	Operations/Staging	Environmental
Negative publicity	Unsuitable suppliers	No parking/transportation	Bad weather
Incorrectly targeted promotion	Wrong combination of suppliers	Site/venue not obvious	Economic decline
Unsuitable PR company	Entranceway not enticing	Site has undesirable event history	Other events at same time for that audience
Incorrect timing of press releases	Site not enticing	Tickets difficult to obtain or lack of response to invitation	Local authorities place last-minute restrictions
Swamped by another industry event	Entertainment not attractive to target audience	Entrance fee too expensive or cheap	Traffic congestion
Wrong staff members or volunteers talking to the press	Incompetent event designer	Queues too long	Sickness outbreak
Unsuitable press contacts	Previous event by same company didn't work	Entrance difficult to find	Includes a national or ethnic/ religious holiday. Attendees out of town.

Figure 7-2
The Fault Tree

DOCUMENTATION

At the various meetings with the stakeholders, it is important to document the risks. A risk analysis sheet, shown in Figure 7-3, can be used. Part of this process is to assess the likelihood of any risk. Use Table 7-1 to assign a likelihood rating to each identified risk. The risk can then be mapped on a graph according to its probability of occurrence and its severity. Figure 7-4 illustrates a simple risk impact graph. The event manager should realize, however, that giving a mathematical value to the probability of a particular risk can give the false impression of mathematical accuracy in an area that is really qualitative prediction—a risk in itself.

For example, one risk to consider is that someone will die of natural causes at the event. If a death should occur, the event manager will of course

Event Risk Analysis

Name of Event :　　　　　　　　　　　　　　　　　　　　　Date :

Prepared by :　　　　　　　　　　　　　　Version

	Identify	Likelihood Rating	Consequence Rating	Contingency Plan	Responsibility	Action/ Response	When	Code
External Risks								
➢ Location								
➢ Economic								
➢ Environment								
➢ Weather								
➢ Competitors								
Administration								
Financial								
Marketing and PR								
Information flow								
Health and Safety								
Security								
Crowd Management								
Arrival/departure								
Site/venue								

Figure 7-3
Corporate Event Risk Analysis Spread Sheet

have to drop what he is doing and immediately attend to this situation. The effect on the event can be very large. The likelihood of a death occurring will depend on the type of event. It is more of a possibility at an event that has a large attendance of older people, such as a retiree reunion luncheon, than it is at an event aimed at young adults. For most events this risk will be high on the left-hand side of the graph.

Table 7-1 Likelihood Rating

Level	Descriptor	Description
A.	Almost certain	Event is expected to occur in most circumstances
B.	Likely	Event will probably occur in most circumstances
C.	Moderate	Event should occur at some time
D.	Unlikely	Event could occur at some time
E.	Rare	Event may occur only in exceptional circumstances

Source: AS/NZS 4360 Standard for risk management.

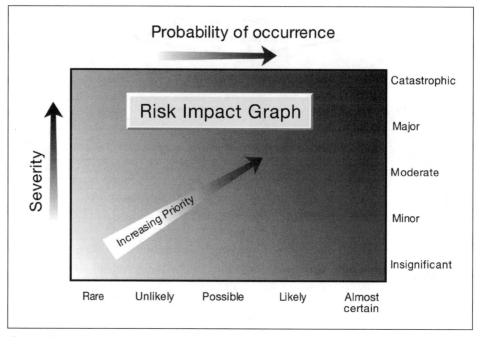

Figure 7-4
Corporate Event Risk Impact Graph

We have included a real-life situation at the end of the chapter. Included with the case study is the analysis chart used by Explosion Lighting to assess the associated risk. The company president, Mike Cerelli, advised us the company always completes the risk analysis prior to the submission of the proposal. This is done for two reasons. First, the analysis can identify the influence on other areas, which we will discuss next. Second, it can impact the cost and the feasibility of the event element.

INFLUENCE DIAGRAM

Any one risk may have effects all throughout the event. To assist in identifying these effects, the event manager can use an influence diagram, which comes from the science of systems analysis that is discussed in more detail in Chapter 6. Figure 7-5 illustrates a simplified influence diagram for securing the services of a major talent for an invitation event late in the planning process. In this case, the major talent is a leading politician; however, it could be an entertainer, sports star, or well-known speaker. The effects of this last-minute choice will be felt throughout the event.

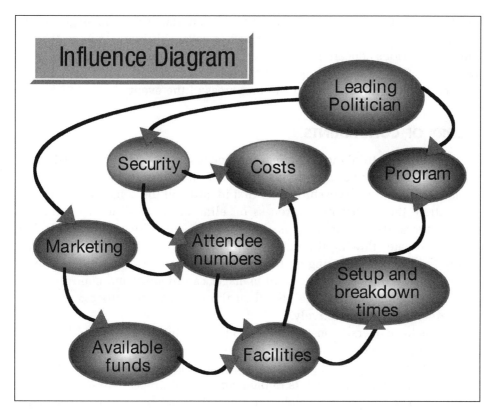

Figure 7-5
Simplified Influence Diagram

The influence diagram is merely a sketch; however, it can assist in clearly thinking through the ripple effect of any risk. The paths shown in the diagram are only for illustration. In fact, the connections can be very complex. Let's follow one of the paths on the diagram: Once the leading politician agrees to attend, the marketing for the event will have to change, which will in turn affect the attendee numbers and the invitation response. An increase in audience numbers will mean a change in the facilities—room size and setup, audiovisual equipment, food, or even the venue itself. These changes, and the fact that the person is famous, will have an effect on the security plan. The increases in these elements will increase the cost of the event, which could cause the project to go over budget. Also, the changes in the facilities will mean a new schedule for the setup and the breakdown of the venue. In turn, these changes and the new talent will affect the production schedule and, therefore, the overall program of the event. Hopefully, successful marketing and the projected increase in visibility will convince senior management or finance to transfer funds from another area to cover this increase in costs. This could be a serious concern if the budget is firmly set and the next level of management or finance will not approve the increased allocation of funds. In that case, cost would have to be cut in other areas of the event.

THEORY OF CONSTRAINTS

A useful style of thinking in project management that can help in risk management is the theory of constraints. In its simplest form it states that the way to manage a project successfully is to first identify all the constraints and then concentrate the management process on eliminating or at least controlling these constraints. An analogy is that of a variable-width water pipe. The amount of water flowing through a pipe will be a function of the narrowest part of the pipe. By focusing on how to expand that constriction, the flow of water can be improved. If the event manager can identify and control the future constrictions—or constraints—then the management process can work more efficiently and effectively.

Events have overall constraints—stakeholder objectives, venue, deadlines, and budgets. However, a manager using the theory of constraints looks for constraints in the management process. Whereas overall constraints are externally imposed limitations, constraints to the management process are internal. This is discussed in Chapter 9, which introduces Web enabling to event management. For example, a communication with everyone in a project will be constrained by the computer literacy of the participants. If 99 percent of the staff and suppliers can use the Internet chat function, but 1 percent can't use it, then the 1 percent will be a constraint on the event management process. By identifying the weak links in the chain early in the planning process, the manager can strengthen the chain. Not identifying the weak links is treated so seriously in the critical chain project management thinking that it is regarded as the major reason projects fail.

RISKS IN COMBINATION

Once the risks have been identified, the event manager should look at how the risks may work together. Each risk individually may be manageable; in combination, however, they may require a different strategy. For example, the effect of a major change in ticketing policy may be manageable. However, this change, combined with the withdrawal of a major sponsor, may be catastrophic. The effect of risks in combination was illustrated recently with the "ticketing fiasco" at the 2000 Olympics when both of these changes occurred at the same time.

CONTINGENCY PLAN

An outcome of the risk analysis process may be an integrated plan of action in response to a major problem. This contingency plan is held in reserve and put into action only if a major risk becomes a reality. This viable alternative to the current plan helps to remove the last-minute panic when a problem occurs. Just having a contingency plan available can assist in the implementation of the project baseline plan. The contingency plan should contain responsibilities, a chain of command, and procedures to minimize or contain the impact. With the contingency plan ready in the background, the major decision then becomes when to activate it.

An example of contingency planning occurred during a recent World Trade meeting. Some of the international companies who had offices nearby had an integrated plan of action if major security breaches developed and if the demonstrators targeted their businesses. This included extra security, communication lines, and evacuation procedures.

Crisis Management

IT WILL HAPPEN

At some time in your career, you will have to face a crisis. A working definition of a crisis is that a situation, if left unattended, can quickly lead to a major disruption of the event or its cancellation. During a crisis, all the communication planning is put to its ultimate test. The quality of your information is always important, but in a crisis, time is of the essence. For this reason, rapid access to relevant information is crucial. During a crisis, the event manual is truly evaluated. The site plan, map, good signage, and contact list become very important elements. The fact that the staff forgot to put north on the site map suddenly goes from an oversight to a disaster.

AUTHORITY

The lines of authority will often change quickly in a crisis, and the event manager has to be aware of who will be in charge. Stakeholders that have paid little attention to the event will suddenly become involved. The event manager may have been dealing with a company's vice president of marketing only to find that the CEO steps in when a crisis occurs. If outside emergency services are involved, the corporate event manager will be regarded only as an advisor in the situation.

THE MEDIA

If the crisis is newsworthy, the press may become involved. If so, the corporate public relations officer or the representative of the corporate public relations firm should handle the press. Whatever is reported will reflect on the stakeholders, the corporation, and the event for years to come. The press will seek out any human interest or tragic story from the staff. The reporters will be very aggressive in their pursuit of information. The corporate event manager and especially the independent event manager should decline to make any statements to the press. Rather, the event manager needs to be concerned, calm, and considered, but focused on dealing with the crisis rather than the press.

During this time, the public relations representative and the senior staff will be looking to the event manager to provide the factual information and documents related to the event. The source of all information has to be as centralized and accessible as quickly as possible. The documentation discussed in Chapter 3 and the event manual discussed in Chapter 10 are both critical at this time.

Postevent Risk Management Report

Part of the event shutdown procedure is debriefing the staff, collecting any incident reports, and gathering any other information that is pertinent to future liability issues. This may include photos, video footage, and the names and telephone numbers of witnesses. However, data gathering for the risk management report is only one portion of the shutdown procedure. The other part of the process is the use of the report to measure the success of the risk management process.

Setting up a knowledge management system that can capture and process this information will enable the corporate event office to learn from each event. The system can be used to develop guidelines and procedures to prevent or to deal with future crises. It can also highlight areas where professional counsel would be beneficial, such as in this scenario: An employee was asked to stop at the post office for her manager on her way to get lunch at a local take-out restaurant. On her return to the office, the woman was involved in a car accident. Not only was she sued, but her corporation was also sued because she performed company work while driving her personal auto. As a result of this litigation, the corporation instituted a program through human resources to inform all employees about the legal implications of their actions.

A Risk Management Example

The following example will show you how one vendor involved with corporate special events approaches risk management. Mike Cerelli, president of Explosion Lighting Company in Philadelphia, is well versed in the risks associated with corporate events. Mike's company specializes in fireworks displays and production lighting. He says, "Dealing with risk turns one into a detective." Mike described his process for assessing the risk associated with a particular event.

Mike's client was planning a large event in Philadelphia, Pennsylvania. The opening ceremony included a light show on a 250-foot barge, followed by a boat parade and choreographed fireworks final show. The client required stages, dancers, and white fabric sails on the barge that would be anchored to the sea wall in the Delaware River. A second barge would be used to house the automated light fixtures that would project images onto the sails and would be choreographed to a prerecorded sound track. The great sails would reach 60 feet in height and various widths up to 250 feet. Mike estimated that it would take two cranes at 120 feet high and 80,000 pounds each to rig the sails.

Some of the risks involved in this project required much attention to detail. Could the barge hold the cranes plus the generators, over 2,000 pounds of fabric, a stage, and approximately 20 people for a total of 195,200 pounds? Could everything withstand the wind pressure? Could the crane arm withstand winds from 10 to 50 miles per hour?

Mike stated that identifying many of the risks involved in his projects comes during the proposal and design stage. His lead designers, managers, and technicians meet with the corporate event manager to identify the objectives and the needs and then begin the task of identifying the risks associated with those requirements. The identification process includes not only the client meetings, but also a road trip to the site for measurements, photos, and discussion with the venue staff, and finally a series of technical and design meetings.

Mike would not want to have a proposal accepted and then find himself in a lawsuit because he could not execute the agreed proposal. He indicated that every event is different and requires special attention to risk analysis. All risks must be considered and validated. One of his challenges in the event described above was to obtain documentation from the barge company that the barge could support the weight. In the event of a catastrophe, the documentation would be required by all parties involved.

Mike reminds us, however, not just the physical risks need to be assessed but also the risks involved in changes in plans. What contingencies are needed in case the client changes the date or changes the proposed stage production provided by another vendor? What implications does that have on his element of the event? Mike stressed that everyone involved should have a complete understanding of the event, not just his or her own area of responsibility. Everyone must see the big picture and the connection between all of the elements. He says, "No matter how many times we discuss the project, additional risks always arise. We feel that we must always be focused on managing the risks of our projects, from the first call to the last light put back into inventory."

If the development of event management follows a course similar to the development of any profession such as engineering or medicine, risk management becomes a vital tool at a certain stage. Event management as a profession and particularly corporate event management has now reached that stage. No corporate event manager can practice without knowledge of the procedures and tools of risk management. This knowledge is important, not only for safety issues and future possible litigation, but also in terms of quality management and keeping that competitive edge. This chapter was only an outline and should be used as a signpost to go deeper into a subject that is essential to the corporate event office.

Wrap Up

1. Corporate events are vulnerable both to physical risks that can put the corporation and the event planner in a legal situation and risks that can change and jeopardize the success of the event.
2. The corporate event manager must maximize the opportunities and minimize the risks to the company.
3. Risks may arise at any point in the life cycle of an event.
4. Risk management professionals specializing in events can assist in identifying, evaluating, communicating, and controlling risks.
5. Risk identification tools, such as the work breakdown structure, a fault tree, documentation, and influence diagrams, can help in managing risks.

6. Individually, risks may be manageable, but risks in combination require a different strategy and require more skill.
7. A contingency plan helps to remove the last-minute panic when a problem occurs.
8. Postrisk management processes should include the capture and process of incident reports and other relevant risk information to establish a knowledge management system. The systems can be used to develop guidelines and procedures to prevent or deal with future crises.

Instruments

Berlonghi, A. *Special Event Risk Management Manual.* Dana Point, Calif.: Alefondus Berlonghi, 1990.

Chapman, C., and S. Ward. *Project Risk Management: Processes, Techniques, and Insights.* New York: Wiley, 1997.

Collins, T. *Crash: Learning from the World's Worst Computer Disasters.* London: Simon and Schuster, 1998.

Goldratt, E. *Critical Chain.* Great Barrington, Mass.: North River Press, 1997.

Kharbanda, O. P., and E. A. Stallworthy. *How to Learn from Project Disasters.* Aldershot, UK: Gower, 1983.

Kliem, R., and I. Ludin. *Reducing Project Risk.* Brookfield, Vt.: Gower, 1997.

Leach, L. *Critical Chain Project Management.* Boston, Mass.: Artech House, 2000.

Tarlow, Peter., *Event Risk Management.* New York: Wiley, 2002.

Points for Discussion and Practice

1. Choose a recent event and create a fictitious risk analysis sheet.
2. Convene a risk identification meeting for an event. Using a whiteboard to record the ideas, use brainstorming as a technique to identify risk.
3. List all the things that can go wrong at a selected event. Select some of those and create a fault tree.
4. Imagine a major change to an event, such as adding a corporate hospitality dinner, and draw a one-page influence diagram.
5. Use the Web to research recent event disasters related to:
   - Fireworks displays
   - Crowd control
   - Financial disasters
   - Food and beverage
   - Alcohol
6. Describe the difference between a crisis and a disaster.

CHAPTER 8

Contract Management

THIS CHAPTER WILL HELP YOU:

- Articulate the role of contract management within corporate event management
- Differentiate and use contracts traditionally required for corporate special events
- Establish a contract management process for a corporate event
- Establish specifications for suppliers of corporate events
- Identify and resolve problems of corporate event contracts

It is not surprising in such a young industry that so little information is available on event-related contracts and even less on corporate events. In the past, much of the negotiation and deals were done on an informal basis, which allowed a degree of latitude with the deal. In the modern business and legal environment, this informality is no longer good enough. The corporate event office may be completely responsible for contracting and thus will have all the legal responsibilities that this implies. If it does not originate the contracts, then the office will more than likely have to consult with both the contractor and the legal department, and will have to assess the contracts coming from the legal department of the host organization. You would be participating in the contracting process and could create a situation in which your corporation is involved in a legal suit based on contract-related circumstances. The inescapable conclusion is that the corporate event manager has to know the whys and wherefores of contract management. This chapter provides a base from which to explore an important function of the modern corporate event office. Because the event industry is so fluid, the concept of variations and claims is introduced, as well as some common problems that can be found in corporate event contracts.

A contract exists when an offer is made and accepted. The contract may take different forms, such as a written document, a digital document (sent via E-mail or on a CD-ROM or computer disk), a fax, or a verbal agreement. Some corporations require that the legal department review all contracts. Other corporations have standard contracts crafted by the legal department, and the vendor is required merely to fill in the blanks where indicated. The legal department must review and approve any variations to these contracts. The larger the corporation is, the more likely that it has a process in place that outlines the details from negotiation through specification to administration or control.

Essential to Projects

The basis of all corporate event management documentation is the contract. The contracts are the goals and objectives of the event frozen in time and are the responsibility of the corporate event manager. Each contract specifies who will do what, when it will be done, for whom it will be done, and in some cases how it will be done. The contract can be as detailed as an entertainment contract or as simple as a letter of agreement or a purchase order. However, as every corporate event manager says, "Write it down." Without a contract, the event would be based on what everyone remembers as the arrangements. This may work for small informal events, but the moment that suppliers, the public, or any government agencies are involved, written agreements are mandatory. This is particularly true in the case of corporations.

A contract is mutually binding and can be brought before the courts. Many people feel that corporations have deep pockets and that they can be sued for millions, making the plaintiff instantly rich. One only has to look in the newspapers and magazines to validate this fact. A recent book, *Whiplash! America's Most Frivolous Lawsuits,* by James Percelay (2000), is not only an interesting look at frivolous law cases, but also serves as a reminder of how costly a lawsuit can be to a corporation. For this reason, agreements cannot be taken lightly and need the full attention of the corporate event management.

Contracts are not the glamorous part of the corporate event industry, and very little has been written about them. In project management, on the other hand, contracts are recognized as central to the correct procedure for project planning and implementation. The engineering and software industries have put a great deal of thought, evaluation, and testing into the contracting process. The corporate event manager can stand on the shoulders of these giants and take advantage of lessons learned from the failures and successes of contracts in these other areas of project management.

Contracts are common throughout project-based industries, and as a result a variety of terms are used to indicate the parties to the contract. In this chapter the terms *supplier* or *vendor* are used to indicate the supplier of a resource. The *resource* can be a service, such as accounting, or goods, such as lights or balloons. In general, the resource will be a mixture of services and goods, such as catering. The resource can also be called a *deliverable* and is an outcome of a process. The *principal* is the company that receives the goods and service. The *client* can be the sponsor or owner of the corporate event, or it can be the event management company. The *contractor* is the provider of the service or goods.

The ideal situation in corporate event project management is shown in the illustration in Figure 8-1. To take an analogy from engineering, the project manager regards the vendor as a black box. How the vendor accomplishes the

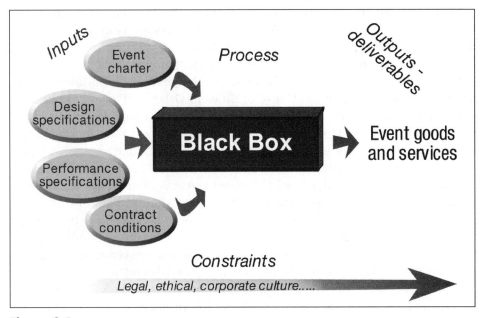

Figure 8-1
Black Box View of Corporate Event Project Management

deliverable is usually of no interest to the project manager. Only the results matter. As described in Chapter 6, this attitude is an object-oriented approach to management. This ideal situation is reached only after many years of working together with suppliers. The limitation of the black box model is the assumption of a straightforward mechanical link between the specification given at the beginning of the process and the actual deliverable. The unique and changing nature of events precludes such a simplistic model.

Although the black box analogy works quite well for the discussion of how the vendor accomplishes the task, the discussion of what is desired by the client is a different story. The contracts between a professional event planner and the corporate client might indicate that the event is a party with swing music in the ballroom on May 1 with 400 people, but it won't indicate how the event planner will accomplish the task. On the other hand, the contract with the supplier is very specific.

Mark Sonder, CSEP, is president of Mark Sonder Music Bookings and Productions World Wide and ViewPoint International Destination Management Services, with offices in New York, Los Angeles, Las Vegas, and Washington, D.C. When Sonder executes a contract with a musical group for a corporate event, the contract is very specific. The contract includes the specific location, date, time of the event, length of the sets, lengths of the breaks, the specific support provided, the travel arrangements (including the class of airline reservations and the specific description of the hotel accommodations, if required), and any specific requests by the venue or the client.

In spite of Sonder's excellent project management process and attention to detail, contract concerns can still arise. Sonder related the following story about a recent booking at the House of Blues in Orlando, Florida. He had negotiated a detailed contract, including all of the above items, between a client and a musical group. Upon his arrival for the event, a venue representative advised Sonder that the House of Blues' corporate headquarters was very protective of its logo and artwork around the theater and backstage. Headquarters did not permit the use of any still or video cameras of any type whatsoever, even if individual artists gave their written permission. In light of this newly revealed restriction, elements of the program would be impacted, including a "meet-and-greet" photo session. As the talent representative, Sonder was required to make sure that the musical group satisfied the venue requirements and that the objectives of the event were still met without infringing on anyone's rights. Sonder quickly arranged a meeting between the venue representative, the client, and the client's attorneys for an open discussion of the restrictions and their options. The group drew up an addendum release from liability to the contract. After they double-checked the language in the document, the parties to the contract were rounded up for signatures. The "meet-and-greet" session was still able to take place with the guests; however, it was located in an area where no artwork or logos would be captured in the photos. Imagine the stress on everyone because this requirement did not surface until just hours before the event. Had the event planner or the client investigated the restrictions, this requirement could have been included in the contract. To Sonder's credit, he had a project management process in place and the correct telephone numbers handy. Therefore, he could think clearly and develop a viable solution in a stressful situation.

Event-Specific Contracts

The business world has all kinds of contracts. What separates the corporate event contract from others is the overriding importance of time. A contract with a supplier, for example, is generally not an ongoing arrangement. It is a single occurrence that cannot afford to fail. If the goods delivered are not of the quality stipulated, the corporate event manager rarely has the time to look for another supplier before the event. For this reason, the contract and its administration have to be planned to the finest detail. This is not to say the contract has to be a bulky document with every contingency written down. It is a physical impossibility to contain all the possibilities in the contract. The contract is not an end to itself, but a method of making sure the client's objectives are met. This means that once an agreement is made, it has to be administered. Good project management will include time for a legal review of all contracts. Time for review is time well spent.

One area that frequently causes problems is the hotel contract. The hotel sales office sells the exhibition space and associated room nights, while the hotel catering and operations staff ensures that the event is implemented as stated in the contract. In the case of one *Fortune* 500 corporation, unfortunately, the production company that had worked with the marketing department failed to specify the name of the function room and the exact move-in and move-out times in the contract. This oversight resulted in many hours of unpleasant discussion with the hotel sales representative and the hotel manager when, in an effort to accommodate another event, the hotel sales representative told the corporation that they were moving several of their meeting rooms and attempted to pressure them into a later move-in and earlier move-out than originally planned. The result would have been inappropriate rooms for the activities planned and exhibits that were not set up in time for the opening of the exhibition hall. They reached a positive outcome to this situation for the corporation but not without a great deal of stress and a creative solution proposed by the corporate event manager who was engaged after the hotel contract had been signed.

Some organizations have a "just get it done" attitude. Consequently, a fast-paced marketing manager may not see in advance the pitfalls of overlooking the details in his or her haste to secure an attractive site. The corporate event planner's role is to point out the possible implications of leapfrogging the required steps in the project management process.

Jonathan Howe, an attorney who is well known for his work in the meeting and event field, recommends that the corporate event manager be as specific as possible. He says that 12 A.M. should be used rather than 12 midnight and that the exact date be used rather than "2 days before" or "30 days before." The specificity eliminates the risk of misinterpretation.

The corporate event manager should carefully follow these key concepts:

- Ensure that all contracts conform to local, state, and federal regulations.
- Determine the time frame for final execution.
- Prepare originals for each signer and use the signed originals as the official document, not facsimiles.
- Create a separate checklist to track the approval process for all written agreements.
- Identify arbitration and dispute resolution methods.

Types of Contracts

The corporate event industry is no different from any other project-based industry when considering the types of contracts available. The two most important contractual relationships for the event are between the suppliers and the independent event planner or management company and between the client or sponsor and the corporate event management team. The resulting contracts can take different forms based on the fee structure. Three types of contracts are used in the event industry: cost-plus, fixed-price, and incentive.

COST-PLUS CONTRACTS

A cost-plus contract is either a cost-plus-percentage contract or a cost-plus-fixed-fee contract. In this case, the contractor passes on any costs directly to the client. It is a common contract made between the event company and its client/sponsor, and can be set up fairly quickly. The event company charges the client a percentage of the gross amount (total cost of the event or a markup)—a percentage or straight fee on each of the elements of the event—and bills the client for the other costs. The event company's overhead could be absorbed by the fixed fee or could be a separate cost to the client. The event company can also structure this so that it is paid on an hourly basis, with the office costs included in this rate. The cost-plus contract means that many of the risks are borne by the client. The client assumes that the contractor will get the best price for the goods and services. If a dispute arises, these contracts often lead to detailed auditing of the event costs.

A unique implementation of the cost-plus-fee contract was negotiated by an independent corporate event planner, Brian Acheson, CSEP of VIP Events, Inc. in Dallas, Texas. In most cases, Acheson's company writes the contract and then contracts with the corporate client, but Acheson is not the agent of the corporation. Therefore, the client must sign the contracts for all elements of the event. In these cases, Acheson is paid a fee that is a percentage of the overall cost of the event and includes any other costs that he might incur. In this unique case, Acheson's contract with a large corporate client named him as an authorized representative of the corporation. Acheson's attorney and the corporate attorney negotiated the wording of the contract to ensure that it could be used to carry out the intent of the contract. Since the corporate client designated him as their authorized representative, his signature then bound them to contracts in their name. In this case, Acheson bought the item in the corporation's name and then, if VIP Events did not pay the bill, the client was obligated to pay for the item. Acheson had a financial signature authority limitation for the event. So he couldn't purchase a hotel or a sporty new car, because that was not within the scope of his authority. This contracting process made things much easier for everyone, as there was no waiting for corporate legal decisions or even for his client to sign the contract before the vendor was authorized to begin the work. The contract was signed in the name of client X by Acheson. This allowed flexibility for all concerned, and it took away monetary responsibility if the corporation folded or decided not to pay Brian for his services. This also expedited the execution of contracts with suppliers. It streamlined the entire process. Brian decided where the money went in the budget, and when people got paid. In this scenario, the corporation paid the vendor for the cost of the item plus they paid a fee to Brian for his services and any other costs that he incurred. Therefore, it was still a cost plus fee contract. The unique feature of the contract was the enablement of Brian to act as an agent of the corporation. His reputation for excellent program management skills won this level of trust for him.

FIXED-PRICE CONTRACTS

In a fixed-price or lump-sum contract, as is suggested by the name, one price is determined for the whole resource. It allows the supplier or contractor the freedom to use its own subcontractors to produce the deliverable. It transfers the risk of variation in cost to the supplier, who must pay all the costs out of the fixed amount. This is the most common bidding contract. In this type of contract, the goods or services have to be carefully described, and the corporate event manager needs to know the market price of the goods or services. Therefore, time and money are required to develop the bid. Any changes in the requirements, such as a change of venue, may be very costly to the corporation.

This type of contract can have both positive and negative implications. An independent event planner who did his homework and crafted a bid for some theme-specific giveaway items that would provide a nice profit for himself yet satisfy the corporate client would gain a sense of satisfaction. The money would be well earned based on his skill. An event planner who did not prepare for price increases based on unexpected international political situations, however, would end up with unsatisfying results. The event planner would have made a low bid to win a corporation's business, cutting his margin too close. When a political situation arose, he would take a sizable financial loss, because he would be unable to obtain the specified items at the original planned cost. The corporation would hold him to the original contract as they already would have issued the signed contract and the associated purchase order.

INCENTIVE CONTRACTS

An incentive contract or a percentage share of profit is common for entrepreneurial events or corporate-sponsored events that have an admission price. The entertainment supplier, for example, might get a "percentage of the door." Incentives can be included in the cost-plus or the fixed-price contract. If certain cost or schedule targets are met, then the contractor or supplier gains an extra fee. This contingency amount is important in corporate special events or when the resources are needed earlier than allowed for in the planning as it can be used as an incentive.

MIXED CONTRACTS

Many contracts are a mixture of the three types described. A venue could be contracted for a fixed fee plus costs with a percentage of the profits. Allowing the vendor to benefit from the financial success of the event often means a reduction in the fixed fee. Put simply, it spreads the risk. The ability to negotiate these types of mixed contracts to the satisfaction of all the parties is an art form. Without the necessary skills, the negotiation process can take up a lot of time and result in a loss of goodwill. As mentioned before, it is advisable to secure the services of an attorney with experience in the corporate event field, especially in the case of unique contracts.

The Contract Management Process

The management process, illustrated in Figure 8-2, involves negotiating the contract and the contract terms, including the all-important specifications of the deliverables. Once the terms are agreed upon and the contract is signed, the contract must then be administered.

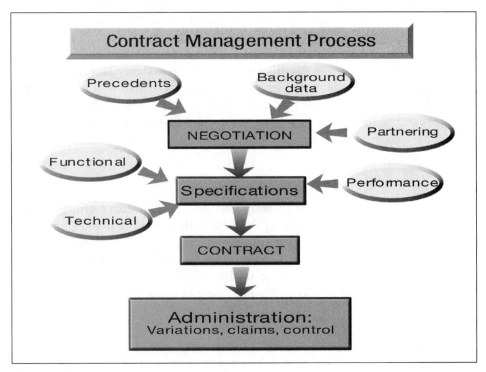

Figure 8-2
Inputs, Process, and Outputs of the Contract Management Process

NEGOTIATION

The basis of all corporate event negotiation is a mutual understanding of the goals of the event. This could be called the mission statement or corporate event charter. Much of the ongoing negotiation is persuasion and motivation, rather than enforced decisions. The corporate event manager may need to persuade the suppliers to arrive a bit earlier or the staff to be more polite, for example. Contract negotiation is a more formal version of this skill. Any mistakes in the contract can have serious consequences.

Background

Preparation is essential for a good outcome from the negotiation process. Background information on the suppliers and their style of business will assist in understanding what can be negotiated, as well as how far to go. Each of the suppliers has its own terminology to describe its services. The event manager needs to understand this terminology. For example, the term *setup* means something quite different for information technology suppliers than for staging suppliers. The preparation should include consideration of the event constraints and variables. The constraints could include the stakeholder objectives, deadlines, and intangible aspects of the corporate culture. The variables can be the three parts of project management: time, content, and cost. Time variables—certainly not the deadline—may include delivery and pickup. Cost variables may include payment schedule, discounts, penalties, and bartering. Content variables can include the quality and quantity of the deliverables. Juggling these variables to the benefit of the corporate event objectives is an important part of corporate event management and requires a good knowledge of trade-off analysis.

Precedent

As precedent is such a powerful argument, any similar successful contracts can be used and referred to during the negotiation. This is a good reason to make sure that the contract doesn't set a precedent that may be regretted at a later time. Reducing or increasing fees is far more difficult once a precedent has been set. Precedents can also be useful in crafting the specifications and terminology for special effects and other unusual event elements.

Partnering

The overriding factor in any negotiation is perhaps the attitude of the parties. A successful corporate event should be seen as a win/win situation or a mutual benefit to all parties. Hence, the concept of partnering with the vendors or suppliers, rather than just negotiating, is important. Coming into the negotiations with a command-and-control attitude, particularly when dealing with specialists, will only impede the process. The suppliers, such as the caterers, sound engineers, designers, and security, should feel they are contributing to the success of the event. With this in mind, attentive or active listening to the other party is an essential skill. Determining the other party's expectations and needs and hearing the more subtle indicators can come only with experience in this area. Every negotiation has covert as well as overt goals. The other party may have subtle reasons for certain negotiation positions, which the negotiators need to understand. Don't drive a very hard bargain; consider other factors. Remember, the lowest cost is not always the objective. The service required to provide a memorable corporate event can mean a lot more than a few dollars saved. A vendor who feels "cheated" may seek to achieve his or her goal by cutting back on services or by providing a lower-quality product. In the end neither person has won. Take the case of the new corporate event planner who wanted to impress his boss with his negotiation skills. He pushed very hard to get the caterer to reduce the price. He was very satisfied with his achievement—until his guests complained that the portions were so meager they planned to stop at a fast-food restaurant on the way home. Needless to say, it was not a memorable event. One of the advantages the event industry has over other industries is that, at least most of the time, it is exciting. Most suppliers and their staff like to be involved, and they want to showcase their skill or product.

SPECIFICATION AND EVALUATION

The specifications are a written description of the required product or service and will be referred to in the contract. The suppliers will use the specification document to estimate a price and to bid for the contract. For unique corporate events using nonstandard products, the specification may be the guide for the creation of the product. Many of the problems in contracting arise from the way the specifications are written. Too often they describe the deliverable in terms the corporate event manager understands rather than making it clear in the language of the suppliers.

The product or service can be described in terms of:

Function of the resources to enable the event to occur successfully. For example, "The lighting should allow the catering and staging personnel to operate under clear light and during the dance time provide exciting disco-type lighting."

Technical description of the product or service. For example, "The contractor will supply and set up fifteen parcans, three lighting trusses, one mixing desk, associated cabling, and personnel."

Performance of the goods or services at the event. For example, "The lighting will illuminate the whole arena for the first two hours with clear but soft lighting and change to disco style for the next two hours."

Technical and performance specifications can be very detailed. To prevent any misunderstanding, the specifications should contain all three types of description. The specification should be written as clearly and concisely as possible. Diagrams are an excellent communication medium. The floor plan or site map is probably the most important diagram. However, too much detail can be a risk, because the supplier may miss the important aspects of the event in the smog of data.

In a multiple bid for the contract, the corporate event manager will need to evaluate all the bids. Project management uses a number of formal rules for this process. Perhaps the most common is to create an evaluation grid or matrix. Across the top of the grid are the key specifications and down one side are the various suppliers. The grid is populated with the data provided by the various suppliers. Another method is to use a weighting system. The criteria are weighted according to their importance to the event. The cost is not the only factor and frequently is not the most important factor. It is certainly strongly weighted, but the ability to deliver a quality product on time, vendor reputation, vendor knowledge of the client, or experience in the venue or city may outweigh the cost.

The capacity of the supplier to deliver the goods or services is an important consideration in awarding any contract. Although one supplier will win on the various criteria, the supplier may well have been using the bid to enter a new field. This is called *buying the bid*—that is, putting in a low bid and undercutting the competitors as a way to enter the industry. The event manager should check the supplier's true financial viability and the supplier's ability to produce the required product or service. Credit agencies, banks, and industry associations can do the financial check. Some corporate event managers recommend speaking to the supplier's employees as one way to determine the vendor's current financial viability.

Administration: Review and Control

Corporate event planners often think that once the agreement is made and the contract is signed, the hard work is done. For some suppliers this will be true. However, the event planner would be foolish to think that the words on paper and the possibility of legal action will make all suppliers comply with the contract terms or with the intangible "spirit of the contract." Also variations in the event planning will almost certainly occur. The event planner must walk a fine line between interfering with the supplier and allowing the supplier the freedom to provide the resource according to the terms of the contract.

The administration of the contract includes:

Briefing all the contractors. Most event management companies or corporate event managers will require preevent meetings to clarify any changes, orient all the suppliers, and explain any uncommon event conditions or special corporate requirements. Further briefing sessions or meetings may be needed. The meetings are part of keeping the communication channels open. In the case of large corporate events the meetings are usually held weekly at the beginning of the event life cycle and become increasingly more frequent as the event date approaches. The core team participants are often required to submit progress reports using the designated corporate project management forms.

Setting up procedures for contract review with tasks and responsibilities. When any changes occur in the event planning, the contract will need to be reassessed. This is applicable for the client contract as well as the supplier contracts. Some method of control may be necessary for any cost-plus contracts to make sure that costs are correctly reimbursed. In some cases, a separate corporate office is responsible for the inspection of contract implementation.

Establishing trigger events or milestones that indicate the success, or otherwise, of the supplier staying on schedule. Often, if a problem develops with the supply of a resource, the corporate event management will be told at the last minute. An inspection process must be in place at milestone events to ensure that a preventable crisis does not occur.

Maintaining a general "firm but fair" attitude about fulfilling the contract terms. The event company or the corporate event manager and all suppliers should know they must abide by the contracts. This accompanies a procedure for the approval for any changes.

Forming a contract administration team. Large corporate events may set up a team to develop a contract administration plan that includes a quality assurance guide and inspections.

The degree of administration of the contract will vary, depending on such factors as:

The uniqueness of the event. Special one-time events requiring unique or unusual combination of products and services will need close monitoring. The uniqueness of the corporate event may be reflected in nonstandard contract requirements.

The experience and skills of the contractors. The aim of most event companies is to have suppliers that are autonomous, need little monitoring, and produce the deliverables to cost, on time, and to quality.

The confidence of the client or sponsor in the event management's abilities. This intangible quality plays an important part in the whole corporate event management.

The magnitude and the visibility of the event. Some corporate events, such as large industry exhibitions, are critical to the future success of the company. These corporate events can make or break the business for the following years, and therefore the progress is monitored very carefully.

Contract Variations

Changes are inevitable, but not all the possible changes can be foreseen in the negotiation and the awarding of the contract. These changes could be external to the event and therefore uncontrollable, or come from inside the event organization and, if known, controllable. The origin of variations to contracts can be divided into the following categories:

External and unknown: Natural disasters, exchange rates, new legislation, client volatility

External and known: Inflation, building work

Internal and unknown: Sickness, staff conflict

Internal and known: New suppliers coming on board, increase in staff

With the correct project management structure and procedures in place, most of the minor variations will be taken care of by the management units or teams that have that element of the event as part of their responsibility. For example, small changes in the event venue design may be decided by the staff responsible for that part of the event. This style of management is part of empowering the staff to take responsibility for their section of the event. Only when the variations are significant to other areas of the event, and in particular affect the objectives of the event, should they come to the attention of the corporate event manager.

CHANGES/CLAIMS

The correct procedure must be in place to control any modifications to the agreement. The request for a change in a condition of the original contract needs to be evaluated and approved, and this whole process must be properly documented. Large corporate events may necessitate the use of change requests, also called variance claims, and approval mechanisms. The effect of any contract change on the event as a whole, as well as on its many parts, needs to be estimated. The decision for variation and the effect on the event has to be communicated to the affected parties. The document templates or forms used for this procedure are filled in with such information as:

- Contractor's name
- Description of change
- Adjustment to fee
- Effect on the event
- Authorization signature
- Any necessary coding or file reference numbers

In some corporations, a new contract is required if the changes to the original contract are significant. In that case the whole process, including the legal review, must be repeated.

Besides considering the process to approve changes and the impact of those changes on the overall event, the event planner must also consider the impact on the vendor when a corporate client makes a change. A properly written contract will protect the vendor from any adverse effects of changes made by the client. The vendor must understand what should be included in the contract. Brian Acheson, CSEP, of VIP Events, Inc., of Dallas, Texas, related the following story regarding a properly written contract.

Patti, a new corporate event planner, spent a great deal of time with a caterer planning a special dinner for the senior staff of the marketing department and several key clients. She wanted to ensure that the dinner was not just, as we refer to it, chicken with peas and baked potato. The caterer went to great lengths to obtain special recipes from the key client's region of the country. One of the recipes selected was for a pumpkin walnut soup requiring two days to prepare. On the afternoon of the day before the event, Patti called the caterer with second thoughts about the soup. She had decided to change it to a more conventional soup, such as cream of tomato or perhaps onion soup. The caterer said he would be happy to make the change, but Patti would be required to pay for the ingredients and the labor to prepare the pumpkin soup that was now simmering in the kitchen. Patti was very irritated with the caterer and could not believe that he dared to charge her when she represented a corporate account. But the contract was on the side of the caterer, who had included a clause stating that any changes within seven days of the event would be charged to the client. This was fair and protective. The caterer had purchased and prepared the ingredients in good faith and could not resell the soup to another client at this point. Clearly, the caterer should not suffer a loss of profit because the client changed her mind.

BREACH OF CONTRACT

When a breach of contract cannot be solved by a claim and negotiation, the parties may resort to legal action. A breach of contract can result from actions by the event staff, so the staff must be aware of the legal risks of any actions. If the conditions of the contract are broken or the intent of the contract is not carried out, then the event company or the corporation can find itself in court. At these times, the importance of effective event documentation and filing becomes apparent.

Common Problems

A basic element of good risk management of contracts is to learn from the most common past mistakes. Most contract problems stem from the unique nature of events and the pressure of the event deadline. These include:

- Too much time spent on negotiation and awarding of the contract compared to administration of the contract
- Lack of sufficient knowledge regarding the event element to properly craft the description of the desired product or service
- Lack of contract knowledge, including common law
- Not realizing the implications of a variation in the contract on all areas of the event (i.e., not using a systems approach)
- Settling for a cost-plus contract, as they are quick to establish
- Not requiring the suppliers to make timely progress reports
- Not realizing that both bidding and administration are costs to the event
- Lack of effective briefings and meetings to facilitate a full understanding of the intent of the contracting parties
- Not settling disputes
- Not obtaining a signed release form at the time of any dispute settlement
- Not asking questions when the description or intent of an element in the contract is unclear
- Not getting any changes in writing or initialed by the authorized party

All parties to the contract should ensure that the people signing it are authorized to do so. Sometimes egos get in the way in corporate life, and some people assumed to have signing authority, in fact, do not.

As an example of how a small omission or inclusion in a contract can cause significant concerns or benefits for the client or the supplier, consider the following scenarios provided by Brian Acheson, of VIP Events, Inc., of Dallas, Texas.

The jurisdiction determines whether items such as gratuities or liquor are taxed. For example, as of this writing, gratuities on events are taxed in Washington, D.C., but not in Dallas, Texas. Restaurants and caterers, however, don't always know the rules related to their industry. In the first scenario, an event planner based in Washington, D.C., wrote a contract with a restaurant for a recognition dinner for a corporate client. The corporate client had indicated that a set budget had been approved for the event and that no additional charges could be submitted against that purchase order once it was issued and the contract was signed.

Consider the impact when the event planner discovered that the restaurant had not included the tax on the gratuity. In this case, the dinner was for 1,000 attendees at $100 per person. At 20 percent, the gratuity would be $20,000, and at a tax rate of 10 percent, the tax on it would be $2,000—an amount that could easily pay the cost for a small band or for a disc jockey for the event. Just as easily, this amount could make a significant cut into the event planner's fee or be cause for concern so that a letter would be placed in the file of a corporate employee. Therefore, the contract should have contained detailed information regarding the gratuity and the tax.

When the omission came to light, the corporate client felt that it was the responsibility of the event planner to pay the tax on the gratuity, as it was her responsibility to be aware of the tax and to execute the contract properly. Further, the event planner's contract with the corporate client did not include a clause regarding errors and omissions. The event planner, however, felt that it was the responsibility of the restaurant to make her aware of the gratuity and associated tax. After many hours of negotiation, the corporation paid the tax (it was less expensive and better public relations than the litigation process); however, the corporate client vowed never to use the event planner again.

In the second scenario, the contract for a $500 show hosted by a disc jockey contained the clause that the disc jockey and the corporate client were not responsible for the hearing loss of the attendees; the purchaser would make the final decision regarding music volume. (Some people stand in front of the speakers all night, and they will come away with damaged hearing. That's why the DJ is always behind the speakers. No one could stand in front of that noise for 175 days per year without the risk of losing his hearing.) In the third scenario, a western corporate event planner who had contracted for a famous but very loud rock group, was grateful that she had included the hold-harmless clause regarding the music in her contract with the corporation, the venue, and the rock group. When one of the attendees claimed to have developed a hearing loss as a result of dancing in front of the rock group, the court ruled in favor of the corporation and the event planner, as she had included the hold-harmless clause in her contract.

Finally, music contracts should include a clause indicating that the music provider will obtain all of the music licensing permissions. In North America, ASCAP, BMI, and SESAC license the use of most copyrighted music. Singing a copyrighted song without paying a fee to the proper organizations can result in a copyright lawsuit.

Contract Finalization—Acquittal

At various times during the organization of a corporate event, all the contracted agreements will have to be acquitted. This is part of the general event shutdown process. Hopefully, all the contractors receive their final payments and any claims are amicably settled. The corporate event planner must check all the contracts so that no residual obligations are pending. All the related documents, including any change/approval documents, schedules, and staff reports, need to be indexed and filed. The corporate event planner should include a thank-you letter with any final payments.

This chapter is not an in-depth exposition of contract law; rather, it is a guide for the corporate event manager, who should always seek legal advice before committing to any contract. An attorney who specializes in corporate event contracts will be particularly beneficial, as he or she will be more familiar with the industry-specific circumstances and can save more money than the fee for services rendered and can provide peace of mind. As Chicago attorney Jonathan Howe says, "A well-written contract can be your best friend."

Wrap Up

1. Select the appropriate type of contract for the event and the vendor.
2. Be specific regarding date, time, move-in and move-out information, function, technical description, and performance.
3. Get everything in writing, including any changes or additions to the original contract.
4. Allow time for the contract to be reviewed by an attorney versed in event contract management.
5. Set up and follow procedures for all of the contract administration activities.
6. Anticipate change and establish procedures for effecting a change.

7. Include time and resources to properly conclude the administration of the event.

8. Consider taking a course in business law to familiarize yourself with possible risks.

Instruments

Cleland, D., ed. *Field Guide to Project Management.* New York: Van Nostrand Reinhold, 1998.

Kerzner, H. *Project Management: A Systems Approach to Planning, Scheduling, and Controlling,* 6th ed. New York: Van Nostrand Reinhold, 1998.

Martin, M., et al. *Contract Administration for the Project Manager.* Pa.: Project Management Institute, 1990.

Project Management Institute. *A Guide to the Project Management Body of Knowledge.* Newtown Square, Pa.: Project Management Institute, 2000.

Points for Discussion and Practice

1. Create a contract negotiation scenario and have the participants role-play the client and other contractors. Establish a time limit and an objective and negotiate a simple letter of agreement. What variables are negotiable? What are the constraints?
2. Choose and create a list of contracts that a corporate event would require.
3. Using the three types of specifications, create a specification sheet for each of the contractors for a corporate event.
4. Give examples of cost-plus, fixed-price, and incentive contracts, and an example of a mixture of these categories.
5. Create a template for a variation claim form.
6. Create a list of unique corporate event elements that would require special wording in the vendor contract (e.g., mechanical bull riding in Texas).
7. Interview an independent corporate event planner and an internal corporate event planner, and discuss a list of "must-include clauses" for their contracts.

CHAPTER 9

The Web-Enabled Corporate Event

THIS CHAPTER WILL HELP YOU:

- Articulate the importance of the Web to corporate event management
- Use the process of Web-enabling
- Create a Web presence for a corporate event
- Assess the current state of the event's visibility and suggest improvements

The fluidity of modern business is no more apparent than in the exploding use of the Internet and corporate intranets. As an event is often a onetime occurrence, the corporate event planner can take full advantage of the latest developments in the Web to become a player in the New Economy. However, this advantage can be fully realized only if the capabilities and limitations of the Web are part of the thinking and decision making over the whole planning and life cycle of the event. This approach, called Web-thinking, is beginning to permeate the event industry.

Integration

To Web-enable an event is to fully integrate the resources provided by the Web into all the functions of event management. Although the term *Web* is used to mean the World Wide Web, a subset of the Internet, most of the techniques described in this chapter can also be used on a company's internal intranet and on an extranet, where a select group is allowed access to a specific area of the company intranet. In all these cases, the Web browser has become the standard method of communication. Of course, E-mail is also used to communicate on a one-to-one basis or to send messages to the entire corporate event team, especially in this global economy where team members may be from many different time zones.

Web-enabling is greater than the two-way process of sourcing from the Web and displaying on the Web. The use of the Web is regarded as far more than a tool for promotion, information research, and communication. Those elements are only a part of the use of the Web in the life cycle of an event. A Web-enabled event has Web thinking permeating vertically and horizontally throughout the management and throughout the life cycle of the event. To truly use the power of the Web effectively, the webmaster (the person responsible for the corporate Web site) must be involved from the beginning of the planning process.

For example, the webmaster and corporate media services or the outside vendor responsible for the graphics should work together on the logo, as the Web will provide both constraints and opportunities on its design. Its colors and layout should be designed so the logo can be downloaded quickly and easily recognized on a computer screen, which presents colors differently than a press presents them using paper and ink. As the logo will have a world presence, it must be discernibly different from logos around the world, yet in the case of a corporate logo it must also convey the appropriate corporate image in both color and design. The constraints and opportunities provided by the Web cannot be an afterthought. They must be fully synthesized into the feasibility and planning of the logo. The logo is but one small part of corporate event management. However, it illustrates that Web-enabling pervades, influences, and surrounds all processes, functions, and tasks of the event.

Today, everyone wants to participate in the new technology-driven economy, and members in the event industry are no exception. More and more corporate event managers and suppliers are using technology every day. According to a May 2000 article by Shoshana Leon of *Event Solutions Magazine,* there are several reasons why so many event-related Internet sites have emerged recently. Leon stated that the most significant one is that event managers and suppliers want to take advantage of the many resources that the Internet has to offer. She states, "Now is a great time for event professionals to take advantage of the tools and resources that are available on the Internet to make the event planning process easier, faster, and more efficient. There are so many different Web sites out there, most of which offer services free of charge or at a minimal cost, to help in all stages of the event planning process from finding vendors and sending on-line invitations to purchasing party favors and managing event data and logistics."

Table 9-1, an outline of the Web-enabled event, shows the benefit of the Web to the various areas of management. Each area of web management can be divided into three categories. Each column in the table provides examples in each category.

Table 9-1　Internet and Management Functions

Management Functions	Examples of Data In (Web data collection)	Process and Services Used	Examples of Data Out (Data distributed via the Web)
Idea Theming Feasibility	Web searching for similar events Stakeholder history Legal constraints	Web search using portals Professional community Web rings	Draft proposal Request for ideas and assistance
Planning	Supplier (vendor) information Sample bid documents Expressions of interest	Web (conferencing E-mails Establish electronic filing and compatibility including filing on the Web	Internet-based software Scenarios
Marketing and communication	Competitive analysis market research data	FTP (file transfer protocol), communication procedure, virtual communites	Web site for event participants Information—rules and regulations Training staff and familiarization Password-protected event manual
Implementation	Participant, attendee registration Report Forms	Creating documents with the Internet in mind— save as HTML Form creation and CGI scripts Auction sites for sale of event equipment	Map on Web site Progress reports to stakeholders Ticket sales Logistic information On-line newsletter
During the event	Chat with participants, performers, speakers	Streaming video	Web cam Virtual tour Last-minute news and announcements
Postevent	Collating E-mails and reports Collating evaluations	Data mining Archiving	Reports to stakeholders Finalization to suppliers

The Development of the Internet

In the information technology literature, three generations of Web site development are recognized. This is mirrored in the event industry. The first two generations can be described as *Information Out*. The aim was to tell the public or attendees about the event. Due to technical restrictions, the first generation was just information, designed much the same as a brochure or flyer. In some unsophisticated cases, the text appeared just as it would be seen if typed on a sheet of paper. The second generation took advantage of the graphics and linking capability of the browsers and provided Web-enabled graphics that could be properly displayed on a computer screen and quickly downloaded. The single-page brochure was replaced by multiple-page sites and hyperlinked accordingly.

During the second generation, many event managers regarded the event's Web site with a "cargo cult" expectation: Once the Web site was operational, all kinds of riches would come. Unfortunately, they were disappointed by the lack of response. It wasn't long before they realized that a Web site is not like an advertisement on TV or radio. Participants have little reason to actually go to a Web site, assuming they can even locate it. The Internet is more like a TV with over 10 million channels. As Corbin Ball states in his "Three Golden Rules of Web Site Design," the site must be easy to find. In the case of an event that is available to people outside of the corporation, the site must be listed with the five major search engines (AltaVista, Yahoo, Lycos, Google, Internet Explorer), which represent 90 percent of the Internet traffic. In the case of an internal corporate event, the Web site location must be broadcast through the company E-mail, the daily Web-based news site, or a paper-based corporate communication.

The current generation of Web sites can be described as *Information In*. The aim is to get users to the Web site and keep them there long enough to gain information from them. The third generation of Web sites is characterized by:

- The use of forms to capture information. These forms might request registration or payment information.
- Targeted information to the user. Although the Web site contains far more data than it did in generation one or two, the information is in linked packets so that the user is not overwhelmed by the data.
- Simplicity of the Web site. That is, it loads quickly and is easy to navigate.
- Integration with all other areas of event management. The look and feel of the Web site is similar to the theme of the event and reflects the corporate identity of the client.

These third-generation Web sites help corporations, associations, government agencies, and event management companies to be more efficient and effective and to save thousands of dollars in the process. In the corporate event business, many deadlines are immovable. Finalizing registration is one of those deadlines. Event planners spent many sleepless nights first trying to determine what was written on the paper registration documents, since many people scribble. Then they had to key in the information on the computer registration documents. All of this work had to be completed by the deadline. It was very time-consuming and prone to errors. Now companies use third-generation Web sites to capture the information entered by the attendees. For those companies without the staff or funding to create and manage their own on-line registration, companies like seeUthere.com are cropping up all the time. For a fee, the site offers interactive invitations, RSVP tracking, on-line ticketing, and event promotion. Whether you create your own registration site or you use a service, labor is decreased and accuracy is increased as the attendees enter their own information. This eliminates many phone calls and creates a happier event participant—not to mention less stress for the corporate event planner.

The third generation of Web sites could come about only after the growth of the Web and the necessary technology. One person who was quick to realize the value of the Web for event registration was Donna Westin, Xerox Corporation's manager of incentive travel. Xerox was an early adapter, implementing a Web-based system in 1996 for the 1997 President's Club incentive trip. The North America Systems Group President's Club is the largest incentive travel program for Xerox employees. This big project spans eight different waves of back-to-back trips to accommodate the approximately 1200 winners and their guests. Westin and her team have the responsibility of reaching and motivating the employees, as well as managing the corporate sales incentive event itself. Every year, they were overwhelmed with registering the winners and fielding the thousands of associated questions, especially as the date of the event grew closer.

Several years ago, Westin realized that the internal company's intranet was helping with communication in other areas, and she decided to find a way to take advantage of the power of the technology at her fingertips and reduce the stress for herself and her team. She knew she needed a professional to assist her in that task, so she contacted Xerox Information Systems and Northwest Incentives in Minneapolis. The two companies worked together to develop a Web site that would be used to provide ongoing information and status reports, as well as facilitate registration for the event. The Web site is linked to all of the elements of the event.

Every January the sales representatives are given targets for their performance. At the end of the year, those who qualify go on an incentive trip sometime during the following March to May. As soon as the sales reps return home from the current trip, Westin puts the next year's trip information on-line. The sales reps who use laptops in their day-to-day work can check on the latest information about the trip anytime and anywhere 24 hours a day, seven days a week. Throughout the year, information, including pictures of the site and trip extension details, is updated and expanded, building the excitement. As the employees qualify, their names are added to a banner that runs across the bottom of the homepage. This adds to the competition and provides an incentive for sales reps to work hard to get their names on the banner early.

The registration process is much simpler and smoother than it had been before it became Web-enabled. The homepage contains a box where the sales representatives enter their employee number. If the entered number matches one of the numbers in the database of qualifiers, the sales rep is then linked to a registration page that carries a banner reading, "Congratulations . . . You are a winner!" The employee inputs the requested information, which is downloaded daily to the corporate travel agency's database. The old process was slow and cumbersome and had many opportunities for errors. The closer the date drew for the event, the more hectic the pace became for Westin and her team.

The new Web-based system has greatly improved the accuracy of the information and increased the satisfaction of the employees. The data about the winners gathered on the Web site is then used for mailing labels, rooming lists, and other trip-related documentation. This eliminates hours of rekeying information and streamlines related processes. Westin estimates that the new process is saving Xerox Corporation $5,000 to $10,000 in mailing costs, not to mention a reduction in stress for Westin and her team. It has also improved employee communications and satisfaction. The site continues to be improved year after year. It currently includes links to hotel information, trip dates, rules, registration, program events, extension information, feedback, passports, help, and common questions and answers. Westin is sold on the idea of a Web-enabled event, and she and her team have been getting lots of compliments both internally and externally on the successful implementation.

Tools

The event industry most adept in Web use is within the exposition and meetings sector. Possibly because much of their clientele is in the information business, such as academics and information technology, they have led the way in Web-enabling for event planners. A major part of the work involved in the meeting industry is attendee tracking. This is a fairly simple task for computer software to handle. This element of the industry is relatively stable, from the planning to shutdown. Many of the ideas and tools used by exhibition and meeting-planning professionals can be transferred to other parts of the event industry. The most obvious is the on-line registration described in the Xerox example.

The most commonly used Internet tools help the event manager to:

- Enable attendees to register on-line
- Track registration statistics
- Create customer profiles
- Host virtual trade shows
- Host an interactive Web site with pages personalized to individual attendees
- Plan and coordinate submeetings and produce a timetable automatically
- Automatically send invitations and reminders to all or a select group of invitees

Many of the tasks in the above list can be outsourced to organizations that provide such services as:

- On-line product demonstrations
- Real-time on-line reports about registration and ticket sales
- Detailed attendee profile reports for future marketing efforts
- Legal and risk tip information
- Meeting industry tips, such as room-rate negotiation
- Listings of events
- Web conferencing

You may need to purchase more than one software program or engage more than one service provider. In the case of a small firm based in Washington, D.C., a $500 software event registration and planning package did not meet all of the requirements. The event planner purchased the package with high hopes of a streamlined process for a corporate annual recognition dinner. He hired an assistant to set up the event, using the software provided, and to input hours of information. When he tried to implement the chairman of the board's requirement that one member of senior staff be seated at each table of employees, the software could not enable the request. It was capable of tracking the RSVP confirmations; however, it was not flexible in its ability to arrange the seating at the tables. The lesson from this story is that you should ask for a trial copy of software early in the planning stages to test it against the event requirements.

INTERNET SECURITY

Although on-line registration is one of the fastest growing areas of Web-enabling, some people are still apprehensive about registering on-line for events with an associated cost. Thus, you need to advertise the type of Internet security your Web site uses. Many people are misinformed about security over the Web. The fear is exacerbated by the stories that appear from time to time in the news whenever an Internet hacker invades corporate intranets or when a virus is on the loose. One should always be wary when downloading anything from the Internet and should also be familiar with the articles written about the negatives of Internet "cookies." People who don't work with the Internet every day become fearful of the unknown. We would like to dispel some of the fears and help the reader communicate the real information about Internet security.

First, making a purchase over the Internet is actually safer than making a purchase in person at an establishment. Why is this so? E-commerce vendors, corporations, and major trade show/exhibition organizers use software on their Web site that is classified as secure socket layer. This software ensures encryption (secure coding) of your credit card information for transmission over the Internet. You can identify sites that incorporate this software by the closed padlock or unbroken key that appears on your browser. The Internet address is also an indicator of security. Any address that starts with "https:" rather than "http:" is secure; the *s* in the address is used as a security identifier. Further, banks and credit card companies limit liability for fraud to $50 provided the credit card holder notifies them of the suspected fraud. Many credit card companies recommend customers use a separate credit card for on-line business transactions, as it is easier to distinguish those transactions from in-person purchases. Whether the transaction is intracompany for an incentive trip extension or upgrade, or it is for an external business transaction, these precautions make good sense.

Second, viruses are not as common as many would believe. The software available today, such as McAfee VirusScan and Norton AntiVirus, offers continuous updates and alerts. However, to take advantage of the protection this software offers, the user must follow good computer hygiene and frequently download the updates for virus protection data files. This good habit will reduce the user's security risks. Further, vendors have a commercial interest to keep their Web sites clean. Backing up files is also a good practice, not only for protection against a virus, but also so that you will have a backup of the entire corporate event plan and associated documentation. The virtual office is no different from the physical office, and a copy of important records is valuable in either format.

You can obtain more information about Internet security from the vast collection of books, magazine articles, and web sites on the topic.

E-MAIL

One of the most powerful tools of Web-enabling is the use of E-mail. It has become so common so quickly that it seems like second nature to most corporate event managers. However, that is not to say that it is used efficiently for events. Ensuring the event team is trained in the use of E-mail can save a lot of time and trouble because E-mail for events differs from general E-mail. E-mail training should include a discussion of the following points:

- Keep E-mails concise. Too many words dilute the strength of the message.
- The information in an E-mail—particularly for organizing operations and logistics—should be addressed to the correct person who has the ability to act upon it. Copy only those who have a need to know, not everyone on the team. It is highly recommended that you put the content in a bulleted list format using numbers and headings. This process will enable you to receive a correct reply and provide you with the ability to track decisions. All of the preceding implies a list of tasks exists. A task is an action with an outcome. In the management of events and their deadlines, extraneous words take up time. Therefore, key words are used or a numbering system so that the outcomes can be matched to their corresponding tasks.
- Put all the sender contact details in the signature. Most E-mail software has a facility for the sender's contact details to be automatically placed at the end of the message. Many people who use internal E-mail (intranet) don't use this feature, as everyone in their company knows them. They then assume it is the same for external E-mail.
- Put the subject in the subject field. Many corporate event planners and vendors juggle multiple events at one time. In an effort to clear their electronic in-basket, the "Hi" messages get deleted before they are read. E-mail must have the real subject in the subject field. This practice also enables the reader and subsequent readers to follow the thread of a series of E-mails. For example, if you've exchanged a number of E-mails about the sound system, you can sort all your E-mail by subject and quickly locate those relating to the sound system. One corporate event planner learned this lesson the hard way. He failed to incorporate the topic in the subject field of an E-mail. Unfortunately, it was his request

for the exhibit booth designer to include a sound system. Each thought the other had handled the requirement. As the booth was being erected at the show, he discovered that he did not have a sound system. After lots of scrambling and some additional cost to expedite the request, the sound system arrived in the nick of time. This situation could have been avoided using the hints and tips described in this text.

The team has to realize that the nature of event E-mail is dependent on the life cycle of the event. Crisp, decision-oriented E-mail is essential when the event nears as no one will have the time to read extended messages. However, in the early planning stages and after the event, personal messages are a good way to establish and maintain a team spirit. By advocating crisp messages, we do not mean that courtesy should be omitted from E-mail. Good manners are always appropriate and are even more meaningful when many transactions take place electronically rather than face-to-face where body language and voice tone can convey a friendly work relationship.

Implementing Web-Enabling

The process of effectively Web-enabling the corporate event office must be done systematically with an eye to future growth. The four sections of the preliminary analysis are shown in Figure 9-1.

AUDIT

What is the current state of the software and hardware available to the corporate event? The cost of the information technology (IT) department—hardware, software, and the expertise to develop and maintain the systems—is high. New technology develops at a rapid pace, but companies cannot install completely new systems every six months. Therefore, most IT departments are a hybrid of old and new hardware and software. The older technology systems, often termed *legacy systems,* can provide a major constraint on Web-enabling an event. Many of these systems are really conglomerations of various software programs and procedures rather than a true system. They have grown organically over the years, with bits and pieces added to them. The IT departments have always wielded much power because they understand the esoteric knowledge of technology, and they may not want to let go of this power. Also, most IT departments have been kingdoms of their own and subsumed within the corporate finance department of a corporation.

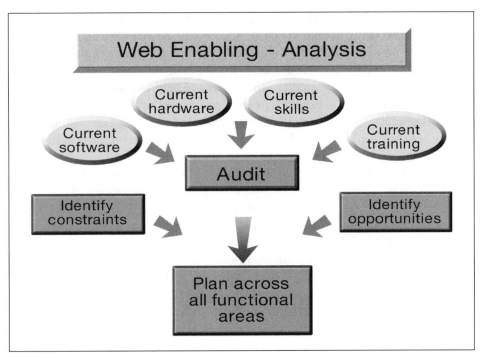

Figure 9-1
Inputs and Outputs of the Web-Enabling Analysis

The process and the existing systems often get in the way of progress. For example, most IT departments usually maintain a waiting list for applications, including Web-based applications, to be added to the system. Addition of a new program requires programming or technical assistance. A conflict exists with the formal queuing process for development and the urgency of the Web-enablement to go to the front of the line to meet the immovable date.

Another reason the IT department might be apprehensive about supporting the addition of new software is the lack of time to test it in an isolated section of the computer to ensure that it will not negatively impact or corrupt other critical applications. Most of the companies that develop software packages for Web-enabling events are aware of this requirement and have solid programs, but other programs exist that could spell trouble for the corporation.

Working side by side with the IT department to conduct an audit will determine what resources are available for Web-enablement and for training the event management team members as required. Some corporations, such as Boeing Corporation, have a Web mentor. Boeing is quite leading edge, and their Web mentor assists other departments in the development of Web-based resources, such as producing the corporate on-line newsletter and linking new Web pages to the corporate Web site. Not every corporation has the resources of Boeing, Xerox, Exxon, AT&T, and other major corporations. Depending upon the size of the corporation and its level of sophistication, many people in the office may be fully conversant with one aspect of the Web, such as chat or Web searching. The disparate development of the Web has resulted in a fragmentation of skills across the workforce. The people with these skills need to be recognized and encouraged to assist the process.

The audit includes assessing the Web capabilities of the various software systems in use. Are they Web compatible? For example, many of the latest software programs are "seamlessly integrated" with the Web. The data that is entered into these programs is automatically ready to be placed on the Web. For those who do not have internal resources within the corporation or the event planning company, outside resources are available to assist with everything from Web page design to Web hosting, as well as the entire event management process. Trade magazines such as *Event Solutions, Special Events Magazine, Corporate Meetings & Incentives,* and *Successful Meetings* provide relevant articles and timely updates on the latest in the industry.

IDENTIFY CONSTRAINTS

The weakest link in the chain can bring the entire Web-enabling project to a halt. This weak link will prove the downfall of any system. If it is a person, then that staff member must be retrained or assigned to another job. The skills that the staff members need in order to be included on this critical chain must be proven skills, not just stated skills. Otherwise, management may not find out a staff member is exaggerating until it's too late to correct the problem.

Some of these weak links identified by various event managers include the following:

- The CEO or senior executives in the company are unfamiliar and distrustful of the Web. Those with the most power over Web-enabling are frequently the least comfortable with it. This is a major problem in many organizations and can lead to all kinds of difficulties, including assigning the wrong person to be in charge of the process and lacking the ability to assess the success of Web-enabling. In the latest literature on software projects, this problem is called *management antipatterns* and is recognized as a major obstruction to the introduction of new software.
- The corporate culture is not hospitable to the Web. This can cover a variety of issues, both obvious and hidden. Issues to consider here are the

pervasiveness of the use of the Web and technology in general in the corporation. How do other departments view the IT department? Is the department considered helpful or immovable?

- The corporate marketing and communications department has control over the Web content. Marketing managers see the Web in a different light from corporate event managers. This problem reflects the more general problem of marketing departments organizing events even though their major skills lie elsewhere.
- The IT department is too slow to upload or change any aspect of the Web. Often the department regards the Web as its domain. Wresting control from the IT department can be hard. Also, IT people have a different concept of deadline than corporate event managers do, so communication can be difficult. IT employees more frequently think in a linear process whereas event managers are always in a multitasking mode. These weak links do not exist in every company but rather are examples of the most common weak links identified by event managers.

All event staff must be familiar with the Web. A short training session demonstrating such procedures as "save as HTML" may help. Often staff members will say they are familiar with the Web when they mean that they have used it, rather than possessing a true working knowledge of it. In an ever-changing system—well demonstrated by its growth—the people most likely to have relevant skills are those who play with the medium. Unstructured navigation, similar to the European explorations of the New World, is sometimes the best and only way to learn. Therein lies the reasoning for the metaphors regarding exploration to describe the use of the Web.

IDENTIFY POSSIBILITIES

The possibilities of the Web and corporate events are infinite. The ideas and techniques will not necessarily come from inside the corporate event office, the event company, or even the specialist event area. The first place to look, however, is the successful Web-enabled event. Public events and events that rely on promotion will have a strong Web presence. Web developments take place so fast that the smart event company will scan all other Web-enabled industries for ideas and applications suitable to events. Even the Democratic National Convention of 2000 used the Internet to plan and implement its event. The most important tool for Web research is the right Web search engine. Belonging to various discussion groups and Web rings can also assist. For example, various project management discussion groups have archived material that the corporate event manager can mine for ideas. Identifying innovative possibilities is akin to the creative thinking process outlined in Chapter 6. The event manager should make connections between aspects of the event or its attributes with attributes of the Web.

CREATE THE PLAN

The final step in the Internet-enabling analysis is to produce a plan that integrates the Web across all areas of the corporate event. The plan needs to fit in with the overall event plan. First, the event manager must determine if the Web structure will be constructed into one or two sites. The event may require a site available to the attendees, whether that's the general public or only internal attendees, as was the case with the previously mentioned Xerox incentive event. A separate but linked site with password security would be available to the event project team. The basis of the plan for the team site will be the folder or file system. As pointed out in Chapter 3, at the current level of Web development, the filing system should be an image of the paper filing system. The tree structure of the folders could follow the work breakdown structure. This tree structure then can be linked to the Web site to allow simple file comparison and transfer. A similar structure used throughout the event will also facilitate information retrieval and staff familiarity with the system. Introduction of the Web system after the event plan has been established will rarely work.

Web Presence

The presence of a Web site will depend on the type of corporate event. An internal event may be placed only on the company's intranet. An exhibition may require exposure only in a specialist industry. If the client or sponsor requires wide exposure, then the Web site needs to be designed and administered so that it has a Wide Web presence through multiple marketing channels. The Web presence is possibly the event's widest exposure. Therefore, every aspect must command attention from users. These elements are a function of the web site's ability to be located and the ease of navigation once it has been found.

The event manager should use the following Web presence checklist to ensure the Web site:

- Is designed for the public and is clean and easy to navigate
- Is listed in search engines, placed on industry lists, and cross-linked to relevant sites

- Contains a hit counter
- Uses various marketing techniques to obtain and retain users
- Is legible for people with disabilities
- Contains current information

A helpful method of designing a web site for the general public is to use personas. In much the same way as the theater uses characters, personas are imaginary people with real-life characteristics. Rather than designing the web site for a faceless, nameless person who is the average person of the target market, the web designer develops the web site for a person with the fully developed characteristics of the intended audience. So when you are designing a web site for corporate employees, you would think of one or two real people. There will be trade-offs of the content and form versus navigability of the web site when using personas. For example, the sound equipment supplier Joe Smith may not be the least bit interested in the moving images. He may just want to quickly get an idea of how to get the gear in, when it is needed, and a general view of the event. Dr. Margaret Doe, who will be attending a seminar, will, on the other hand, be very interested in the professionalism of the event as reflected in the design of the web site. However, it will be worth the trade-offs, because the site will be more useful and effective. One must remember that someone who is accessing the web site can go straight to the area that interests him or her. It is only the click of a button away. This is unlike a hardcopy brochure, in which the reader needs to look at the entire brochure before finding the relevant information.

The Virtual Office

The Internet, with its simple widespread communication and storage, has given rise to the concept of a virtual office. It is not surprising. Most decisions are made over the phone or by E-mail so that it really doesn't matter whether the team is next door or half a continent away. The existence of the event portal, a one-stop Web site that contains information and links to suppliers, means that many functions of a physical office can be supplied over the Web. In the past, easy retrieval of documents via the Web versus security was a concern for event planners. A locked filing cabinet in a physical office implies there is some level of security; that is, the entire world cannot read the documents contained in the drawers. However, current levels of security software contain passwords and encryption, so the locked metal file cabinet is losing its usefulness. Inexpensive, simple conferencing software and IRC (Internet relay chat—a form of person-to-person communication over the Internet) can allow parties anywhere in the world to make decisions simultaneously. Now that security and the physical functions of the office, as well as internal and external communications, can be enabled via the Web, all elements are in place to establish a virtual event office.

Corporate event planning can now be worked on 24 hours a day and even with an event team distributed across time zones. Is there then any need for a conference room? Whether face-to-face communication can be replaced remains to be seen. Building and maintaining trust is particularly difficult over the digital media. Also, integrity of information has to be established and maintained. Subtle aspects to trust and integrity may require true personal interaction. As a result, face-to-face meetings become precious in the corporate event management process. They often include a social element so that a team spirit can evolve through personal interaction. This is particularly important across cultures, both corporate and social. The virtual team's digital relationships need to have some social aspect. Informal Web communications such as chat rooms and special interest groups may assist in creating understanding among the geographically distributed event team. The message board, similar to the original bulletin boards and a useful tool in corporate event management, combines the ability to provide the latest general information with messages to individual staff members or attendees.

EVENT MANAGEMENT SOFTWARE

Project management software has the advantage of being widely used and available off-the-shelf. However, its disadvantage is in giving the appearance of certainty when, in fact, certainty doesn't exist. Event managers have attempted to use various packages of project management computer software to organize and streamline the event management processes; however, a simple mathematical calculation can show the limitations of this type of software. A single part of an event—such as the setup of a venue—may entail over 100 tasks. This means there is a maximum of 5050 relationships between the tasks. If you add an extra task, that number increases to 5151. Although all these tasks may not be directly related to each other, the number of relationships that might change is enormous. Also, the type of relationship may change.

Event managers use the concept of the black box to reduce the complexity of this system. This is useful for only one extra task, however. Between the initial plan and the actual event, myriad changes will occur. If the event manager uses the black-box concept, the event company will spend more time entering data than actually running the event. The more fluid the event environment is, the less useful the current project management software. This type of software is far more suitable for a stable event environment, such as in the meeting and exhibition industry, where it can be used for event planning and presenting a summary of the event to the stakeholders. That is not to say that suitable software will not be developed for other types of events. Advances in complexity and fuzzy logic may produce such a product. The corporate event office or the event company has to do a realistic assessment of the return on investment with regard to software. Also, some major corporations will specify that only certain project management software will be supported. This is especially true in the case of companies that outsource the support of the personal computers and software used by their employees. Some corporations have also standardized on particular project management software packages, and the reports or charts and graphs these packages output are required to be submitted to the managing executives at specific milestones in the project management process. If the specified package cannot meet your event management needs, then you can agree to supply your own support and use the software on personal computers that are isolated from the main software packages (such as the corporate billing program), or you can outsource all or a portion of your software needs.

To find out the current state of software, you may simply conduct a Web search. When reviewing software, recall the all-too-familiar warning to the experienced corporate event manager: The seller is not the same as the maker. The people who rent out the venue are from the marketing department, and their goal is to make a sale. They probably won't be there on the day of the event. The event manager will have to deal with the operations people on that day. The same warning is necessary when evaluating software; the seller of the software is generally not the developer or the person who operates the help desk. For a more detailed discussion of software, refer to the book *Special Events, Twenty-First Century Global Event Management,* by Dr. Joe Goldblatt, CSEP (Wiley, 2002) or research the trade journals or Web sites such as Corbin Ball Associates, www.corbinball.com.

Web Site Guidelines

An internal or external professional should create the corporate event Web site. Spending a few more dollars in this area can make the difference between success and failure. Also, the IT department needs to be involved to ensure adequate server space for the desired information and the expected incoming information.

Most of the information that would normally be sent to event participants and suppliers by fax or by postal mail (now referred to as *snail mail*) should be included on the event's Web site. The following guidelines specify for corporate event managers the types of information the different groups will expect to find on the Web site. These guidelines are not exhaustive and, with the rate of change in this aspect of event management, need to be updated regularly. However, they provide a starting point to assist the Web-enabled event.

THE SPLASH PAGE AND THE HOMEPAGE

If a Web site's homepage is considered to be similar to a book's table of contents, then the splash page is the book's cover. The homepage will contain all the links to the relevant information about the event. Although the only real function of the splash page is to link the user to the homepage ("Click here to enter!"), the purpose of the splash page is to grab the user's attention and immediately communicate a feel of the event's theme and style.

Not all Web sites use a splash page, but instead send users directly to the homepage. To determine whether your event's Web site should have a splash page, consider these questions:

- Is the splash page attractive, interesting, and engaging, and does it enhance the event's theme and style?
- Does the splash page load quickly?
- Can the user quickly get to homepage, which contains the relevant information?

The splash page could contain one of the following items:

- A photographic collage of past events, giving an indication of the style of the event and type of people who attend
- Quotes of interest
- Program highlights, or photos of star performers, speakers, and celebrities
- The client's and other sponsors' logos (and perhaps linked to their sites)

The homepage itself should contain links to the following items:

- Registration
- Tickets
- The program
- A map of the event site or venue
- Media releases

- The latest news on the event—including, for example, press clippings
- Audience/attendee/guest information
- Supplier and performer (artist, competitor, or exhibitor) information

ATTENDEES, PARTICIPANTS, SPECTATORS

Attendees, participants, and spectators using the Web site will expect it to contain the following items:

- A search function
- A program of the event, often as a downloadable chart or spreadsheet
- A map of the event site and a locator map (downloadable and printable)
- Tips linked to transportation timetables and preferred travel agent
- A registration form
- A guide to accommodations, linked to the local tourism bureau
- Parking and other facilities on-site such as ATMs and rest rooms
- Special facilities and ADA services, for example, wheelchair- and stroller-friendly events
- Child care facilities
- Ticket information, including
  - Ticket prices
  - Where to buy tickets
  - Early Bird tickets
  - A downloadable order form
- Frequently asked questions
- The dos and don'ts, for example, no pets
- Essential phone numbers
- Contact information, which can also be used to collect information from the user

VIPS, SPEAKERS, ARTISTS, COMPETITORS

The Web site should contain the following information for VIPs, speakers, artists, and competitors:

- A map of the site from their point of view, emphasizing staging areas, greenrooms, training or practice areas, rest areas, and personal effects lockers
- Performance, competition, and speaking schedules
- Rules and regulations

- Contacts for staging requirements
- Ticket or corporate ID badge policy
- Accompanying personnel policy
- Special parking area information and directions

SUPPLIERS, VENDORS, SUBCONTRACTORS, EXHIBITORS

The portion of the Web site for suppliers, vendors, subcontractors, and exhibitors should be succinct and to the point and would contain the following operation information:

- A printable site map from the point of view of site operations and logistics, including the sizes and locations of entrances/exits, booths/tents, electricity outlets, and obstructions
- A locator map for the venue
- Bump-in (load-in) and bump-out (load-out) times
- Schedules of drop-offs and pickups
- Schedules of the event program—or a link to that part of the Web site
- Contacts on the day
- Rules and regulations, including necessary insurance and union regulations
- Catering/rest area for suppliers
- Ticket policy, such as "no free tickets"
- Accreditation or identification needed, registration method, and place to enter the event site

EXHIBITORS

In addition to needing all the above information, exhibitors will also need the following:

- Downloadable exhibitor information pack
- Three-dimensional view of the exhibition area so that the exhibitors are familiar with the site before arrival
- Links to freight forwarding and shipping agents, insurance agents, security, stand builders
- Model of an ideal stand design
- Video of last exhibition
- Specialist loading and unloading information—ramps, docks, weight restrictions, floor loadings, forklifts

Gathering and Distributing Event Information via the Internet

Many corporate event planners look at the Web only as a place for researching information in the planning stage or for registering attendees prior to the event, but the Web can also be useful for distribution of information both during and after the actual event. An excellent example is a major manufacturer's sales conference that took place in 1999. In years past, the event manager was sending E-mail messages and making phone calls up to the eleventh hour in order to gather the presentations in time for printing, which was done at headquarters and shipped to the event site. However, this event was different. With the emergence of E-commerce print shops, the event manager established a PowerPoint master for the presentations. She set up a secure Web site for the speakers to submit their presentations. Because she had arranged to ftp (file transport protocol for Web-based transmission) the presentations to a printer in the event city, she was able to grant a little more time for the presenters to polish their presentations. Both presenters and attendees were happy as the printed material matched the last-minute edits. She was also able to accommodate attendees who registered at the last minute. Just a quick phone call to the local printer resulted in extra copies of the presentation binder delivered to the event site. Following the event, she posted the presentations on-line on the corporate intranet. The sales representatives were able to download the presentations and customize them for their clients. The corporate event planner won kudos with the corporation as she saved hundreds of dollars on the shipping costs of the materials and enabled personalized presentations that the client felt helped secure more business.

Using the Web as an Event Site

The Web is part of the corporate event business from both sides of the desk. Not only can the Web help to enable an event, but the Web can also be the reason for the corporation to hold an event. Consider the case of a client of P. W. Feats, an event marketing, design, and management company located in Baltimore, Maryland. This example shows not only how the Web was an opportunity for an event, but also how following a process ensured a successful event.

One of the largest food service distributors in the United States strategically decided to embrace the Internet by moving its entire $580 million equipment and supply business to the World Wide Web. To launch this new E-commerce division, a series of events was designed and produced to address creatively the client's goals through an integration of elements including technology, design, décor, and company brand reinforcement. It required choreographing four unique events, including serving a breakfast to 15,000 Wall Street rush-hour commuters, ringing the New York Stock Exchange (NYSE) opening bell, an analyst presentation in the NYSE boardroom, and a cocktail reception held on the stock exchange floor.

P. W. Feats was challenged by only five weeks' notice to design, plan, and organize all four events. Tractor trailers, a JumboTron, a tent village, staging, and all other event elements had to be moved into and set up on a narrow street in lower Manhattan within twelve hours. Only 45 minutes were allowed to set up the evening cocktail reception. Events had to be broken down and set up simultaneously. To be successful, P. W. Feats's timing had to be flawless.

The initial proposal included a comprehensive design and layouts; complete element and responsibility descriptions; production, installation, and dismantling schedules; and budgets for every aspect of the entire event. It addressed each challenge in detail. Each event had its own project manager and production team, and all parties involved were contacted, provided a schedule of their responsibilities, and included in preproduction planning. Event elements were prepackaged by setup area and loaded on a first-need, first-out basis. Personnel were familiarized with and assigned to specific setup zones.

The strict adherence to the intricate and involved schedule for these events rendered the following results. Analysts repositioned the company's stock rating from "buy" to "strong buy," and the price increased by almost two full points. The client received national and international news exposure on stations such as CNN and CNBC, and following the coverage, a new key international business partnership was initiated within 48 hours.

The simple economics of competition demand that if a corporate event office or independent event company does not take advantage of the Web and all the company could gain from it, then the company will go out of business. Web-enabling is not an extra arm of promotion or marketing; it affects all areas of event management and underpins all functions of the corporate event project management system.

Wrap-Up

1. Web sites are now in the third generation. They have moved beyond information out and information in to fully enabling an event via the Web.

2. The Web can save time and money, and can improve processes.
3. A variety of Internet tools are available for event planning and management.
4. Tasks can be outsourced to specialist firms that deal with specific event resources and services.
5. The Internet is a safe and effective means of organizing and implementing an event.
6. E-Mail can speed communication and decision making, but it must be crisp and well organized.
7. Most corporations have a hybrid of legacy and new software systems. The event planner must validate the status of current hardware, software, and technical support before incorporating the Internet into event plans.

8. The weakest link in the chain can bring the entire Web-enabling project to a halt. So, weak links must be identified early.
9. For the Internet to be used effectively, its use must be a part of the initial planning process, not an afterthought.
10. Web sites should be designed and administered for an effective Web presence.
11. Off-the-shelf software must be evaluated early in the event planning stage to ensure that the capabilities match your requirements.
12. The Web can not only enable an event but also be the reason to hold a corporate event.

Instruments

Brown, W. *AntiPatterns in Project Management*. New York: Wiley, 2000.

Cooper, A. *The Inmates Are Running the Asylum*. Indianapolis, Ind.: Sams, 1999.

Ball, Corbin. "Three Golden Rules of Web Site Design." *Corporate Meetings & Incentives* (February 1999): 29.

Ligos, Melinda. "Point Click Motivate." *Successful Meetings* (May 1999): 81.

Project Management Institute. *Project Management Software Survey*. Newtown Square, Pa.: Project Management International, 1999.

Reynes, Roberta. "Xerox Corporation—Winning on the Web." *Corporate Meetings & Incentives* (November 1998): 31.

Tiwana, A. *The Knowledge Management Toolkit: Practical Techniques for Building a Knowledge Management System*. Upper Saddle River, N.J.: Prentice Hall, 2000.

Just start; any of the five major search engines, such as AltaVista, Google, Internet Explorer, Lycos, or Yahoo, can help you find sites to assist you with event planning.

Points for Discussion and Practice

1. Create a storyboard for an event Web site.
2. Using popular software, create a simple Web site for an event.
3. Search for sites that advertise corporate events, and note all their features. Compare them with the checklists in the text.
4. Find corporate event services and list what is offered.
5. Find corporate event management discussion groups.
6. Use a Web search engine to find information on antipatterns, and discuss how this can assist in the process of Web-enabling an event.

CHAPTER 10

The Corporate Event Manual

THIS CHAPTER WILL HELP YOU:

- Articulate the use of event manuals as a corporate event management tool
- Recognize the various purposes of event manuals
- Create a manual for a corporate event
- Set up templates that can be used for all corporate events
- Establish a comprehensive checklist system for corporate events

---

The corporate event manual is a record and summary of an event. Successful corporate event managers traditionally keep their own manuals as a way of organizing all of the various elements that go into an event, and use their manuals to hold key documents, such as schedules, forms, copies of contracts, and checklists during the building of an event. After the event is over, the manual is archived and provides a historical record of the event. This manual then becomes part of the intellectual capital of the corporation.

The type of manual described above would be used for one large, multifaceted event. For the manager, a critical function of the manual is to hold and store checklists. For each new corporate event, the checklists can be assessed and refined, adding additional checklists as necessary. This chapter concludes with a number of sample checklists that can be used as thought starters for developing your own checklists for your specific event.

For the manager, the value of having archival records of important lessons learned is proof enough for creating and keeping manuals. The late Marianne Brittingham of Vienna, Virginia, shared the following: "I learn all sorts of tricks about making these types of events run smoothly every time I do one. I always save my control books as reference. I have a bookcase full and every now and then I pull one down, jog my memory, and save myself learning some of these lessons over again."

This chapter focuses on the "event operations manual," a packet of the critical information that is distributed to each person involved with the event. Experience has proven this to be a best practice and key enabler to successful events.

These manuals are used for orienting staff and should hold all documents related to putting the event together, and most important, give instructions for the game plan while the event is running.

Types of Corporate Event Manuals

The corporate event manual can serve as both a list of procedures to successfully plan and implement a corporate event, and a record of the procedures used to execute the event. The organizational skills used to set up a manual at the beginning of a project help the manager to visualize the key elements of the event and, in this way, help the manager to develop an initial plan. Many large companies have operations and logistics manuals with procedures and checklists that can be adapted and used in similar events around the world. This is particularly true of corporations launching products in multiple countries simultaneously.

Although there are many types of event manuals, most will fit into one of four categories. The manuals that are created or adapted for an event will depend on the event's size and complexity, as well as on who is going to read and use the manual. For example, there may be a manual for the media and those concerned with the media on the day of the event and a different manual for those concerned with the audiovisual requirements.

1. **Master event manual:** This type of manual contains key documents that will show you how to organize a corporate event. It might include the company philosophy or branding strategy. This manual contains various templates or forms that can be easily adapted to the various types of corporate events. It also includes the corporate policy regarding the request for proposal (RFP or RFQ), vendor relationship, corporate payment pol-

icy, contracting processes, legal review processes, corporate guidelines on types of events permitted, and the ethical and social standards for each type of event. It may contain sections written specifically for a type of corporate event, such as an exhibition or a seminar.

2. **Report manual:** This type of manual focuses on the history of the corporate event and most likely will be compiled during the planning and implementation phases of the event. It will be a corporate record of the processes used to organize the event, as well as a record of the event itself. Often, a version of this manual will be given to the various stakeholders.

3. **Operations manual or production manual:** This type of manual is the day-to-day working manual for a specific corporate event. It is the output of combining elements from the master manual with the requirements, constraints, and variables of the specific event. It will contain a section that describes how the event fits into the strategic objectives of the corporation as well as the objectives for the event. If the event is a live show or a corporate video broadcast, it will be called a production manual.

4. **Staff manual:** As the corporate event staff does not need to know the details of all procedures and of every checklist, they often keep a smaller manual related to their specific tasks and assignments. "Just give me what I need to know to be able to do what I have to do," said one staffer at Celebrations Event Planning. "Key documents related to my specific responsibilities are critical, but, at the same time, I need to have the big picture too—I need to have a feel for the whole event if I am to help it be successful," she said. Therefore, security would have a security manual, registration would have a registration manual, etc.

Of all the areas of corporate event management, the exposition industry has created the most comprehensive event operation manuals. These manuals can take the corporate event manager from the first concept of an exposition, through the suggested marketing schedule, to sourcing venues, and even show the manager how to create floor plans. As these manuals are going to be used with different operation teams, such areas as common terms and definitions and a plan for the filing system (both digital and paper) become important sections of the manual. These manuals can be set up on the Web or the company intranet and become part of the knowledge management system.

Corporate event project management is primarily concerned with the manual used by the event management team and event operations staff. There are many different types of events; therefore, there are many different types of operations manuals. Each type of operations manual would include the appropriate documents and checklists for the specific type of event. The manuals for the Olympic Games would stress acceptable methods of interacting with people of different cultural backgrounds. The operations manual for corporate training, on the other hand, would have an entirely different emphasis, as would an operations manual for a press conference or a corporate picnic.

In general, the corporate event manual is the documented outcome of the project management process. Each of the functional areas can contribute an aspect to the manual. The various functional areas of corporate event project management, whether a competitive sports event, a seminar, or a sponsored arts festival, need constant monitoring. Control documents show a written record of all monitoring activities. They act as a record of the event, as well as a method of communication. A systematic approach to this enables the event manager to learn from each event. A system enables comparison and therefore improvement. The outputs—the documents—can form the material version of the knowledge of the corporate event. The contents of the manual would depend on its purpose. An operations manual used to build and run the event would be different from the manual given to the sponsors. Figure 10-1 illustrates how a collection of documents related to the event build the event manual.

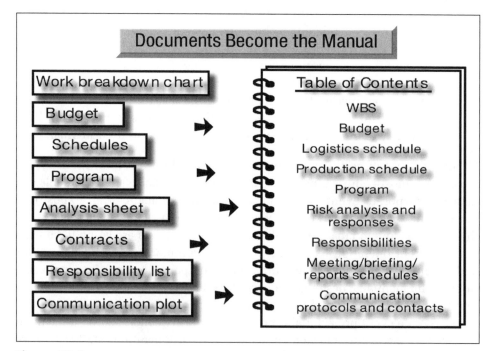

Figure 10-1
Table of Contents of the Corporate Event Manual

Event Operations Manual (EOM)

The corporate event operation manual can vary in its content. It is the result of the project management process, combined with experience and advice—no matter how informal or un-stated. Figure 10-2 illustrates this process.

John Oppy has conducted many seminars, conferences, and product launch events for Xerox Corporation. He suggests that the documents in the event operations manual be organized based on their frequency of use rather than alphabetically. He also recommends that tabs in the manual have titles that will facilitate the quick location of documents. Plastic sheet protectors can be of assistance for the purpose of organizing information, since they enable grouping documents related to a specific item, with the most recent document placed on top of the stack in the protector. This process has helped Oppy avoid errors resulting from lost or outdated information. According to Oppy, the key documents that must be included in the Event Operations Manual include the:

> ***Audio Visual list**—A table that describes audiovisual requirements, including what equipment is required, the time the*

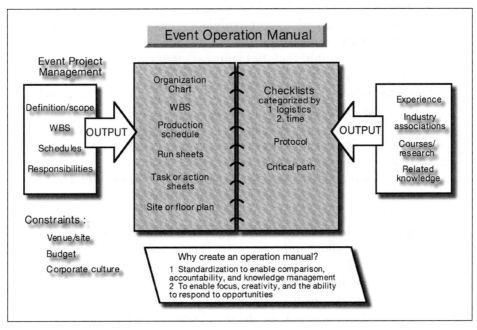

Figure 10-2

Origins of the Documents for the Operations Manual

equipment is needed, the room name and number, the contact person, when the room is available to do the setup, a cross-reference for the electrical requirements, and the strike date.

Electrical list—A list similar to the audiovisual list. However, the electrical installation or the setup of the generator is typically set at the start of the event. The electrical installation is a milestone that enables other setup work to begin.

Move in schedule of an event—A schedule based on the agreement set in the venue contract. Ensure this information is well documented using specific detailed dates, times, and room names.

Participant registration list—A list used to track all registrations for the event. It can also be used for a variety of logistical purposes, such as ensuring transportation arrangements for all attendees.

Session titles, rotation plans, and special requests—A one-page brief reminder of the schedule, including times and location of each activity.

Rotation Schedules—Detailed session schedules for each group of attendees, including their room number or location and times.

Memos—A collection of documents that provides a paper trail of the event and enables you to validate requirements and justify your changes or decisions, if you are challenged.

Notes—A section that includes your personal comments and other minute details, including reminders.

Lab schematics—Layouts for furniture placement, electrical, and equipment position, audiovisual placement. This does not necessarily have to be completed using sophisticated computer graphics. Often a hand-sketched layout will satisfy the requirements of the staff who will be using the documents.

Session outlines—A collection of the session outlines for staff reference. The outlines are usually included in the conference overview package for the attendees.

Conference plan and session design document—In the case of conferences and training events, development of the session content will help determine the final success of the session. You should require that the session content developers submit an outline with measurable objectives, as it will assist you in keeping them on track for the development of their materials. The measurable objectives requirement makes the creation of evaluations logical and easy. This process allows you to coach the people who are inexperienced or who are not proficient in developing presentations.

Financials—An Excel spreadsheet is a helpful tool. It can be used to track the budget each month before the event. At the close of the event, when the master venue or event company bill is finally reconciled, the budget can be easily revised using this software.

Evaluations—The evaluation is a summary of the opinions of your event participants and guests. The evaluation report provides you with the evidence you need to improve the quality of future events or to obtain funding for a similar event in the future.

CORPORATE EVENT OPERATIONS MANUAL CHECKLIST

The corporate event operations manual is used on the day of the event. The checklist below is for a specific corporate event's operation manual. If this checklist is put on the internal corporate Web site, then it can be adapted to other corporate events. Perhaps the most powerful commands on a computer are copy, paste, and delete. These commands allow the manager to easily use a master checklist and adapt it to a specific event.

Manual Design

The design of the corporate event operations manual must be well produced to encourage easy and effective use.

- It should be strongly bound, with a colorful plastic cover so it can be used and found on the day of the event.
- The cover should include the event logo.
- It must have tabs listing the individual program elements (phases) for quick reference.
- It should contain a contents page that also lists all tabs.
- Finally, it should include a quick reference index.

Contacts and Key Logistics

- The office and cell phone numbers for all key personnel.
- The headquarters' location and hours of operation.
- The information telephone lines for the event.
- The performer contact list—it is helpful to break the list into units by stage or room.

- A short list of contacts specifically related to the day of the event. This is helpful, as the entire list of contacts can grow quite long for a complex event.
- The names of key venue management personnel.
- A written procedure for locating lost persons or property.
- Telephone numbers for emergency services, such as medical, ambulance, fire.
- The telephone number and location for police.
- Security contacts, locations, and details.
- The location and telephone number for first aid.
- The telephone number for road and traffic authorities.
- The telephone number for transportation and parking personnel.
- A list of all radio channels.
- A guide and list of codes for two-way radio operation.

Production

- The event summary, including time, action, and location of each activity.
- The map of the event venue and site.
- The production schedule for each location.
- The move-in and move-out and setup schedule, including date, action, suppliers, and crew list.
- The crew (backstage) schedule, including load-in and load-out times.
- The catering requirements for the event production staff.
- The accommodations for the event production staff.
- The information booths and map of their location.
- The security information to control the event.
- The security brief describing the role and scope for security.
- The photocopies of all credentials and information concerning their inspection.
- The task responsibility list, including description, location, who is responsible, and comments.
- The action sheets, including date, time, action, and position.
- The rest room locations and hours of operation.
- The parking information and map.
- The road closure schedule and maps.
- The bus (event transport) schedule and map (of route).
- A guide for service quality with the public and guests, including cultural issues.

- Examples of frequently asked questions, including the locations of Automatic Teller Machines (ATM) and first aid locations.
- Copies of the incident report form and directions for completing them.
- The risk scenarios and how to implement them.

Media Information

- A description of the location of the media facilities and the media center.
- A preview schedule, including media briefing times and locations.
- A list of where and how to acquire visual images of the event.
- The event fact sheet
- A concise summary of the event background

Creating the Event Operations Manual (EOM)

The corporate event operations manual is a communication medium from the event management team to the event staff and volunteers. It contains information to enable the smooth operation of the event. As with all communication, the event office is responsible for ensuring that the content is accessible and understood by the reader.

The first questions to ask are: Who is the audience? What do they need the EOM for? Creating a number of personas—as described by Alan Cooper in his 1999 book, *The Inmates Are Running the Asylum*—can assist in answering these questions. Personas are virtual people with real-life characteristics, representing the people who will be using the manual. For example, Kay, the floor director of a closed-circuit corporate television broadcast, will use the EOM for the schedules and set layouts for the program. If the event manager designs the EOM with Kay in mind, the EOM will contain all of the information she requires in a format that she can use to perform her tasks. Knowing when the manual will be used is also important. It could be designed as a backup to what is already known—that is, as a reminder, for emergency situations, or as the basis of all corporate event operation information. It is generally a combination of all three.

Unlike many other types of operations manuals, the EOM will be used for only one event. So having an alpha, beta, and gamma copy to be tested out is a luxury. In other words, the manual cannot be improved by trying it out on the event—it has to work the first time it is used. This means that the risk factor is high. Therefore, comprehensive planning of the design and content of the manual is imperative.

DESIGN

Given the variety of people using the manual and the rigors of an event, the manual should be made of sturdy material. Most corporate event managers use a hardcover three-ring notebook. A colorful cover will help it be easily spotted and less likely to get lost. For outdoor events, a slight rain shower can dissolve ink and produce a wonderful Rorschach test image. Therefore, a plastic cover and waterproof ink is recommended; photocopies and laser prints are waterproof. The clear plastic sheet protectors not only keep the documents clean and dry but also allow previous copies to be stored in the same protector as the current version. The cover should also feature the event logo so it will not be confused with other manuals. The clear plastic covers enable colorful logo sheets to be inserted in the front cover.

When setting up the manual, think of these aspects: In an emergency, how quickly would the relevant information in the manual be found? Would Frank, the security guard, or Chang, the new staff member, be able to locate the information quickly? Depending on the reason for the manual, the speed and ease of finding information can vary. Colored sections, colored tabs, a contents page, and an index can all be useful.

CONTACTS

Emergency contact numbers generally take precedence over all other contact numbers. They need to stand out in the manual and should not need to be looked up in an index. However, what happens if no phone is nearby, or if the user is out of cell phone range, or, as often happens in an emergency, if the phone circuits are jammed? The location of emergency services needs to be included, and an alternative service needs to be described, for example, runners (bicycles are very handy in outdoor events, whereas electric carts are used in large indoor venues) and/or two-way radios.

When organizing events that include families, knowing the location of the lost children tent is not enough. Every staff member and volunteer needs to know the procedure to follow when children are lost, and this procedure should be described in detail in the manual.

If phone numbers are different for the days of the event, then an "on the day" contact list needs to be included.

An important fact to remember is that a corporate event that takes place within a city or town affects all kinds of services. The contacts for the local traffic authority and even the military forces, such as the National Guard, may need to be included. To save employees having to answer innumerable questions, an information telephone number may be set up. However, this number is of little use unless all the staff knows the number; make sure it is in the manual. The contact numbers of the management of the star acts, such as the keynote speaker, can be very important if any changes to the program occur.

Does everyone know how to operate the two-way radios? Don't assume everyone is going to remember. A summary guide to their operation can become a lifesaving procedure.

PRODUCTION

Event Summary

Time, action, and location may be obvious to the event manager, but the more staff and volunteers that are involved, the less time the event manager has to explain to them the overall event. A summary in the manual can be a real time-saver.

Map of Event Site

Visual language is a powerful tool in the event manual. When someone wants to know where the rest rooms are, you can point to them on a map or floor plan far easier than you can explain their position. With a map or floor plan, the reader can choose how to get there. The manual may include a number of maps: a locator map (i.e., where, generally, the event is being held), a map emphasizing the access points and infrastructure for the suppliers, a map of the emergency paths, and so on. A variety of maps are usually required for an event. The reader and purpose of the map should be kept in mind when you are producing the maps or floor plans of the entire venue for the event. Ensure that all the maps, or a scaled version of them, are placed in the EOM.

Schedules

The schedules for the day of the event can take different forms depending on the size of the event. These schedules have to be created as part of the corporate event project management process, so placing them in the event manual is no extra work.

The Event Specialist Staff/Crew

The crew, consisting of event staff and volunteers who bring the event to life, need a variety of schedules to coordinate their work so that their work doesn't clash with other activities on the site. For large corporate events, the crew accommodation and catering information may need to be in the manual.

Security

To assist with event security, the location of security officers should be included in the manual, as well as when and where security briefings will be held, and a copy of all required security passes. Special security procedures need to be included, for example, how to resolve gate entry disputes, or what to do when people try to get in without an invitation. In recent years, corporate competitors have made more frequent attempts to enter internal corporate events, particularly in the case of training or product launch exhibitions held in a public location such as a hotel or convention center.

An example of how valuable it is to have a photocopy of event credentials in the EOM is shown in this example. Ellen, a professional corporate event planner, had recommended to her client that unique color-coded badges should be used for an internal product announcement at a well-known Dallas hotel. Ellen had placed color copies of the eight different badges in the production manual. On the day of the event, three people from a competing company attempted to enter the auditorium for the keynote speech and product announcement. Security had been properly briefed, and took the three men aside. They used the manual to validate that the employee badges they were wearing were not official. The corporate client and the authorities were then called in to handle the situation. White-collar crime is a significant risk and can cost the corporation millions in lost sales. In this case, the process and the documentation were extremely valuable. Needless to say, Ellen was complimented on her professionalism, and she has continued to successfully manage many more events.

Task List

Some corporate event manuals are primarily a combination of the task responsibility list (TRL) and the action sheet. These clearly state who is responsible for what, and when and where it is supposed to happen. They are the final stage of a work breakdown structure and are vital for the efficient management of corporate event operations. The action sheets may have exact times, such as start and stop times, or more general times, such as peak hours when staff and volunteers are most needed. The latter is useful if the staff or volunteers have finished their assigned tasks early and wish to assist one another in an understaffed area.

Questions at Events

A "Frequently Asked Questions" section in the front of the manual will assist the smooth flow of the event. For example, of all the questions asked at events, "Where is the rest room?" in every conceivable language certainly is the number one question asked! Remember, the men won't know where the women's facilities are (and vice versa), so explicitly note both locations in the manual. A list of the other frequently asked questions should be given to all event staff members and volunteers.

Transportation Information

Transportation information is mandatory if the attendees are to arrive in a safe condition and in a happy mood. Include maps and more maps. For a parade, the road closure schedule is essential. In particular, correctly scheduled placement and removal of barricades can produce a smooth event. If some barricades are removed and let the traffic through only to be stopped at another barricade, it can quickly create a gridlock.

The Guests

The correct procedure for dealing with the general guests needs to be included in the manual, particularly if you have volunteers. Those who do not work in the service industry can easily become flustered and frustrated with guests' demands. An easy to find "Frequently Asked Questions" section in the EOM can help keep everyone calm and contribute to attendee satisfaction with the event. In countries with people of many different cultural backgrounds, you would be wise to include a section on cultural sensitivity.

Very Important Persons (VIPs) may require special handling, so notes detailing all this should be included in the EOM. In the case of executive communication exchanges or hospitality suite events, the VIPs may also be hosts. A senior executive of a well-known technology corporation required that one week prior to any event, the event manager supply a manual containing a biography, photo, and important business information on all of the VIPs expected to attend the hospitality function or sponsored event he was attending. He would diligently study the manual and astound the guests with his wonderful ability to recall faces and facts. Now his secret for success is known, but his identity shall remain our secret.

Safety Procedures

The correct procedures should be summarized in the manual for safety and other related procedures. Also, the manual may need a page or two for incident reports with adequate space for answers to questions and the date, place, and time to be filled in. Sufficient space will enable a complete report detailing all of the facts. Capturing specific details at the time of the incident can be especially beneficial to corporations in this litigious society. People will fail to recall facts accurately weeks after the incident, let alone the years it may take before a liability case comes to court. Accurate documentation could save the corporation thousands or perhaps millions of dollars.

MEDIA INFORMATION

The corporation event operation manual may need to contain a separate section for the media. In particular, describe the facilities available to the media (cabling, outside broadcast van) and the location of the media center. If the event will have live broadcasts, the briefings schedule and the event highlights can be very important.

DISTRIBUTION OF THE EVENT OPERATIONS MANUAL (EOM)

The manual should be distributed to staff and volunteers well before the corporate event so that they have time to familiarize themselves with its contents. Put on the front page "Bring this manual to the event." Even so, a few spare copies should be available at the event.

Checklists

A checklist enables the event manager to ensure that all of the smaller tasks associated with an element will be completed. Checklists can be used at any stage in the event planning, execution, or shutdown process. Its use in order to focus on the task at hand cannot be surpassed.

Below are a variety of checklists for different aspects of corporate event management. These checklists have been compiled from the experience of many corporate event managers. Although by no means exhaustive, these checklists will provide a good beginning for new corporate event managers to compile their own checklists. Checklists can be found in other parts of this text for signage, the event manual, and the Web. Other checklists can be found in the book *Festival and Special Event Management* (1999). It includes checklists for shutdown, ticketing, queues, and attendee transportation.

Figure 10-3 shows a map of checklists from the Web site of one of the author's (Bill O'Toole): www.epms.net. The event manager can easily search other Web sites, such as those belonging to suppliers, universities, government agencies, and so on, for checklists that can then be customized by the event office. These checklists can be adapted to future events and downloaded by any of the staff or participants. Checklists consist of a minimum number of words, since they serve as memory joggers. Frequently, there are a number of

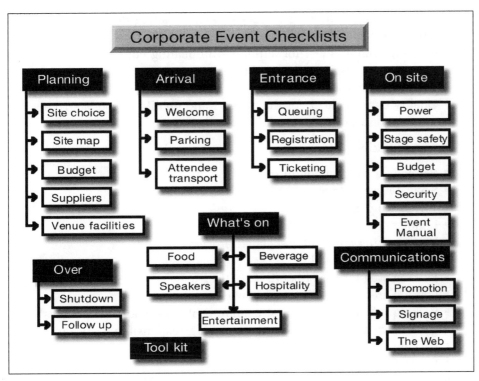

Figure 10-3
Schema of Checklists

tasks to be completed for the items. The more words there are on the checklist, the less it will be used. So, keep it succinct. The detail can be found in one of the event manuals. The idea of the checklist is to ensure that nothing has been missed.

Planning/Suppliers

- Suppliers' specific conditions: date, time, and description of goods.
- Insurance—public liability, staff, and so on.
- Supplier specific safety regulations, for example, fire marshal (for fireworks supplier), correct permits.
- Logistic needs for suppliers at the event, as well as to and from the event.
- Overall supplier schedule; check clashes and check with venue or site on logistics such as loading dock times.
- Individual schedules for suppliers, showing arrival and exit times.

- Supplier maps, showing entrances, exits, loading docks, and other facilities and specific sites of interest
- Communication sheet for suppliers, indicating contacts for the day of the event and emergency numbers.
- Payment schedule
- Quality control check for the number and quality of goods arriving and leaving venue/site.

Arrival/Parking

- Venue/site parking conditions.
- Security for parking areas.
- VIP parking area.
- Limousine pickup and drop-off area.
- Valet parking area and associated process.
- Parking area for trucks.
- Parking area for ticket booth activities.
- Parking areas, including lanes, marked.
- Parking information in guest communications—maps, program sales.
- Giveaways and souvenirs—where, policy, responsible party, etc.
- Parking attendants.
- Overall sinage.
- Obtain and set up road barriers to facilitate traffic flow.
- Tow trucks—availability, access, etc.
- Turning circles and passenger drop-off points that are clear and well marked.
- Shuttle service—schedule, locations for pick-up and drop-off.
- Safe pathways to the event and event exit points identified.
- Briefing for running sheet, listing expected arrival of groups and coaches.
- Cash flow.
- Uniforms.
- Protective clothing for designated personnel.
- Tickets for sale or free issue.
- Lighting.
- First aid, fire extinguisher.
- Communications—radio, etc.
- Waste management.
- Staff briefing schedule.
- Staff meeting area (sheltered).
- Staff checklist, arrival and leaving times.
- Name tags.

Entrance and Registration

- Registration mailings and follow up.
- Speakers' handouts.
- Information packets—bus timetables, taxi numbers.
- Name tags in alphabetical order (first organized by organization, corporate division, or country, if applicable).
- Attendee bags: giveaways stored for easy access.
- Correct and clear signage.
- Visible registration desk.
- Storage area for boxes and additional supplies, giveaways, equipment, etc.
- Staff:
  - Organize staff for registration.
  - General staff briefing.
  - Staff briefed on VIP protocol.
  - Arrival and exit contingencies—late and early.
  - General daily information for staff, for example, rest room, breaks, first aid.
- Messages and organized message board.
- Meeting stakeholders, for example, security, key hotel staff, Master of Ceremonies, AudioVisual.
- Map of layout of attendee registration area for easy access.

On-site/Power

- Type of power: three-phase or single-phase.
- Amount of power needed, in particular at peak times.
- Emergency power.
- Position and number of power outlets.
- Types of leads and distance from power source to device.
- Correct wiring of the venue (old venues are often improperly grounded).
- Incoming equipment volt/amp rating.
- Safety factors, including covering leads and possibility of electricity ground leakage as a result of rain.
- Local and state regulations regarding power.

Security

This list is meant only to assist your event management and is in no way a definitive list. Security can be a major risk management factor and requires utmost care and the correct information. We recommend that you seek professional advice.

- Entrances and on-site areas
- Equipment security before, during, and after event
- Cash security
- Crowd control
- Communications systems and backup
- Security time schedule and briefing time and place
- Incident reporting procedures
- Security budget
- Sourcing and selection of security company
- Special security needs of VIPs, entertainers, and others
- Chain of command
- Visibility and personal appearance
- Integrating security with federal, state, or local police and emergency services

Food

- Caterers, staff, volunteers
- Test kitchen facilities
- Food
- Cutlery, dishes, packaging
- Serviette/napkins
- Power and gas
- Generators
- Safety
- Waste management
- Refrigeration
- Caterer briefing
- Menu check
- Schedule to caterers
- Serving order for sit-down dinner
- Payment
- Queuing
- Cash registers
- Booth setup
- Dress for staff
- Specialty food
- Contingency plan—weather, alternate catering

Beverages

- Money collection, float, electronic funds transfer, point of sale, ATMs
- Licenses

- Price—cash registers
- Staff—appoint manager
- Staff training, including state and local laws regarding age verification and handling of intoxicated guests or clients
- Refrigeration, ice, ice machine
- Uniforms
- Utensils
- Signage—promotional material
- Dispensers, alcohol selection
- Queuing space
- Staff identification
- Waste disposal bins
- Washing water
- Security
- Glasses, cups
- Coasters
- Lighting
- Rest rooms
- Power contingency
- Cleanup plan

Entertainment

Entertainment includes keynote speakers, performing artists, and sports stars.

- Arrival of stars confirmed
- Greenroom, rehearsal, and dressing room
- Catering
- Sound check
- Costumes
- Stage area condition
- Run sheets checked by entertainment
- Hair, makeup
- Accommodation
- Check Audiovisual, props
- Artists/entertainers' guest lists
- Transportation
- Photograph and video on-site
- Aisles and access areas clear
- Run sheet to technicians
- Front-of-house staff and conditions checked

On-road Event Checklist

- Route approval
  - Traffic management
  - Emergency response plan—police, fire, ambulance, security
- List of participants
- Order of participants
- Confirmation of date and time
- Task force and committees setup
- Meetings scheduled
- Corporate event manual created including production/run sheets
- Information distributed to participants
- Equipment needed
- Staff required, trained, and uniformed
- Entertainment—secured and scheduled
- Confirmation of subcontractors, including cleaning, waste, catering, transportation
- Method of transportation during the event
- Media strategy—including camera sightlines and security
- Notification of impact—shops, residents
- VIPs secured and operation impact measured (e.g., extra security)
- Contingency plan, including weather
- Assembly area secured, marked out, and equipped
- Disassembly area prepared
- Barricade setup and breakdown schedule
- Briefing times established
- On-site communications check—handhelds, mobile phones, bullhorns, sound system
- Debriefing and site check

The Corporate Event Manager's Tool Kit

Even experienced corporate event managers often overlook the final detail: assembling a tool kit for the day(s) of the event. John Oppy, of Xerox Corporation, shares his tool kit checklist for a sales event focused on a product launch:

John's Conference Tool Kit

Aspirin
*Assorted small screwdrivers**
Band-Aids

CDs—10 blank
CD-ROM read/write drive
Cable to lock down the laptop so it does not grow legs and walk
  away from the control room
Cell phone—at least one
Computer—laptop model
Duct tape—10 rolls (I use it for everything, even as packing tape.)
Felt-tipped markers
Floppy disks for computer
Knife for opening boxes*
Leatherman tool*
Network cables marked with my name
Power strips marked with my name
Pager that works inside the venue
Tape measure
Tweezers*
Walkie-talkies
Zip disks—10
Zip drive for computer

In addition to the list provided by John Oppy, you may want to consider including items from the following thought starter checklist. You can adapt your list by combining items from these lists and adding any items that may be required for the specific type of corporate event you are planning. You can then delete what is not necessary for a particular event.

- Communication
  - Handheld/walkie-talkies
  - Loudspeaker or other similar device
- Equipment
  - Camera (small)
  - Electrician's screwdriver and pliers*
  - Flashlight (small one)
  - Gaffer tape
  - Swiss army penknife*
- Information
  - Clipboard
  - Event operation manual or
    - Schedules

*Be careful in packing your kit for travel to the event. The asterisked items must be placed in checked luggage. Since September 11, 2001, they are confiscated if carried on the airplane.

- Contact numbers
  - Incident report sheet
  - Plenty of pens
  - Spare paper
- Money
  - Cash (and change)
  - Credit cards
- Weather
  - Hat
  - Raincoat
  - Sunblock
  - Sunglasses

The corporate event operations manual represents the distilled knowledge of the event. The type of the event manual will vary according to its function. With the use of software and the Web, they can be easily created, improved, communicated, adapted to all kinds of events, and stored for future events. Not to use a corporate event manual is to lose a valuable communication tool and an essential part of the event knowledge. The checklists, like the manual, are the written knowledge of the corporate event management that is used on a day-to-day basis. Every event can contribute to the corporate event office's checklists so that they grow and improve with use.

Wrap Up

1. The corporate event manual is a documented record and summary of an event.
2. There are many types of manuals, but, generally, they can be classified as one of four types—generic, report, operations or production, and staff.
3. The emphasis of the manual is directly related to the type of event being planned.
4. The manual should be well organized so that it will be easy to locate important documents when needed.
5. Checklists can be used as memory joggers to ensure that all of the smaller details are not overlooked.
6. A well-stocked tool kit can be extremely useful when you are on-site at an event.

Instruments

The texts listed below all have extensive checklists that can form the basis of the event office checklist. The World Wide Web has extensive checklists. Visit conference and meeting industry Web sites to find their venue checklists.

Epple, A. *Organizing Scientific Meetings.* Cambridge, UK: Cambridge University Press, 1997.

Goldblatt, J. *Special Events, Twenty-First Century Global Event Management.* New York: John Wiley, 2002.

Malouf, L. *Behind the Scenes at Special Events.* New York: John Wiley, 1999.

McCabe, V., B. Poole, P. Weeks, and N. Leiper. *The Business and Management of Conventions.* Brisbane: John Wiley, 2000.

McDonnell, I., J. Allen, and W. O'Toole. *Festival and Special Event Management,* first ed. Brisbane: Wiley, 1999.

Points for Discussion and Practice

1. List the limitations of using an event manual.
2. Construct an outline for a paper corporate event manual. How can this structure be transferred to the Web? Would it be the same? How can the structure be adapted so that it works in both media?
3. Create a checklist for the event elements shown in the schema in Figure 10-3 but not listed in the checklists above.
4. Search the Web for event manuals.
5. Compare the operation manuals on the Web with the corporate event operations manual. What do they have in common and what are their differences?
6. Create a Web-based checklist schema for your events.

CHAPTER 11

Costing, Procurement, and Cash Flow

THIS CHAPTER WILL HELP YOU:

- Describe the value of costing in the corporate event project management system
- Implement estimating and cost control techniques
- Implement the methods of procurement
- Assess the ability of suppliers to meet corporate event specifications

---

Cost management is one of the most important areas and the least studied by event managers or their staff. Perhaps this explains the continual problem between corporate events management and finance departments of some companies. The event team uses terms that are foreign to the average accountant, and accountants use terms that are foreign to many event managers. The goal of this chapter is to give corporate event managers the necessary terms and methodology both to systematically control the costs of an event and to be able to talk to the finance department or the corporate controller in a company. *Costing* is a common term in project-based industries and, like so many of the terms used in this text, is gradually becoming part of the accepted language of events. Costing is the estimating of event costs, establishing a baseline or budget, controlling those costs, and documenting and reporting the process. The budget to put on an event can be made up of a bewildering variety of costs. One minute the event manager is negotiating with a caterer, and the next minute the event manager is contracting for the entertainment, and the next, arranging for additional corporate staff. The only way to control such a situation and properly estimate, evaluate, and allocate the cost of an element is to understand how costs are classified. Once you determine how to allocate a cost, then you are able to apply standards for making cost comparisons and for estimating the appropriate amount of funding needed for that element. By analyzing the costs of an event, the manager will be in a far better position to negotiate a good deal to gain the most value for the element and to account for the overall event budget.

The estimating flowchart shown in Figure 11-1 illustrates the various elements of the costing process.

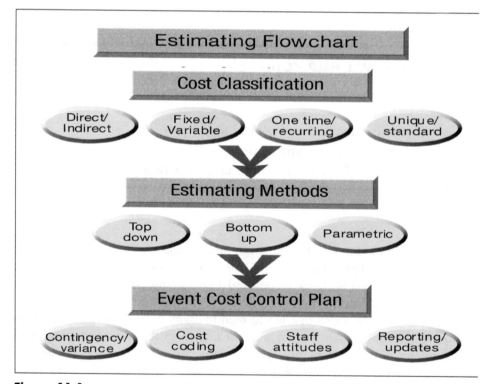

Figure 11-1
Estimating Flowchart

Cost Classification

DIRECT OR INDIRECT COSTS

Perhaps the most common division of costs is into direct and indirect costs. Direct costs are those that are specifically incurred by the project, such as hiring staff, catering, renting the venue, and obtaining specific insurance for the event. Indirect costs are the rest of the costs, such as event management office expenses and general insurance. The indirect costs are also called overhead expenses; they are the cost of the event support. The direct costs can be calculated fairly easily as they are often quotes from suppliers and standard rates for labor and rentals. Part of the art of event management is to allocate the indirect costs correctly. For the sake of cost estimating, they may be expressed as a percentage of direct costs.

UNIQUE OR STANDARD COSTS

The division of costs into unique and standard is of great interest to the corporate event manager as unique costs can have a high risk. Standard costs are those that are normal within the industry. They are easily computed and therefore generally have low risk. However, as the event is meant to be special, the unique aspects of the event may incur unknown costs. For example, the use of a special lighting setup with lasers and the latest in digital control may require a number of quotes to gain an idea of the costs. The uniqueness of the setup may hide additional unplanned costs. Although unplanned costs may be covered in the agreements with the suppliers, the corporate event manager may not have time to start again if further costs associated with the element are found.

FIXED OR VARIABLE COSTS

Fixed costs stay the same no matter what happens at the event. Variable costs will change; they rise and fall depending on known aspects of the event. For example, the cost of the catering at an invitation or ticketed hospitality event will vary according to the number of people who attend. The variable costs have the greatest opportunity for the event to go over budget; therefore, new corporate event project managers or independent entrepreneurs who focus their business on the corporate world should expand their knowledge in this area.

ONETIME OR RECURRING COSTS

Recurring costs are those that repeat during the life cycle of the event and therefore need to be scheduled into the cash flow. Onetime costs are generally found at the beginning of organizing the event, although they may be staggered over the life cycle to assist in cost control. Typically, costs will be divided only once into a security deposit, a payment before the event, and a final payment after the event. The payment schedule may not be fixed; therefore, it is an important negotiating point with suppliers and clients.

To illustrate these cost divisions, Table 11-1 shows some costs and how they can be classified. The administration costs, such as general staff wages, photocopying, and telephone, will vary according to the size of the event and the profile of the event; therefore, administration is a variable cost. Because these costs are absorbed into the general administration of the event office, they are indirect costs. Administration costs will recur over the event project life cycle. As the costs are standard, they can be estimated fairly accurately. The event security will be a variable cost as it depends on factors such as the size of the event and the VIPs in attendance, such as performers, speakers, or corporate senior staff. It will be a direct cost to the event and is generally a onetime fee. Event security has now become a standard cost and can be estimated accurately.

LOST OPPORTUNITY COSTS

The corporate event manager must consider the costs of lost opportunities. Concentrating on one event may cause the independent event company to turn down many smaller events. A corporation may have to choose between events based on budget or the process capability of the staff. The corporate event manager may compare the cost of losing the next-best opportunity to the cost of the one chosen. Lost opportunities can have political and financial costs. If the marketing manager is told the event office cannot support his event be-

Table 11-1   Cost Classification

Cost	Fixed	Variable	Direct	Indirect	Onetime	Recurring	Unique	Standard
Administration		Yes		Yes		Yes		Yes
Proposal development	Yes		Yes		Yes			Yes
Sponsor decoration	Yes		Yes		Yes		Yes	
Security		Yes	Yes		Yes			Yes

cause it is managing a large human resources event, either he may choose to go to an outside event planner and never return to the corporate event office for his requirements or he may choose to discuss the issue with upper management indicating how his event has a more compelling effect on the corporate bottom line.

Estimating Costs

Estimating the cost of an element is a mix of art and science. It is almost impossible to estimate event costs with 100 percent accuracy. Since it is necessary to establish some type of budget, the effective event manager must make an educated estimate based on past experience and currently known facts. To make the best possible estimate, the event manager needs to understand the different methods used to estimate the costs. The various methods may be used together or used at different times in the planning process in an endeavor to increase accuracy.

For large, complex events, establishing the budget is a specialty area. The best estimated costs become the baseline that can be used as a guide for planning, monitoring, and financing the event. Any changes to this baseline need to be authorized by the client or the client's manager. The baseline is necessary in the changing corporate event environment, as the effects of any change in cost need to be managed.

For example, the cost of a change of venue is an important consideration in the selection of a venue. The event manager can make a good business decision only if the estimate of costs related to a change of venue has some degree of accuracy. Fortunately for the event planner in one midwestern bank, she had prepared detailed requests for quotations with very specific information regarding her upcoming event. As a result the bids from her suppliers were realistic. When the venue of choice suffered severe damage as a result of hurricane George in 1998, she was able to accurately forecast the cost of relocating the event to another venue and to remain within her budget.

ESTIMATING METHODS

The type of estimating method that is used depends upon the particular type of event and the available information. There are three types of estimates—top-down, bottom-up, and parametric. The event manager may use one or a combination of all three methods to arrive at the best estimate of costs for an event. The following is a brief description of each type.

Top-Down Estimating

In top-down estimating, also called analogous estimating, event managers base estimates on their experience in managing similar events. How much would a standard product launch cost? These kinds of estimates are only a ballpark figure as the event managers rarely consider the unique costs of the event in any detail. For a corporate event manager to know what is normally spent on an event is a valuable starting point in cost estimation. It gives the client or sponsor at least a cost envelope.

Bottom-Up Estimating

In bottom-up estimating, the cost of the whole event is assumed to be the sum of the cost of its parts. This sensible assumption is limited by the amount of time and data necessary to work out the estimate. At some time during the event, however, this process has to be implemented, as it is the only real way to keep control of costs. The procedure is to use the work breakdown structure (WBS) to analyze the event into its cost centers. The cost of each of the lower levels of the WBS is estimated through quotes and experience. These are then rolled up into a cost for the whole event.

Bottom-up estimating is a simple matter in theory, but the process can become complex as the event nears, because many changes may occur as the event evolves into its final form. However, most major corporations hold the event manager or management team responsible for adhering to the budget. Discussions with corporate event managers indicated that many of the event managers' bonuses or merit raises were tied to their ability to produce an event on or below budget. Therefore, budget reports are included in the weekly core team meetings. One-on-one meetings usually occur between the vendor or team member, supplier, and event manager as budget-related changes occur. Corporations are becoming stricter about adherence to budget as most have no slush fund and all funds must be accounted for in the overall corporate budget. The finance department is also conscientious about requiring documentation.

Parametric Estimating

In parametric estimating, the overall cost of the event is assumed to be related to one element, a parameter, of the event. For example, standard exhibition costs are related to floor space. Concert costs are related to the number of attendees. Hospitality events, where catering is the major focus, are calculated as a per-head cost. The accuracy of this type of estimating will depend on the direct relationship between the event characteristic or parameter and the event as a whole. A critical mass point may occur where that relationship is no longer directly proportional. For example, once an event goes beyond a certain size, the relationship between cost-per-head catering and the event cost as a whole is no longer applicable. The event may need a larger or an additional venue and new or additional caterers.

WHEN TO ESTIMATE

The three estimating methods can be used at different times over the project life cycle. Unfortunately, the most-accurate cost estimates are needed for the feasibility study, when the least amount of data is available. However the cost estimation is performed, the general rule is that the estimate becomes more accurate as the event date nears. Initial estimates are the rule-of-thumb or analogy estimates. The initial estimate will be based on experience, similar events, and the identification of the major cost items. The degree of accuracy could be 50 percent either way. The corporate event planner will need to take into account the client history, which could include asking the following questions: Does the client change its mind often? Does it have experience in events? Will the staff change during the event? What is the overall corporate culture? Parametric modeling where a major indicator parameter is identified and costed may be beneficial to the corporate event planner in preparing the initial cost estimate.

An increasing number of clients require detailed estimates. This is particularly true of the finance department. With the increased focus on budget responsibility, however, this is also true of marketing and human resource departments. (Finance will keep them on their toes!) The need for detailed estimates can result in an impact on the event content. If the estimate is too detailed, then the event manager may not be able to change the content when there are changes in other areas, such as a change of venue or a change due to weather. On the other hand, once the client relationship is well established, the event manager may be given carte blanche on the event within certain parameters. That does not mean that once the trust is established, the event planner can order excessive gifts for the attendees or expensive champagne without concern for the budget or discussion with the client. The event manager must still stay within the established guidelines. In some cases the client will sign a signature authorization up to a certain spending limit.

CONTINGENCY

Many things can occur during the planning stage of an event that are beyond the control of the corporate event manager. For example, a paper mill strike could cause the cost of invitations to increase beyond the original estimate. The addition of a celebrity speaker could cause the cost of security to be increased. Inclement weather could create the need for a marquee tent at the venue's entranceway or for additional staff with umbrellas to greet the guests. If the schedule needs to be accelerated, contingency funds could be used as an incentive for the staff. For example, they could be paid a bonus, from the contingency fund, if they can complete the work ahead of schedule.

The contingency fund is the allowance for unknowns and is part of the cost of the whole event. The amount of the fund should reflect the accuracy of the estimating procedure but is generally around 10 percent of the overall budget. Experienced clients will expect some sort of contingency fund; however, other clients may make the corporate event planner fight for it. The contingency fund should not be used as an excuse for sloppy cost estimating.

EXPLANATIONS

When presenting the cost estimates to the client or other stakeholders, the corporate event planner should include the method used to arrive at the figures and their degree of accuracy. This can be expressed as an estimate plus or minus a percentage figure. For example, decoration might cost $20,000 plus or minus 10 percent. A detailed estimate would be accompanied by the work breakdown structure. The event manager should also include background and supporting information. This would include an outline of the assumptions underlying the figures, for example, the exchange rates for international events or the inflation rate for future events. Marketing initiatives tied to the millennium celebrations provide a good example. Planning for those events began as much as ten years in advance. The inflation rate was used to calculate the venue rental fees and hotel accommodation fee structures. In fact, one New York hotel was booked before ground was broken for the hotel construction. Thus, an explanation that the estimate was based on comparable rates plus the rate of inflation would be included in the presentation to the client.

Cost Control

Once the costs are estimated and a baseline plan of the budget created and approved, the event office needs to have in place a procedure to control those costs. The basis of cost control is to recognize possible deviations from the baseline and to respond in an effective way. The response may be to mitigate the effect of changes or to change the baseline. A deviation from the plan may be a onetime cost change or may be indicative of a trend resulting in significant cost overruns. The latter is especially important in large-scale projects and is estimated through a process called trend analysis. Further detail on this topic can be found in Bent and Humphreys's 1996 book, *Effective Project Management through Applied Cost and Schedule Control.*

The difference between the estimated or budgeted cost and the actual cost is called the *variance.* If progress reports as mentioned above are required by the client, then the variances need to be calculated and may be used to indicate a trend. A positive variance means that the actual costs are greater than the projected cost. A negative variance, when the actual cost is less than the budget, may indicate a problem with the estimation methods. Sophisticated project management software packages can be used for this aspect of costing, but for most events this is a bit of overkill and can result in more time being spent on cost control than on running the event. A simple spreadsheet can easily indicate a variance.

Perhaps the most important control system is the informal one of a *cost-conscious staff.* No matter what formal systematic controls are put into place, someone will always have to be responsible for keeping the event on track. When the staff and volunteers make suggestions or decisions, they must realize that cost is a significant factor. Besides the staff, all the suppliers must realize the importance of keeping to the budget. The event management must always evaluate the often competing aims of creativity and cost. Too much emphasis on the dollars could be at the expense of the end product. This is often the problem when dealing with the client's finance department, which is not familiar with the work involved or the cost of the elements. The event manager must also consider the trade-off between cost, time, and quality. The finance department, of course, looks at the cost, whereas the event office looks at the time and quality.

Properly prepared requests for proposals are most beneficial when the event office must explain to the finance department the need for a more costly element. Many corporate event departments create a design document that includes a detailed description of each element and the value proposition for that element, or in other words, the positive impact of the element on the event. For example, including a song written for an event has far greater value than the actual cost of the writing of the song. Long after the event, people will be humming the song in the hallways of the company. The song will have a lasting, positive effect on the employees and will definitely add value to the event. Without the song, the event would not have the same effect.

BOOKKEEPING—COST CONTROL CODES

A valid description of the variation from the baseline can be derived only from accurate accounts. The description in the form of a report could be generated from software as simple as a spreadsheet or as complex as a high-end project management software system, such as Primavera. Choosing the right software system is part of setting up the event office. Obviously, the chosen system needs to be compatible with the other software systems used in the event planning.

The event manager may set up two accounting systems. One is a commitment accounting system, in which the obligations are noted. This generally informal system lets management know how much money has been committed at any one time. It is interesting to note that commitment accounting is increasingly used in areas where changes to plans may occur. The other system may be cash account or accrual accounting. Whatever system is used, it should be able to give the event management a snapshot of the financial situation at any time.

Basic to project-based industries is the use of a coding system. The codes are generated by the work breakdown structure and provide a simple way to track the cost of resources. Even just adding an extra column to a spreadsheet and using it for a simple code will assist in cost management. For example, the costs of an award night could be set out as AV = audiovisual, CA = catering, AD = administration, TR = transportation, and so on in a similar manner. Transportation can then be subdivided into TR.1 = VIP transportation, TR.2 = guest transportation, and so on. This method allows the data to be subdivided into as much detail as is necessary and to be expanded as the event planning becomes more complex. Some areas may not need to be further subdivided. For example, you don't need to subdivide the audiovisual component if one supplier handles it. The coding system also assists in standardizing the methods used and therefore reduces mistakes due to vague terminology and incorrect spelling. With a simple coding system, the data can be collated, compared, and sorted. The ability to perform these functions is essential for good cost management. The codes can be used on invoices and order forms and contained in file names.

To enable correct data entry into the accounting system, the event team must keep accurate records. For small events, the process may be as simple as making sure that any decisions that affect cost are jotted into a notebook. For large events, the corporate event team needs to develop a standard procedure that will use authorization forms for any changes to the cost baseline. These forms and procedures are referenced in the responsibility matrix outlined in Chapter 3 in the section on documentation. The authorization process and the use of the forms must be communicated to all the vendors, corporate employees, and volunteers. Often in large corporate events, unauthorized persons charge items to the event budget, such as room service, copying or fax services, or package delivery charges for staff or speakers. It may appear to be a small charge that will get lost in the noise at the time, but the event manager can quickly go over budget and consequently be affected in his or her performance review.

CORPORATE EVENT PROJECT LIFE CYCLE (CASH FLOW)

For many corporate events, scheduling the cash flow is a significant part of the cost control procedure. The cash flow schedule shows when and how much cash is coming in and going out over a period of time. The timing for incoming cash may not coincide with the outgoing cash. Of particular concern is the need for further finances and how long before the extra funds are available to the event. In the case of corporate event management, the finance department may take several weeks to establish a budget center and transfer funds to the event budget. In the meantime, the event manager will need to make deposits for major items such as the venue, contract with an outside event planner, or engage a guest speaker or celebrity. Therefore, the paperwork process should begin as soon as the event is deemed feasible.

In the situation where many of the event costs need to be paid before the arrival of any income, cash flow takes on a dominant role in the event planning. To illustrate, let's consider the simple example of an event sponsored by the local government to promote retailers and the general shopping district. The event, called the 12 Days of Christmas Magic, will involve various magicians performing to the public during the 12 days before Christmas.

The spreadsheet in Table 11-2 shows what happens if the event planner's income is paid according to the custom of the client. Given the demands of the suppliers, the net result, shown in the graph in Figure 11-2, is that the

Table 11-2 Initial Cash Flow Table

Weeks Out	Client	Suppliers			Cumulative Amount
	Client A	Stage	Entertainment	Sound	
10	$5,000				$5,000
9		−$4,000			$1,000
8					$1,000
7			−$5,000		−$4,000
6					−$4,000
5					−$4,000
4					−$4,000
3					−$4,000
2	$10,000			−$3,000	$3,000
1					$3,000
0		−$4,000	−$5,000	−$1,000	−$7,000
−1	$15,000				$8,000
Total	$30,000	−$8,000	−$10,000	−$4,000	

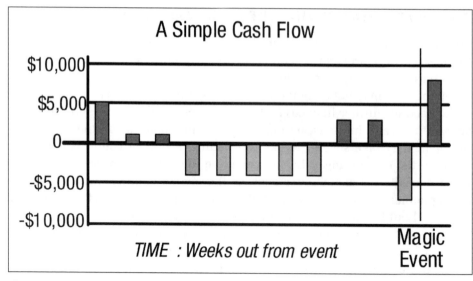

Figure 11-2
Graph of the Cash Flow

event company would have to pay some of the expenses out of its own pocket for at least six weeks. If the payments are negotiated so that the clients pay more up front, as shown in Table 11-3, then this risky situation is greatly reduced. Figure 11-3 shows that the event company is in the black for most of the event project life cycle. This is only a simple example, but it illustrates the importance of the payment schedule.

Another danger area occurs if the client pays the suppliers directly. Event suppliers—in particular, entertainment agencies—may work on a different invoice and payment cycle than the client or sponsor does. A good practice is to have the finance department or the corporate event team member with the ultimate budget responsibility discuss payment terms with the entertainment agency controller. For example, if the entertainment agency bills on the first of the month but the corporate policy is to process invoices for payment on the thirtieth, the entertainment agency may not receive the check in the mail for five weeks or more. Additionally, many corporations require the signature of the event project manager or the internal client before processing the invoice. If the marketing manager has global responsibility, the invoice could sit in the in-basket for two weeks before it is signed and sent to finance for payment. Early discussions regarding payment processes and schedules can avoid disappointments and unnecessary financial stress for the supplier and the corporate event manager.

Table 11-3 Cash Flow Table After Negotiation

Weeks Out	Client Client A	Suppliers Stage	Suppliers Entertainment	Suppliers Sound	Cumulative Amount
10	$5,000				$5,000
9		−$4,000			$1,000
8					$1,000
7	$5,000		−$5,000		$1,000
6					$1,000
5					$1,000
4					$1,000
3					$1,000
2	$10,000			−$3,000	$8,000
1					$8,000
0		−$4,000	−$5,000	−$1,000	−$2,000
−1	$10,000				$8,000
Total	$30,000	−$8,000	−$10,000	−$4,000	

Corporate event sponsorship also deals with cash flow issues. Nonprofit organizations must plan their expenditures on a fiscal calendar just as corporations must. Take the case of a corporation and a nonprofit organization that don't follow the same fiscal calendar. Disappointments and disconnects can occur when the financial calendars are not in sync. The nonprofit organization can miss its quarterly target due to this lack of synchronization. Both parties will benefit from a discussion of the financial calendars when the corporation sponsors a charitable or nonprofit event. The good public relations generated by the corporate involvement with the charity could otherwise be lost due to lack of communication.

Frank DelMedico, an independent corporate event planner, gave a positive example of how good communication played a role in a sponsored event. The corporate client received the benefits of a $10,000 level of sponsorship in exchange for committing a specified number of employees to raise money for the charity. Based on previous experience with other similar corporations, the charity predicted that the average employee would raise $75. During the actual event, some employees and their families raised as much as $1,000 on their own. The event gave the corporation recognition and the charity received the involvement and the funding they desired. Good communication in the planning stages of the event enabled the groups to arrange for the collection and transfer of funds at specified intervals which enabled a positive cash flow.

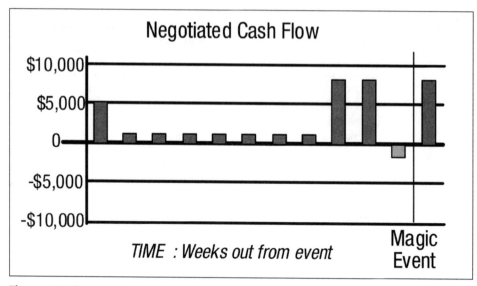

Figure 11-3
Graph of the Cash Flow After Negotiation

The positive outcome of the event on both sides made the request for sponsorship easier the following year.

In another case, DelMedico indicated that a furniture corporation committed a percentage of sales from a weekend of sales in conjunction with a charity fundraising event. The charity provided a photo for the event promotion and a tie-in to the Chicago broadcast of the national telethon. The corporation gained national exposure and increased sales for the weekend. The charity received increased funding. The fiscal accounting period for the furniture store matched the fiscal quarter dates for the charity. Therefore, the transfer of funds occurred at the appropriate time to pay the final expenses of the event and to enable the charity to include the funds raised during the event in the next year's charitable distribution. The match of fiscal quarters made it a success for everyone. If the quarters had not matched and the transfer of funds had occurred after the close of the quarter for the charity, the charity would have missed its goal for the year and the allocation to the charity recipients would have been negatively impacted.

MARKUP AND PASSING ON DISCOUNT

An important consideration in costing is how much the event management company will charge. This charge will depend on a number of factors, including the type of event company, the relationship with the client, and the standard methods used by the client. A systematic approach to event management requires guidelines. These can be structured in a variety of ways, from charging an administration cost as a percentage, to marking up all the costs, to just a straight cost. This will be reflected in the type of contract: cost-plus, fixed-price, incentive, or hybrid. An event company might charge between 10 percent and 30 percent of the gross. An entrepreneurial event management company might take whatever monies remain after the bills have been paid.

Another important consideration is how the event management company will handle any discounts it receives from suppliers. The event management company might not pass discounts on to the client. Conversely, the event management company may regard the discounts given by suppliers as part of its competitive advantage and pass them on to the corporate client as a way of demonstrating good faith. The client may expect this as part of its normal day-to-day business dealings. However, no matter what decision is made on this, it needs to be apparent to the client as any detailed auditing after the event will certainly uncover it. According to Robert W. Hulsmeyer, CSEP, senior partner with Empire Force Events based in New York, "Pricing is moving in the direction of revealing costs plus professional fees. That structure recognizes the event management industry as a profession, the way public relations and advertising professionals are recognized and compensated." The cost plus fee also provides a clearer picture of how the price is achieved, as well as the true value of the element and associated services.

PROBLEMS

The fact that it is almost impossible to have a full rehearsal for an event means that the event manager must be sensitive to actions that indicate a future problem in the area of cost. There can be any number of indicators; however, here are just a few that will help you recognize possible problems.

Lack of product detail: Far more may be involved in a good or service than is realized at first. The standard example of this is the conference venue brochure. Photos of a product to be rented may not show the right level of details necessary to make a good cost estimate. The wise corporate event planner will remember that the performance of the good or service contributes to the success of the event.

Account delays: Due to the normal delays in the accounting procedure, event management may misunderstand the current financial situation. The accounting department will not keep details on an event, as its priorities are different from event management's priorities. The costs may be absorbed into the general costs of the organization. The purchase order/invoice/payment cycle is an excellent method of accurately recording transactions, but it gives rise to unacceptable delays in reporting the current financial situation. The corporate event manager can, however, request a separate budget center for the event and request that the finance department run periodic financial reports to assess the current status against budget. Most project managers keep a log of cost commitments. This may be a simple matter of another column in the spreadsheet showing what amounts have been committed to the specific resources. To know the current financial situation is vital to any negotiations with vendors.

Scope creep: Although scope creep is dealt with in the chapter on the project management process, it needs to be reemphasized here as it surfaces in the costing. The amount of work needed to create the event can expand without the knowledge of the event management until it is too late to take action. This is perhaps the most common problem in project-based industries. The event planner should work out and implement a scope change procedure that requires approval from the event manager. However, the procedure should provide for some leeway when adjustments need to be made. According to Garland Preddy, administrative liaison specialist for the United States Marshals Service, one has to be aware of the history of events. Certain events, whether they are corporate or government events, tend to have a history of scope creep. This is particularly true with events that also have a history of late registration. The event may be planned to have a reception hour and a speaker. The event planner adds small items to the program to generate more interest and to encourage registration. Gradually, the event increases in size until it has mushroomed into one much larger than planned. By the time the true scope of the event is apparent, the planner cannot easily make changes and must pay the associated costs. This can easily happen with a new marketing manager who is nervous that his creative idea will fail and he will be viewed as a failure, so he makes the changes in an attempt to guarantee his success.

Procurement Program

How the suppliers are identified and engaged, as well as the method of coordinating with them, was covered in Chapter 8 on contracts. This section describes the overall method of procurement, the process of obtaining the necessary resources and services to enable the event to occur. The first step is identifying the resources and services. This relates back to the work breakdown structure. Each of the tasks will need resources. For example, a sound system requires labor, specialist equipment, and skills. The contractor may supply most of the resources for a work package or a group of tasks. No one needs to find all these resources for the contractor, because that is why the contractor is hired.

A standard document used to identify the resources needed is shown in Figure 11-4. The document can be used to forecast the use of the resources. These resources can then be scheduled for arrival, use, and removal. However, the scheduling will have to be done in consultation with the suppliers. The cost of resources can be a function of their availability. The cost of renting marquees, for example, may be dependent on the time of year.

Once the resource and service needs are identified, they need to be sourced. The first consideration is whether the event company, the sponsor, or the client already has these internal resources. In some areas (accounting, for example), the client may prefer the event management company to use the in-house services. In other cases, the sponsor will require the event company to use its partner's or parent company's services. Another consideration is whether the

Code	Resource	How Many	Cost	Standard/ Nonstandard Event Manager Notes (e.g., use last year's figures)	Date/Times
AV.1	Flat screen	3	$800 each/day	Standard	2 days
AV.2	Data projector	3	$700 each/day	Standard	2 days
AV.3	Operator	1	$300 each/day	Standard	3 days
AV.4	Video unit	2	$200 each/day	Standard	1 day
CA.1	Catering	For 200	$80/per person per day	Standard	2 days
CA.2	Cocktails	For 150	$35/per person per day	Standard	1800–2130 day 1 (6:00 to 9:30 pm day one)

Figure 11-4
Resource Analysis Sheet

resources need to be manufactured for the specific event or whether they are standard products. In the case of trade shows, the décor in the booth is usually made to order and fits the current theme of the event or the company.

QUOTES

The corporate event manager needs to establish a system for finding the best supplies. The three-quotes method is the most common. However, planning events has so many special conditions that comparing the quotes can be difficult. A formal call for bids or quotes may be needed on large events. On smaller events a quote from the list of preferred suppliers is the most common method. Obtaining an accurate quote is important, because the event manager may have no time to change to a different supplier as the event nears, nor would the event manager be able to cancel the contract. This means that a significant amount of work needs to go into describing to the suppliers exactly what is needed. Just a description of the goods required may not be sufficient, because what counts for events is generally what the resources can do. Thus, the statement of work should clearly describe the goods and services required and should include performance specifications.

The advantage of using procedure and documentation standards is that the standards or documentation can be incorporated into the contract and the elements specified compared to the goods and services when they arrive. The procedures, documentation, and product or service specifications as per the standards may become the basis of later negotiations over fees. It can also be the basis of the knowledge management of the event management company or corporate event management department. Engineering project management companies often have a library of specifications that are adapted to each project. When calling for quotes, the corporate event office or the independent event company is in a similar position to the client, and many of the assessment criteria used in the event feasibility study can be applied. For example, is the provider's business stable? Can it extend the goods or services if required? Will it be able to focus on the event over its whole life?

LEASE, MAKE, OR BUY

Not all resources for an event will be rented. The decision to hire, rent, make, or buy resources for an event will depend on a number of factors, including:

  Return on investment: This financial decision is based on the costs of hiring, buying, and manufacturing and on the resale value and depreciation.
  Legal and other risk considerations: Will the supplier be responsible for the resources?

Schedules: Timely manufacture and delivery, turnaround times, repair and maintenance times.

Quality assurance and change: Will the resources be of the quality needed for the event? If the situation changes, will the resources still be of use to the event?

Future use and storage: Will the resource be useable for future events? What is the cost of storage?

Consider, for example, event management software, more correctly called event planning software. What exactly is the return on investment? Implementing new software has so many subsidiary costs, such as training and new hardware, that a simple cost analysis can be quite baffling. Add to this the knowledge that the software may be obsolete before the event takes place.

TEAM

As not every facet of the resource can be described on paper, the corporate event manager should build a rapport with the suppliers and understand their businesses. The supplier is a critical part of the event team. The corporate event manager needs to be familiar with the items that will be expensive for the contractor to supply. Asking for extra microphones may not be a large cost compared to asking for radio microphones. An extension to a stage may be a minor item, whereas a change in the lighting setup may be a major cost. A common problem with event suppliers is that the department that closes the deal is not always the one in the company that supplies the goods or services. For example, a problem may occur because a salesperson or an account manager makes the arrangement, but the operations, manufacturing, or distribution department actually performs the service or creates the product. In other cases, problems result due to communication errors, as when the supplier obtains an item from a subcontractor. The risk is that the actual supplier will ignore all the unwritten agreements. This can be caught before it becomes a problem by stipulating the responsible party in the written agreement. However, we strongly recommend that all agreements be added to the contract in writing and be initialed by the signing parties.

SUPPLIER CHECKLIST

A cost overrun is often a result of choosing unsuitable suppliers. New events are particularly prone to this risk. The suppliers often become the work units or objects in the project management process and therefore are the building blocks of the event. The event office should assess the ability of the suppliers to deliver. Figure 11-5 is a simple checklist to assess the supplier's abilities to deliver on time, to budget, and at quality.

> • Reliability—in particular, punctuality
> • Experience with events of similar size and scope for the supplier
> • Ability to focus on the event, often one of many
> • Guaranteed quality of product
> • History in the event business
> • Discounting for large orders

Figure 11-5
Supplier Checklist

Costing and procurement affect the profitability of any enterprise. Smart procurement can reduce corporate event overheads and give the event, its management, and the client or sponsor a competitive edge. The methods and terminology outlined in this chapter are used in project-based industries, including Department of Defense contracts and information technology. They have been honed over many years of constant use around the world. The event industry by comparison is in its infancy. Event planners can no longer do costing on the back of an envelope and procurement as a handshake deal. Event planners need to be knowledgeable about best practices and have a systematic and accountable methodology.

Wrap Up

1. Costing is the estimating of event costs, establishing a baseline or budget, controlling those costs, and documenting and reporting the process.

2. Costs must be classified in order to apply standards and make cost comparisons, as well as to allocate the appropriate funding for the element.

3. Costs are classified as direct or indirect, unique or standard, fixed or variable, one-time or recurring, and as lost opportunities.

4. To make the best possible estimate, the corporate event manager needs to understand the different methods used to estimate the costs—top-down, bottom-up, parametric methods.

5. Estimating may be performed at any point in the event life cycle; however, it becomes more accurate as the event date nears.

6. If an estimate is too detailed, it can hamper the event manager's ability to make content changes, when a change in circumstances necessitates a change in content.

7. The event manager should have contingency plans and costs based on those plans, since things can occur that are beyond the control of the event staff.

8. When presenting cost estimates to stakeholders, the event planner should include information on the method used to determine the cost and the degree of accuracy of the estimate.

9. The event office must have a process in place for controlling and tracking costs, as well as for adhering to the budget.
10. Scheduling cash flow is a significant part of the cost control procedure.
11. An event company may charge the corporation based on cost-plus, fixed-price, or incentive, or a hybrid of these methods.
12. The corporate event manager must be vigilant regarding indicators of future cost problems, such as lack of product detail, account delays, and scope creep.
13. The identification of resources required and the overall procurement process enable the event to occur.
14. The use of standards for procedures and documentation in contract preparation provides the opportunity for the event manager to compare goods and services in the contract. The specifications and standards can also be the basis of future negotiations regarding fees.
15. A checklist can be beneficial to the event manager in assessing the supplier's ability to provide the required goods and services.

Instrument

Bent, J. A., and K. K. Humphreys. *Effective Project Management through Applied Cost and Schedule Control.* New York: Marcel Dekker, Inc., 1996.

Points for Discussion and Practice

1. Describe how your event office can instill cost consciousness in your staff.
2. Choose an event and create a work breakdown structure. Use the WBS to:
   a. Create cost centers and cost control codes.
   b. Estimate the costs using the bottom-up method.
   c. Calculate the accuracy of each cost and the accuracy of the total cost.
   d. Create a cash flow table for the event project life cycle. Estimate the cost payment schedule.
   e. Create a resources analysis table for the event.
3. Research the use of commitment accounting or a commitment log for event management.
4. Expand the cost classification table (Table 11-1) to include other elements of event management.
5. Use the Web to research U.S. Department of Defense contracts and procurement processes and regulations (www.defenselink.mil).
6. What are the limitations in using the Web for event procurement?
7. Compare the costing procedures of other project industries, such as construction and IT, to corporate event management.

CHAPTER 12

Demonstrating Value Through Measurement and Analysis

THIS CHAPTER WILL HELP YOU:

- Articulate the value of evaluation measurements to corporate clients
- List types of evaluation processes and instruments
- Describe successful evaluation strategies for corporate events
- Describe the relationship between evaluation and return on investment
- Evaluate a corporate event in terms of return on investment

---

Each year, as the budgeting process for the following year begins, corporate management must determine the most effective vehicle for communicating their messages and achieving their goals. Corporate events are included in this process and must compete with other projects for available funds. Therefore, the project manager must be able to demonstrate that an event can efficiently and effectively achieve the corporate objectives. The event manager must consider how the costs and return on investment (ROI) compare to other options available to the client. How does an event fit into the client's business strategy? How will the event fit into the corporate culture? How can the event manager support the department manager in a request for funding, or how can he or she assist the department manager in the decision-making process with regard to project options? The focus of this chapter is the evaluation process, which provides the data to assist in responding to these questions. Evaluation results provide fact-based information that can be used to communicate the relationship of the value received (the elements of the event and their effect on the attendees) to the price paid (the cost of the event).

Overview of the Importance of Evaluation

It is always a pleasure for the corporate event manager to observe the attendees at an event enjoying the festivities or sharing the excitement of learning new things; however, the achievement of measurable objectives is the basis of future funding and approval for future corporate events. Current standard practice in many corporations is to evaluate every corporate event. A well-designed evaluation process enables the client and the event manager to determine if the event met the desired goals and objectives as well as the needs and opportunities for future events. In many social events, to circulate an evaluation form or to conduct an in-person evaluation would be inappropriate. However, it would be appropriate to monitor the satisfaction level of guests during the event and to send a postevent evaluation form to the attendees' home or office.

Not only is evaluating the event important, but also documenting and justifying your added value as a corporate event manager is an ongoing activity that must be tied to every step of the event project management process. Savvy corporate event managers maintain extensive records that document their consistently positive performance. This information is communicated to the client in proposals, postevent evaluation reports, and letters. The practice builds both client rapport and continued business.

Generally, event evaluations cover two distinct areas: first, content, including speakers, activities, and entertainment; and second, destination, venue, facilities, and services. The primary focus of the event evaluation is to determine how well the content related to the purpose of the event. Content questions provide valuable information regarding the success of each element. The evaluation process provides direct feedback from the attendees regarding the quality of elements, such as the speaker, the topic covered, its value to the attendee, and whether the attendee is interested in future events or discussions on that topic.

The secondary focus of the event evaluation is the fit of the destination and venue to the event. In the early planning stages, the event manager compares a variety of destinations and the facilities available at each destination. These are then rated against a set of criteria developed with the attendee profile, the event content, and activities in mind. The evaluations completed by the attendees reflect how well the chosen destination and facilities hit the mark. The attendees' responses to the questions aid the corporate event management office or independent planner in modifying the profile and in selecting future destinations and facilities.

It is the responsibility of the corporate event manager to plan a program that weaves together a variety of elements, including items such as educational presentations, social activities, meal functions, and recreational activities. The evaluation data indicate how well the event succeeded in this area. The corporate event manager's observations can also add to the data gathered from the attendees. The valuable observations of the planner and staff can provide input for plans for the next event.

Vendors also should be included in the evaluation process. Vendors can provide feedback based on their observations and on the processes used to plan and execute the event. Constructive criticism should receive serious review and consideration. The ultimate goal is to improve upon your processes and your product.

USE HISTORY OR PRECEDENTS TO DEFINE ADDED VALUE

The evaluation results from past events can be useful for determining whether a particular component is needed to make the event a huge success. Researching a company's past events and activities can make its future events more memorable. As a corporate event manager, you must be fiscally responsible and consider whether the value of each activity was equal to its cost. If the element or activity increased the overall value of the event, you can use this data to support including the activity in future events. If there was a sufficient return on investment in terms of a desire for guests to return for future events, evaluation results that indicated the element supported the theme or led to increased sales, then the client should be made aware of the added value of the element.

EMPLOY EXPERTS TO SUPPORT YOUR CLAIMS

If you desire any analysis beyond a mean, an average, or an opinion sample, we recommend that you engage an evaluation professional. Most event planners are not educated in the area of statistical analysis. Professionals can utilize the data in a variety of ways and can provide valuable details regarding the opinion of the attendees. In addition, a professional can work with the corporate event manager and the client to develop the evaluation instrument. This will enable everyone involved to gain the most information and value from the evaluation process. The results can also help you sell your professional event management services for future events or to sell the concept of a value-added element. In the world of corporate events, you can add significant value to your services if they include the ability to perform evaluation services.

QUANTITATIVE AND QUALITATIVE EVALUATION METHODS

Quantitative Evaluation Methods

A survey of the attendees, the number of sales related to the event, and detailed records of other pertinent factors provide an accurate quantitative measurement of the event's value. This is generally performed using an evaluation instrument, usually a questionnaire or survey. The evaluation process can be performed via a questionnaire that attendees complete at the site, a computer survey either completed on-site or posted on-line, or a telephone survey. Most people are familiar with the ubiquitous "bubble form," the type of evaluation wherein the respondent uses a pen or pencil to darken circles (bubbles) that reflect their opinion. Retail stores, doctor's offices, schools, and restaurants use this type of survey to gather information about customer satisfaction.

Careful advance planning for a quantitative evaluation survey is necessary to ensure that meaningful data is collected. If the questions are not worded properly, the resulting data can be expensive and meaningless. Professional help with the construction of the questions is highly recommended. This type of evaluation survey has positives and negatives. On the positive side, it is simple to administer, and it is quick and easy for the attendee to complete. It is usually constructed with either a Likert scale or a semantic differential scale. The Likert scale asks the respondee to choose between several levels of satisfaction, such as *strongly agree, somewhat agree, neither, slightly disagree,* or *strongly disagree.* The semantic differential asks the respondee to choose a word that describes the level of satisfaction. The choice provided is between two opposing terms such as *great fun* and *boring.* On the negative side, this type of evaluation does not allow for personal expression of an opinion outside the parameters of the exact question. It also does not provide any insight into why the attendee selected a particular response. Therefore, you may not be able to get to the root of the dissatisfaction to make adjustments in the next session or the next event.

Qualitative Evaluation Methods

A qualitative evaluation survey is best conducted face-to-face or in focus group interviews. However, when in-person contact is not possible, a well-constructed questionnaire or survey form can be mailed to the attendee. Unlike the quantitative form, the qualitative form contains open-ended questions. This encourages the respondees to reply in their own words rather than forcing them to choose between restrictive categories that may not express their true opinions. This type of questionnaire takes more time to complete, and the data analysis is more challenging to compile. However, it does provide more detailed insight into the attitude of the respondees. A thorough reading and analysis of this type of evaluation can help the event manager discover patterns in the responses, which can provide valuable information for internal evaluations of the current event and for planning for the next event. All findings should be reported to your event stakeholders.

EVALUATION DATA VALUE

Positive data can be used to raise the benchmark for the next event. If this year you used fireworks at the company picnic for added value, then you may have to come up with another activity' or spectacle to give new dimension to next year's event. In sales-related events, an added-value activity can triple or quadruple sales by enticing people to stay longer, buy more, or investigate your product further. This is always a good argument for added-value activities.

The perceived value of an event component may be higher or lower than the actual value, depending on such things as the context in which the data are presented or the personal opinion of the stakeholder. Make certain *in writing* that the event management team knows the *actual* cost and the data indications of the actual value. Elements may be considered a waste of money by some executives; however, the data collected may indicate otherwise. Also, the corporate staff may have a different opinion about the value of an element. Empirical data will help to make a clear business case for or against an element.

The following is an example of how empirical data can provide a positive business case for holding an event. Keith, a corporate event planner for a major technology manufacturer that was in the process of reorganization and "rightsizing," related an excellent example of the value of event evaluation and related statistical data. Keith called the vice president (VP) of marketing to start the planning process for an annual recognition event. The vice president said that he was considering eliminating the event because of recent budget cuts. Fortunately, Keith was aware of the budget cuts and had done his homework prior to calling the VP. Keith discussed the increase in sales and the improvement in employee retention that were directly related to the previous year's event. The VP listened intently and requested a copy of the brief report that Keith had compiled. Upon reviewing the report, the VP determined that the event offered greater value for the targeted audience than other marketing options, such as advertising or direct mail, and shifted his budget to enable the recognition event to occur. The event planner worked with him to substitute elements in several areas to contain the cost and still provide an exciting and memorable event.

Design and Implementation

Although statistical data is very useful, attendees are not readily inclined to complete a questionnaire when they are enjoying an event. Therefore, the corporate event manager must make it easy and convenient for them to complete the questionnaire. Laurence Rudolph, Ph.D., recommends that the questions be specific; that the questionnaire be designed with a crisp, clear layout; that pencils to darken the circles on the bubble charts or pens to write comments on the qualitative instruments be provided; and that collection boxes are conveniently located for the completed questionnaires.

Categories should not be lumped together. Each discrete element should be listed separately. The result will provide the specific data required to perform a careful analysis of the respondent's evaluation. Specific questions yield the most beneficial information. Questions that are too broad or too general in nature probably will not provide any information to assist in the future decision-making process. The client will want to know if the objectives for the event were met and to what degree they were met. For example, did 95 percent of the attendees believe that they could communicate the corporate strategy to their client following the strategy session? This information is a key factor in the decision to hold the event again in the future.

The evaluation instrument must include the objectives of each content module if the event includes speakers or training sessions. Make sure that there are no ambiguous words or sentences used in the construction of the questions and statements. A best practice followed by the authors is to have a test group of the target population or someone in the company, outside of the event management team, read the evaluation questions. The test group should be familiar with the terminology but objective enough to provide good comments. In addition, ensure that the form is coded correctly so that each session or event element is clearly identified. Remember that the "bubble forms" are read by machine. Also, the information may be skewed if the attendees think the questionnaire has been designed for another session or is not relevant to their session or activity. Anonymity is critical, as the respondees may not answer truthfully if they believe that their responses will be communicated to corporate management team.

A short, concise questionnaire will encourage attendees to comply with the request for feedback. One corporation spent a large sum to carefully design a six-page evaluation for a weeklong event. The attendees took one look at the form and decided it was too complex. The corporation received less than a 5 percent response rate on the form, a sampling of information too small to be statistically significant. Usually, one page printed on two sides is the maximum that attendees will complete.

Clear and specific directions ensure that the evaluation form is completed correctly. Remember, often a speaker or a general manager will be the person asking the attendees to complete the evaluation form at a corporate-sponsored event. This person is unlikely to have detailed information on the evaluation instrument or a background in evaluation and statistical analysis. Clear and concise instructions are even more critical for a Web-enabled evaluation.

Design the evaluation instrument with plenty of space. Ensure that the items are clearly numbered and that they align properly. If the instrument contains qualitative questions, then it should allow adequate space for the attendees to state their comments. The typeface should be an adequate size to read legibly. The document should have a crisp, clean, organized appearance. Do not try to squeeze too much information onto the form, as it will serve only to confuse the respondees. Maintain a consistent style to your format. Place qualitative or open-ended questions at the end of the evaluation form. Provide a section for each presenter or speaker in an element. Place demographic questions at the top of the form to ensure that the respondee will provide the information. The information gathered from these questions will aid in benchmarking against the target population profile crafted in the early planning stages of the event. Did those for whom the event was planned attend? Did another unplanned audience also attend? What was the impact? Questions from the previous event can track the trends and enable year-to-year improvement. Marianne, a corporate event planner for a consulting corporation, related an example of such an improvement. The evaluations from one of her conferences indicated that the attendees desired more in-depth technical information on an emerging technology. The following year, she engaged several industry experts for an "Ask the Expert" panel session. It was one of the most popular elements in the conference and an interest generator for the following year.

A well-marked box or other container should be strategically placed at all exits. In some cases, labeled envelopes are provided to the speaker at corporate training seminars or kickoff meetings. The speaker should be advised of any processes for completion and collection. For example, the speaker should allow five to ten minutes at the end of the presentation for completion of the evaluation. Preferably, an attendee can be "volunteered" to collect the evaluation forms and return them to a central location.

One corporate event manager found a clever process to ensure the collection of all evaluations. She asked for a volunteer among the attendees to be responsible for the evaluation collection and delivery to the control room. In exchange for an envelope of collections, she provided a gift certificate to a well-known department store. In another case, she traded the attendees a logo sweatshirt for their completed evaluations. Her bright ideas have netted her positive results. She consistently delivers an event report complete with charts and graphs just two days after the event. Her clients are impressed with her strategies and the valuable information she is able to provide. This information has ensured her contracts for the following years.

The Value of Evaluation

To obtain the greatest impact, tabulate the evaluation data and provide the results to the event management team quickly. This is especially true of your successes, although negatives can often be salvaged if the team can make quick decisions based on this data. During more complex events, such as weeklong conferences and seminars, the most effective time to evaluate speakers is immediately at the end of each presentation. You can quickly tabulate the results and provide feedback to the speakers before their next sessions. This will enable the event manager to reinforce the positives and make adjustments where necessary.

Host "Lessons Learned" sessions with the corporate event management staff and the client immediately following the event. This gives everyone the opportunity to provide feedback on what they observed while the information is fresh in their minds and while everyone can be in attendance. This critical element is usually scheduled as a part of the total event management process. This important activity will capture valuable information for future event planning.

Many major corporations and larger independent event managers create a separate form for the client to evaluate the event project manager and the staff, as well as the vendors. Reports, documentation, and a diary of the event management team performance (a hero or heroine file) can prove valuable when selling the services of the department or the independent event management company. Documented positive publicity about events managed and cost reductions achieved can provide both anecdotal and statistical information regarding the value of the event project manager.

Justifying Event Elements with Facts

Corporate event managers can use facts to justify event elements they recommended or to sell their professional services. The word of the event manager alone may not be sufficient. An event office library of articles and notes regarding events of colleagues or events attended by the event manager serve as good examples and support recommendations to the event management team. A position supported with facts from well-constructed evaluations can make the difference between a positive and a negative response from the client. Data adds professionalism and educates the client.

Valuable information is obtained only with proper planning. Evaluation is an integral part of the corporate event project management process. A well-executed evaluation process can provide the statistical information desired by the finance department. Reports containing the appropriate information in a clear, concise layout can aid a marketing manager or a human resources director in gaining the required funds to hold the event. The corporation views events as a means to communicate corporate messages, generate sales, communicate corporate initiatives, educate staff, reinforce behaviors, and introduce new products. The corporation expects a return on investment and will review the ROI in a number of ways. An opportunity cost is what the organization gives in return for the event in addition to the actual cost of the event. For example, if a salesperson attends a training event, then face-to-face contact time with the client is lost in exchange for the time spent at the event. The corporation will consider the sales generated by the new information or skills gained at the event minus the lost revenue of the time out of the field. On the other hand, the corporation will also consider the goodwill it receives from an event in exchange for the financial cost of the event.

Evaluation data is a valuable resource and must be kept in a secure location whether the data is in digital or paper format.

Dennis Frahman of Xerox Corporate Communications provided what he felt was the best example of a positive return on investment (ROI) with measurable results: the sponsorship of a major exhibit at Drupa 2000, a printing show, during the second half of May 2000 in Düsseldorf, Germany. Xerox sponsored a 60,000-plus-square-foot exhibit in a hall entirely of its own that had over 75,000 people in attendance. The event management office set up show specials and carefully tracked attendance. They found that they had a ROI higher than what was normally achieved through direct mail. The event involved more than 300 individuals and over 15 months of planning. It included a core team of 12 people, located in Europe and the United States, who designed the exhibit, developed supporting marketing communications, acquired the audience, and tracked the results. Frahman states that the successful event was the result of:

Setting clear and measurable objectives up front
Following a structured event management process
Obtaining adequate funding and having the funding remain stable
Maintaining an international team at both the leadership and working level

What made it challenging was:

The time zone variances and cultural differences
No clear final authority, due to multiple parties and paths of appeal

Frahman adds, "You must always know why you're participating in the event and find a way to measure it."

Central to any profession is the ability to forecast. The forecast does not have to be 100 percent accurate; however, it must use measurements that can be compared with alternatives. The projectization of business as described by authors such as Turner (1999) and Gray and Larsen (2000) drive the need to compare projects within a corporation. A pharmaceutical company, for example, will need to choose between a variety of projects to fund, such as product research and development, sponsorship, a conference, or new software. Until an event can be compared with other company projects, it will always be the poor cousin. It is surprising that little or no work has been done on event modeling. The notable exception is tourism events. They contribute a significant amount to a country's GNP and are the focus of a number of studies. In particular, their economic impact and the cost-benefit analysis has been applied to large sporting events and conferences. There can be no doubt of the need for event cost-benefit metrics. How else can a sufficient return on investment be calculated? Event evaluation has little meaning unless it can be used as the basis of forecasting.

An argument often made against using cost-benefit analysis is the intangible nature of many of the benefits. It seems that they can't be measured.

However, this situation is found in all public projects and marketing projects. It is not an insurmountable problem. For example, a pharmaceutical product launch/seminar would look at these benefits:

- Networking with current clients and prospective clients
- Sales
- Brand awareness
- Media exposure

These could be measured initially by:

- Leads and referrals
- Registrations
- Actual sales that are directly traced to the conference
- Media exposure measured versus cost of comparative advertising

Ultimately, a dollar figure must be attached to them, otherwise it is impossible to forecast the results of the next event or to compare the investment in the event with the investment in other projects. The aim of project appraisal by a corporation is the elimination of error by reducing the uncertainty in decisions.

A seminar within a company can be measured by the time saved by the application of the new skills and knowledge learned as an output of the seminar. This can be estimated in terms of man hours and therefore wages saved.

A two-week sales seminar may be directly measured in terms of an increase in sales over a set period of time. However, the true cost-benefit analysis must take into account the opportunity costs of having the sales staff out of action for two weeks. The equation becomes:

$$\text{Event net worth} = \text{Benefits} - \text{Costs} - \text{Opportunity costs}$$

Participation in a trade exhibition can be estimated using the data from past exhibitions and extending it. It is important to weight this data according to the time influence of the exhibition. There may be a positive flow on effect, as business will occur years after the exhibition. There will be a point when the company will pass the payback period—the time when the investment has been returned. For example, a recent product launch cost well over $1 million. The luxury car company involved in the event invited current owners of the previous models and made over $6 million on the sales as a direct result of the event. The payback period ended during the event. The sales after the event contributed positively to the corporate bottom line.

A company incentive event can be seen as reward to staff and as a way of attracting skilled staff. In cost-benefit analysis terms, it may be measured by the benefits of attracting and retaining skilled staff versus the cost of training new staff.

The process of corporate event modeling is:

- *Stakeholder analysis:* This includes internal company stakeholders, for example marketing, sales, finance.
- Defining and classifying the benefits and identifying costs (including opportunity costs).
- Establishing metrics within the guidelines of the business brief.
- Creating a model, including sensitivity analysis and estimating of payback period.
- Forecasting for future events.
- Using the next event to refine the model.

The process of corporate event modeling is shown in Figure 12.1. This process should identify parameters that contribute to the cost-benefit of the event. For

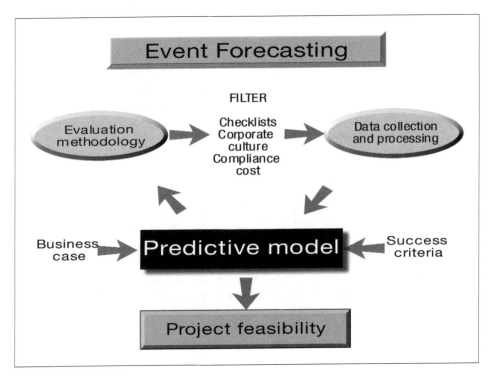

Figure 12-1
Process of Corporate Event Modeling

example, a parameter for an overseas trade event may be the level of contacts made within the country. This parameter will contribute directly to the business success of the event. By using data from previous trade events, the importance of this parameter can be given a dollar figure.

A useful tool in this process is to look at the boundaries—also part of sensitivity analysis. Again, the case of an overseas trade exhibition provides an excellent example. Once the parameters that contribute to the cost-benefit of the event have been identified, then a look at the boundaries will provide an estimate of the cost-benefit effect of a small change in one of the parameters. If more work (cost) is put into attracting higher-level contacts in the host country, will this additional work (cost) significantly contribute to the benefits, and if so, by how much?

In summary, a corporate event should be seen as contributing to the business. It is ultimately concerned with the business proposition. Therefore, evaluation of the event is far more than evaluating its success as an event. It must create a model—metrics—to forecast and make a good business case for future events.

Table 12-1 was created from an informal survey of event managers who attended our project management training workshops. Few of those surveyed had any metrics for comparing the benefit of the events with previous events or other projects within the company.

Table 12-1 Cost-Benefit Survey Results

Type of Event	Benefit	Measure
Public relations	Promotional value Media coverage Awareness	
Corporate events, such as award nights, launches, trade shows, theater evenings, road shows, roundtables, office openings, gala dinners (client entertainment and education), breakfasts, luncheons, forums, social clubs, workshops, conventions, sales conferences, trade booths, media briefings	Increase in sales Lead generation Improve product and company profile Boost staff morale and obtain better results from staff's work Check on competitors (also create a presence) Building relationships (client seminars) Add value	Actual revenue received Media exposure (quality and quantity) Attendance figures (and drop out) Number invites versus number attended ratio Time/money ratio

continued

Table 12-1 *(Continued)*

Type of Event	Benefit	Measure
Association seminars	Informing members of regulations and improvements in efficiency Educating stakeholders	
Internal corporate events (sales staff seminars, staff parties)	Team knowledge Increase in sales Enthusiastic sales team Staff stays with company Growth of sales force	
Recruitment events	Meet event objectives	Recruitment survey—increased interest in defense Count of attendees Postevent analysis
Fund-raising events	Money (fund-raising) Raise profile, image, and goodwill of community Create/raise awareness Build network	Surveys during the event (focus groups, etc.) Research awareness Male/female ratio Business generated Product awareness
Trade exhibition		Attendance Profit/loss
Sports competition		Increase in tourism Media coverage Sponsorship attracted Attendee numbers
Community/public events	Social development Enhancement of community Fund-raising PR exercise Raise level of education and training	Feedback and evaluation Media exposure (quantity and quality) Economic injection into community, determined via survey calculations Lack of public complaints Number of attendees Increase in tourism

Finding a way to measure your success is a fundamental principle of corporate event project management. Now you have discovered a new system for managing corporate events through effective project management. The result of your new system will be measured by the success of your next corporate event. Use these corporate event project management principles and practices to grow your career as well as the entire corporate event management industry. Good luck with your next corporate event project!

Wrap Up

1. Evaluation data provides clear information regarding the value of a corporate event.
2. The primary focus of the event evaluation is how well the content related to the purpose of the event.
3. A quantitative evaluation is usually constructed using restrictive categories and a Likert scale, and provides a measurable assessment of an event.
4. A qualitative evaluation uncovers details and true personal opinions regarding the event. It is nonrestrictive and uses open-ended questions.

5. Design and implementation are critical to obtaining statistically significant information.
6. Evaluation can help the corporate event manager justify event elements or even the event itself.
7. Corporations expect a return on their investment (ROI) in an event.
8. Finding a way to measure your success is a fundamental principal of corporate event project management.

Instruments

Getz, Donald. *Event Management and Event Tourism.* New York, NY: Cognizant Communications, 1997, Chapter 14.

Mules, T. *Financial and Economic Modeling of Major Sporting Events in Australia.* Adelaide, Australia: Center for South Australian Economic Studies, 1998.

National Center for Cuture and Recreation Statistics, Australian Bureau of Statistics. *Measuring the Impact of Festivals—Guidelines for Conducting an Economic Impact Study.* Canberra, Australia: Statistics Working Group of the Cultural Ministers Council, 1997.

Polivka, Edward G. *Professional Meeting Management,* 3rd ed. Birmingham, Ala.: Professional Convention Management Association, 1996.

Snell, Michael. *Cost-Benefit Analysis for Engineers and Planners.* London: Thomas Telford Publishing, 1997.

Wright, Rudy R., CMP. *The Meeting Spectrum: An Advanced Guide for Meeting Professionals.* San Diego, Calif.: Rockwood Enterprises, 1989.

Points for Discussion and Practice

1. Construct an evaluation instrument for your corporate event.
2. Select the best evaluation method for an exhibit at a trade show and for a training program for technicians.

3. Describe how you will determine whether to use qualitative, quantitative, or both a qualitative and quantitative evaluation for your next corporate event.

APPENDIX 1

APPENDIX 1A

Contact Sheet

Last updated <....................> or version # replacing version #-1

<Name of Event and Logo>

Code	Name	Phones	Mobile	E-mail	Fax

Page Number <....>/total no.

<file name> <date ....>

Event Project Management System   epms.net

APPENDIX 1B

Reponsibility List		<Name of Event and Logo>
Code	Person/s	Responsibility or output

Key or Legend

<file name> <date ....>

Event Project Management System   epms.net

APPENDIX 1C

Task or Action Sheet

Last updated <.................> or version # replacing version #-1

<Name of Event and Logo>

Code	Item	Action	Due	Person	Comment

<file name> <date ....>

Page Number <....>/total no.

Event Project Management System   epms.net

APPENDIX 1D

Work Package for <name of contractor or task group>

<Name of Event and Logo>

Last updated <...............> or version # replacing version #-1
Total work period:

Code Task	Description	Begin	Finish	Responsibility			

Page Number <.....>/total no.

Event Project Management System   epms.net

<file name> <date ....>

APPENDIX 1E

Run Sheet for <date and/or place of actions>   <Name of Event and Logo>

Time	Action	Event area	Sound/lights/visuals	Person	Comment	

Page Number <....>/total no.

Event Project Management System   epms.net

<file name> <date ....>

APPENDIX 1F

SAMPLE CORPORATE EVENT RUN SHEET

The following is a sample of a run sheet used for a corporate recognition dinner. The event included various audiovisual components and the chairman of the board, as well as a famous person as speaker. It was very important that the audiovisuals used by the chairman of the board be perfectly timed, so a run sheet of the production schedule was constructed. Note the exact timing listed for the actual ceremony. Also, notice that the schedule indicates who has what responsibility. It is concise and specific. We are happy to report that the event was highly successful.

2002 Recognition Dinner Production Schedule

4/14/02

9:30 A.M.	Event manager arrives for final inspection.
10:00	Tent crew arrives for setup.
2:00	Tent inspection and final item check with Victoria.

4/15/02

3:00	Event manager arrives at Dumbarton House for supervision.
4:00	Audiovisual technician presets audiovisual.
4:30	Beverages are delivered.
4:45	Coordinators arrive at Dumbarton House for supervision. Coordinator completes inspection form.
5:00	Caterer arrives at Dumbarton House for setup.
5:15	Florist arrives with delivery.
6:00	Sean arrives for executive staff support. The George Washington University student and Events Plus of Northern Virginia employees arrived.
6:05	Staff receives instructions and reviews their roles and responsibilities. Staff sets up place cards, programs, and table cards.
6:15	Valet arrives and receives instructions. Musicians arrive and set up.
6:30	Photographer arrives; Sean is available for assistance and direction.
6:40	Founding directors arrive.
6:45	Bob and Nancy (wife), Jim and Karen (wife) set for welcoming. Staff in place at name tag/escort card table.
7:00	Cocktail hour on the terrace and music begins.

7:30	Audiovisual company performs final check and implementation.
7:55	Waiters announce dinner and move guests to dining room tent.
8:05	Chairman speaks (2 minutes).
8:07	President speaks for 5 minutes (will show new Web site here, audiovisual technician ready for cue).
8:14	Dinner is served.
9:12	Head waiter informs chairman when all tables have received dessert.
9:15	Chairman speaks regarding founding directors and history (2 minutes).
9:17	Founder's Award is announced (3 minutes).
9:20	Video of Founder's Award recipient is shown (5 minutes).
9:25	Founding member makes followup remarks (2-3 minutes).
9:27	Chairman makes closing remarks (2 minutes).
9:29–9:50	Music plays while guests depart.
10:00	Caterer cleans and breaks down equipment.
	Coordinator and event manager complete Dumbarton House inspection form when breakdown is complete.

APPENDIX 2

Explosion Lighting Case Study

Risk Analysis Sheet

The Risk Analysis form included in this appendix is the form that was used by Mike Cerelli of Explosion Lighting for the assessment of the risks associated with the event discussed in Chapter 7. Notice that the elements listed on the left side of the form refer to the possible risks associated with the particular event. Notice also that each element has a feasibility and a responsible person associated with it. Finally, Mike noted the objectives of the client on the form so that he could keep the objective in mind as he assessed the risk.

EXPLOSION LIGHTING COMPANY RISK ANALYSIS SHEET

RISK ANALYSIS SHEET / LAST UPDATED														
Production Management/JOB NUMBER:		LOCATION:			DATE OF EVENT:									
Name:	Address:		Phone:		Fax:		E-mail							
Client Needs/Goals and Objectives:														
DESIGN/NECESSITY	ASSOCIATED RISKS		FEASIBILITY				MANAGER							

EXPLOSION LIGHTING & DRAPING COMPANY/LAST UPDATE

BARGE FORM

Production Management/JOB NUMBER: LOCATION:

Name:	Address:	Phone:	Fax:	E-mail

Client Needs/Goals and Objectives:

EVALUATION	NOTES	FEASIBILITY	FOREMAN
Barge surface			
Barge level			
Barge balanced			
Weight of all equipment			
Equipment placement			
Weather			
Maximum allotted wind speed			
Maximum allotted rain/ snowfall			
Maximum water current			
Maximum weather condition combo			
Height/width of sails			
Sail material			
Flame retardant			
Time to ship sails to designer			
Time to create sails			

Sail load	Sail rig points	Rigging device	Attachment of sails to barge	Generators and specs	Cables	Number of people	Stages and stage sizes	Hours worked	Total crew	Overtime	Uniform	Spare equipment	Permits	Politics

Index